Principles and Practices
of Performance Assessment

Principles and Practices
of Performance Assessment

Nidhi Khattri
Alison L. Reeve
Michael B. Kane
American Institutes for Research

LEA

LAWRENCE ERLBAUM ASSOCIATES, PUBLISHERS

1998   Mahwah, New Jersey   London

Lawrence Erlbaum Associates, Inc., Publishers
10 Industrial Avenue
Mahwah, NJ 07430

Cover design by Kathryn Houghtaling Lacey

Library of Congress Cataloging-in-Publication Data

Khattri, Nidhi.
    Principles and practices of performance assessment / authors, Nidhi Khattri, Alison L. Reeve, Michael B. Kane.
        p. cm.
    "The result of a research project conducted by Pelavin Research Institute (PRI) ... under a contract with the Office of Educational Research and Improvement (OERI) of the U.S. Department of Education (contract number RR91172004)"—Preface.
    Includes bibliographical references and index.
    ISBN 0-8058-2970-9 (cl. : alk. paper). — ISBN 0-8058-2971-7 (pbk. : alk. paper)
    1. Educational tests and measurements—United States—Case studies. 2. Competency based educational tests—United States—Case studies. 3. Educational evaluation—United States—Case studies. 4. Educational change—United States—Case studies. I. Reeve, Alison L. II. Kane, Michael B. III. Pelavin Research Institute. IV. Title.
    LB3051.K5115   1998
    371.26—dc21   97–45967
                                                              CIP

Books published by Lawrence Erlbaum Associates are printed on acid-free paper, and their bindings are chosen for strength and durability.

Printed in the United States of America
10 9 8 7 6 5 4 3 2 1

Contents

Foreword

Studies of Education Reform, a U.S. Department of Education-funded examination of 12 of the most important strategies of education reform, was planned in 1990, while I served as Assistant Secretary for Educational Research and Improvement. The set of 12 studies was intended to explore some of the most important areas and issues in education reform—including systemic reform, educational technology, school-to-work initiatives, school-based management, and curriculum reform—that emerged in the 1980s and early 1990s, and to show how those various reforms fit together. It gives me great satisfaction to write this foreword to a book reporting on the findings of one of those 12 studies.

The authors of *Principles and Practices of Performance Assessment* took the opportunity created by the Department's support to conduct what is, to the best of my knowledge, the broadest investigation of the characteristics of performance assessments and their impacts at the school level. In their careful exploration of a diverse set of 16 schools—where teachers and students are using an equally diverse set of performance assessments—the authors explore some of the major issues confronting policymakers and educators as they set about introducing new forms of assessment. Looking at the intersection between the performance assessment and the school, the authors describe:

- The characteristics of the several types of assessment techniques that have come collectively to be known as "performance assessment" or "authentic assessment."
- The facilitators of and barriers to the implementation of performance assessments at the state, district, and school levels.
- The factors that affect teachers' "appropriation" of performance assessments, or, in other words, teachers' ability to take new forms of assessment and adapt them for use in their own classrooms.
- The impacts of those assessments on teaching practice and learning.

The assessments they investigate include those developed and introduced at all levels of the educational enterprise: state departments of education, district offices, and schools themselves, as well as assessments promoted by national groups such as the New Standards Project, the Coalition of Essential Schools, and the College Board. The authors show how assessments initiated at these different levels can vary significantly in terms of their characteristics, how they are implemented in the classroom, and how they influence teaching practice.

Reading *Practices and Principles of Performance Assessment* today, 7 years after the study was first conceived at the Department of Education, I am struck by how topical the issue of student assessment, and performance assessment in particular, remains today. My years as a member and president of the Maryland State Board of Education brought me face to face with many of the issues the authors raise. Their discussions of the trade-offs inherent in any system of student assessment, the imperative that validity and reliability be maximized for new forms of assessment, the intersection of assessment reform with standards-based reforms, and any number of other topics will be of great benefit to policymakers in the process of reconceiving their states' or districts' assessment systems.

The authors' findings about the challenges of developing and implementing a system of performance assessment, and, in particular, about the importance of coordinating the introduction of performance assessments with other facets of the education system, are particularly instructive for those involved with standards-based reforms. The importance of a compatible linkage between content and student performance standards and the assessments used to evaluate students' mastery of that content should be self-evident. Yet, too often it turns out not to be so. When policymakers and educators embark on the process of devising a set of standards, they should at the same time be thinking of how they will assess students' progress toward achieving the levels required by those standards and how teachers will be prepared to teach and assess student work. In my current position as President of the Council for Basic Education, an independent organization devoted to improving education by promoting a standards-based liberal-arts curriculum, I have come up against the challenges of achieving such coordination and alignment among standards, assessments, professional development, and other components of the educational system in our work with a number of states and local districts.

The authors also perceptively discuss the importance of matching the format of an assessment with its purpose. This lesson was one too readily lost in the early enthusiasm for performance assessment. Performance assessments—including student portfolios, demonstrations, experiments, written projects with multiple components, as well as simpler, open-ended response tasks—are powerful tools, both for teachers seeking to understand better students' depth of and approaches to learning, and for the public who demands that students be required to know more than a (fleetingly) memorized set of facts. At the same time, performance assessments, which can be both costly and time consuming to administer, are not necessary to test students' understanding and mastery of all types of valued skills. As policymakers and educators, we tend to lose sight of the system and its purposes, focusing instead on the new method.

The result too often is a mismatch between our purpose and our tools. As the performance assessment movement matures, the importance of this lesson is becoming clear.

This volume makes a strong case for the vital importance of professional development if teachers are to be able to use performance-assessment techniques effectively and if they are to teach students the complex cognitive skills that such assessments, when well constructed, demand. This lesson, too, is one that resonates with my personal experience and the knowledge I gained during my years on the Maryland board. Too often, policymakers forget the human side of the systems we put in place. Teachers, many trained in the old school of assessment, need access to a range of professional development experiences to help them learn to work with performance assessments—including how to develop assessment tasks, how to establish performance criteria, how to interpret the meaning of individual students' performance, and how to build lessons based on what they learn from students' performance on assessments. Unfortunately, there is a tendency among policymakers and the American public alike to undervalue woefully the importance of teachers' professional development. I cannot stress this point too strongly: The hours teachers spend outside of the classroom learning new skills are crucial to the growth of their skills as teachers and, consequently, to the quality of the education they provide to our children. It is an encouraging finding of the authors that some states and districts, as well as some national reform organizations, have recognized the centrality of teachers' professional development to the successful adoption of new methods of student assessment and have responded by instituting extensive professional development opportunities for teachers.

The future of student assessment in America is currently at a crossroads. At the time of this writing, the Clinton administration is promoting the development of a voluntary national test, based on the National Assessment of Educational Progress, to be administered to 4th and 8th graders in participating states and districts. Despite some compromises, the long-term outcome of this controversial proposal remains uncertain. At the same time, states continue to rethink their student-assessment systems. With the growing recognition that no one assessment can accomplish all purposes, the pendulum that swung toward the "performance assessment panacea" almost a decade ago has begun to come back toward center. I expect that as we enter the 21st century, we will see states striving to put in place balanced assessment systems, ones that include performance-assessment components as well as norm-referenced and criterion-referenced tests. We must prepare for the future with our knowledge of the past and the present. This book is valuable to all who begin this journey.

—*Christopher T. Cross*

Preface

Principles and Practices of Performance Assessment is the result of a research project conducted by Pelavin Research Institute (PRI), an affiliate of the American Institutes for Research (AIR), under a contract with the Office of Educational Research and Improvement (OERI) of the U.S. Department of Education (contract number RR91172004). In 1991, OERI issued a request for proposals entitled "Studies of Education Reform." Twelve studies were incorporated under this general heading, each reflecting some aspect of the reform movement that had placed education at the forefront of the national agenda in the late 1980s. PRI was awarded a 3-year contract to study assessment reform, which we interpreted to mean the contribution of performance-based, non-multiple-choice assessments to education reform.

As part of the study, we visited 16 schools across the country that were participating in the development or implementation of performance assessments as a result of national, state, district, or local assessment reform initiatives.

This book begins, in chapter 1, with an overview of the historical and contemporary issues related to assessment reform. In chapters 2, 3, 4, and 5, we present our cross-site analysis and discuss our findings regarding the key characteristics of performance assessments, the facilitators and barriers in assessment reform, factors that affect teachers' ability to use new assessment techniques in their classrooms, and the impact of assessments on teaching and learning. Finally, in chapter 6, we summarize the key findings of the study and the policy and research implications of those findings. Appendix A identifies the specific study objectives and provides an overview of the study design. Appendix B summarizes the case studies we conducted of the 16 schools that participated in our study. Appendix C lists the research questions that drove the study.

ACKNOWLEDGMENTS

The support and participation of several individuals and institutions made this study possible. We are grateful to the state and district education agency personnel and to the principals, teachers, students, parents, and school-board members who devoted large amounts of their precious time to answer our questions and guide us in understanding the issues related to assessment reform. We regret that our promise of anonymity leaves them without the public recognition they deserve.

We also are grateful to David Sweet, the OERI monitor of Studies of Education Reform: Assessment of Student Performance, whose incisive feedback guided our work at every step, and to Ruth Mitchell, who served as Project Manager during the study's initial stages and as Senior Advisor during the later years. Her steady interest in and support of the project was invaluable.

This study also benefited from the participation and general support of the members of our Advisory Committee, including: Dr. George Elford, Educational Testing Service (retired); Dr. Lauren Resnick, Learning Research and Development Center, University of Pittsburgh; Dr. Ramsay Selden, Education Statistics Services Institute; Dr. Karen Sheingold, Educational Testing Service; Dr. Loretta Shepard, Department of Education, University of Colorado; and Dr. Grant Wiggins, Center on Learning, Assessment, and School Structure. In 1991–1992, the Advisory Committee members also included: Dr. Robert Mislevy, Educational Testing Service; and Mr. Sol Pelavin, American Institutes for Research.

We also acknowledge the capable support and contributions of the following individuals: Becca Adamson, Kerry Traylor, Doug Levin, Ray Varisco, Keith Tidman, Gwen Pegram, Sheran McManus, Kimberly Cook, B. J. Horgeshimer, Calvin Hawkins, Michael Garet, Kimberly Gordon, Rebecca Shulman, and Shelley Kirkpatrick, all at Pelavin Research Institute; and Amy Stempel and Stephanie Soper, both at the Council for Basic Education.

—Nidhi Khattri
—Alison L. Reeve
—Michael B. Kane

1

Introduction[1]

This book on the 3-year research project, Studies of Education Reform: Assessment of Student Performance, begins by examining the impetus behind and issues associated with *assessment reform*—a phrase commonly understood to mean the systematic shift at all levels of education organization toward performance assessments and away from multiple-choice tests for instruction, accountability, or student certification. Developing and implementing non-multiple-choice methods of assessing student performance has become a major, and controversial, part of the education reform movement currently sweeping the nation.

Our ultimate purpose in this study was to elucidate the status of assessment reform in U.S. education systems and to offer recommendations for policy and future research. The major objectives of the study were as follows[2]:

- To document and analyze key characteristics of performance assessments.
- To document and analyze facilitators and barriers in assessment reform.
- To document and assess impacts of performance assessments on teaching and learning.

This chapter provides a historical overview of the current movement toward the development and use of performance assessments, outlines the relationship of assessment reform to broader issues in education reform, highlights the technical and measurement questions related to the use of performance assessments, and provides a brief overview of the study objectives and design. The subsequent chapters discuss the findings as well as research and policy implications of this study. The appendixes offer a more detailed discussion of the study design, summaries of the case studies, and a list of the major research questions.

---

[1]This chapter is a modified version of Khattri and Sweet (1996).

[2]The specific research questions are presented in Appendix C.

1

A BRIEF HISTORY OF THE PERFORMANCE-
ASSESSMENT MOVEMENT

The use of performance assessment is not an entirely new strategy in American education. Essays, oral presentations, and other kinds of projects always have been features of elite private education. In many classrooms—both private and public—teachers for years have been assessing student progress through assigned papers, reports, and projects that are used as a basis for course grades. At the national level, the Advanced Placement Program of the College Board from its inception has assessed students by requiring at least one written essay in addition to responses to multiple-choice questions (as well as laboratory experiments in the sciences and demonstrations in music).

What is new in the current reform movement is the emphasis on the use of performance assessments for systematic, schoolwide, instructional, and curricular purposes at the school level and for accountability purposes at the district and state levels. In some instances, proponents of assessment reform view performance assessments as the lever for systemic curricular and instructional reforms at any level of the educational hierarchy.

The present focus on performance assessments as a systematic strategy of public education reform has its origins in three related phenomena, all of which gained momentum during the late 1980s: the reaction on the part of educators against pressures for accountability based on multiple-choice, norm-referenced testing, the development in the cognitive sciences of a constructivist model of learning, and concern on the part of the business community that students entering the workforce were not competent enough to compete in an increasingly global economy.

Given these concerns, education reformers insisted that, in order to function as a lever of education reform, assessments must be based on a generative view of knowledge, require an active production of student work (not a passive selection from prefabricated choices), and consist of meaningful tasks rather than of what can be easily tested and easily scored. Assessment reform also rests, explicitly or implicitly, within the notions that: assessing student performance against established standards is better than against group norms; teaching and assessing problem-solving, critical-thinking, and writing skills are essential for student achievement and growth; and teaching and assessing procedural knowledge, such as the scientific method and writing processes, are as important as teaching and assessing factual knowledge. Thus, in assessment reform theory, all performance assessments must require students to *structure* the assessment task, *apply* information, and *construct* responses, and, in many cases, students must also be able to *explain* the processes by which they arrive at the answers.

An overview of the efforts in U.S. education systems to reform assessment of student performance is perhaps best organized by their level of initiation:

national, state, district, or school. Although this organization is, in some ways, artificial, it nonetheless helps us to impose order on and to understand better a phenomenon that encompasses a wide range of purposes and methods of assessment reform.

National Level

National (nongovernmental and governmental) involvement in assessment reform shares the limelight with state-level efforts. Several national, nongovernmental projects tackling assessment, curricular, and instructional reform have gained national prominence in recent years. For instance, the New Standards Project (NSP), the Coalition of Essential Schools (CES), and the College Board's Pacesetter program have exerted considerable influence on education administrators and teachers across the nation, and have influenced a shift toward the use of performance assessments.

The New Standards Project began in 1991 with the aim of reinvigorating and revamping American education (Resnick & Simmons, 1993). It is jointly managed by the National Center on Education and the Economy and the Learning Research and Development Center at the University of Pittsburgh. The crux of NSP's work involves establishing performance standards and designing curricular, instructional, and assessment strategies. The NSP board, which guides the formulation of performance standards and assessment strategies, is composed of representatives from NSP's partner states and districts, and from professional organizations such as the National Council of Teachers of Mathematics (NCTM), the American Association for the Advancement of Science (AAAS), and the National Council of Teachers of English (NCTE). As of March 1995, the NSP program listed 17 state and 6 urban district partners.

The Coalition of Essential Schools is a national force in its own right. It was established in 1984 at Brown University, as a school–university partnership to help redesign schools. Coalition members now include more than 230 schools that are actively involved in reform. The reform work of the member schools is guided by a set of nine Common Principles, the sixth of which pertains to assessment. The sixth principle states that students should be awarded a diploma only on a successful demonstration—an *exhibition*—of having acquired the skills and knowledge that are central to the school's program. As the diploma is awarded when earned, the school's program proceeds with no strict age grading and with no system of earned credits by time spent in class. The emphasis is on the students' demonstration that they can do important things (Sizer, 1989). Several member schools have fashioned their graduation requirements on this principle.

Performance assessments on the national level have always been a feature of the College Board's Advanced Placement (AP) program—especially the Studio Art Portfolio Evaluation, which has no written or multiple-choice portions.

This evaluation, in fact, is an example of a well-established national portfolio examination (Mitchell, 1992).

More recently, the College Board launched the Pacesetter program, which is being designed as a national, syllabus-driven examination system for all high-school students. It is modeled on the AP examinations, which (with the exception of Studio Art) contain both multiple-choice and partially open-response items. The Pacesetter design incorporates two forms of assessments—classroom assessments and end-of-course assessments. Currently, 60 sites in 21 states are implementing Pacesetter course frameworks and associated assessments in English, mathematics, and Spanish ("Prominent Educators," 1995).

The most visible indication of national-level, governmental involvement in assessment reform came with the passage of the Goals 2000: Educate America Act (P. L. 103-227). Passed in 1994, Goals 2000 offers states the chance to obtain federal grants to develop standards-based education systems. As a result, Congress allocated $105 million in FY 1994 for Goals 2000, and imposed no funding limits through FY 1999 ("Goals 2000," 1994). As of September 1995, 48 states had applied for the U.S. Department of Education's Goals 2000 grants. Although states' initial applications included only general plans regarding how content and student performance standards would be set, future applications will be required to detail how student performance will be measured, in order to assess whether or not students are meeting set standards. The law formally authorizes the National Education Goals Panel (NEGP) to monitor progress toward Goals 2000.

In another national program, Title I (formerly Chapter I), performance assessments—especially portfolios—stand a chance of being included as options for use beyond norm-referenced multiple-choice testing. Congress reauthorized the Title I compensatory education program in 1994. By law, states are required to use the same or equally rigorous standards and assessments they devise for Goals 2000 for monitoring the progress of Title I students, but districts can devise their own standards and assessments as long as they are as rigorous as those of the state. Through these requirements, Title I aims to coax states away from norm-referenced multiple-choice tests and toward more open-ended, performance-based assessments (Olson, 1995).

In addition to the Goals 2000 and Title I programs, the work of several national organizations and professional associations in developing content standards for academic areas has implications for assessment reform. The efforts of many of these groups (e.g., NCTM, The Center for Civic Education, The Consortium of National Arts Education Associations, and The National Center for History in the Schools at the University of California at Los Angeles) in establishing content standards is supported by the federal government. The work of the NCTM, which released the mathematics standards in

1989, has been the most prominent among these organizations and has had the greatest impact to date. Two NCTM publications—*Curriculum and Evaluation Standards for School Mathematics* (1989) and *Professional Standards for Teaching Mathematics* (1991)—are guiding the teaching *and* assessment of mathematics in several states and school districts across the nation. (Published in May 1995, *Assessment Standards for School Mathematics* is likely to be just as influential.) The NCTM standards, for example, promote the evaluation of students' mathematical problem-solving and communication skills through the use of applied mathematical problems. Similarly, documents published by the AAAS, such as *Project 2061: Science for All Americans* (1989) and *Benchmarks for Science Literacy* (1993), have influenced the teaching and assessment of science.

Reports of the U.S. Department of Labor's Secretary's Commission on Achieving Necessary Skills (SCANS), too, have been active in prodding school systems toward more performance-based assessments. After an extensive survey of the business community, SCANS reported that employers and employees share the belief that workplaces must "work smarter" (SCANS, 1991, p. v); for a workplace to "work smarter," its employees must possess certain competencies, such as interpersonal skills, and foundation skills, such as basic skills in reading, writing, and thinking. The SCANS work, in fact, is pertinent to Goals 2000; SCANS competencies, which, among other things, emphasize interpersonal skills and intelligent use of information and technology, have a direct relationship to what students learn in classrooms. The SCANS commission envisioned setting proficiency levels for SCANS competencies and developing an associated assessment system based on demonstrating SCANS competencies through applied, contextualized problems.

State, District, and School Levels

Useful catalogs of performance assessment activity at the state and district levels include *The Status of State Student Assessment Programs in the United States* (Bond, Roeber, King, & Braskamp, 1995) and *State Student Assessment Programs Database (1993–1994)* (Council of Chief State School of Officers & North Central Regional Educational Laboratory, 1994). Also helpful is a survey of local district activity by Hansen and Hathaway (1991). These catalogues highlight the growing popularity of performance assessments. Information about activity at the school level is more difficult to obtain, because it is circulated largely via word of mouth, through professional networks, or by an occasional journal or newspaper article.

Similarly, there are many small, pilot, or research and development efforts underway that may be funded by state agencies or even by the federal government through its national research centers and laboratories. For example, the National Center for Research on Evaluation, Standards, and Student Testing

(CRESST) at the University of California at Los Angeles and the North West Regional Educational Laboratory are involved in research on the development, implementation, and effects of performance assessments. These small, local efforts are very much a part of a national trend, but they are difficult to catalog in a systematic fashion.

States. Developments at the state level are more dramatic than are those at the national level. States committed to performance assessments as public policy are slowly increasing in number. For example, in the 1993–1994 academic year, 38 states used writing samples to assess student writing proficiency, 25 included performance-based items in their assessment systems, and 7 included portfolios (Bond, Roeber, King, & Braskamp, 1995).

In the late 1980s and early 1990s, a number of states (e.g., California, Connecticut, Maryland, Vermont) became trailblazers in the development and implementation of more innovative performance-based assessments. Currently, the most notable of these states are Vermont, Kentucky, and Maryland. Vermont, perhaps, is the most innovative of them all, being the first to fully implement a portfolio-based performance assessment system in writing and mathematics. Kentucky and Maryland also administer performance events once a year. Other states, such as Oregon, were not far behind in designing and implementing ambitious performance-based assessment systems. However, despite the great deal of energy going into these reforms, public backlash in some areas has given rise to a hostile climate for such reform endeavors. California's bold move with its California Learning Assessment System (CLAS), for example, was vetoed in 1994 by Governor Pete Wilson. The program ended under an avalanche of criticism from parents that the assessments required their children to read distasteful materials and invaded family privacy by asking intrusive questions. (The future of Oregon's plans for assessment reform is also uncertain.)

Most states experimenting with performance-based assessments are explicit in their desire and intention to use the new assessments to influence instruction in the direction of conceptual, holistic teaching and learning, in addition to being interested in program evaluation.

There is some evidence that the use of performance assessment systems has achieved the aim of influencing instruction in the desired direction. For example, Vermont's surveys show that teachers have changed their instructional approach to align with project-based, holistic teaching (Koretz, Stecher, Klein, McCaffrey, & Diebert, 1993), and Kentucky teachers have changed their instructional strategies as a result of Kentucky's system of portfolios and performance events (Kentucky Institute for Education Research, 1995). Evaluation of data collected from teachers in these two states indicates that teachers are asking their students to write and to work together in groups.

However, most other evidence is anecdotal and is best established in terms of teacher performance rather than in terms of student achievement.

In summary, states have exhibited an extraordinary variety of responses to the advent of performance assessments, from a whole-hearted embrace of portfolios to an apparent lack of interest in new assessment methods. Thus, identifying the factors that facilitate the development and implementation of performance assessments was clearly a challenge for this study.

Districts.   Assessments being developed at the district level are not as visible as those at the state level because the scale of the reform efforts tends to be smaller. Nonetheless, several districts have taken the lead in developing and implementing performance-based assessment systems and are getting national attention for their efforts. For example, the San Diego City Schools in California are a hotbed of activity. The district leads the Southern Consortium of the California Assessment Collaborative with money provided by the California legislature for districts to experiment with performance assessment.

Another example is the public school system in Pittsburgh, which is famous as the site of ARTS PROPEL. It has a Syllabus Examination Project (SEP), 60% of which is based on performance assessments (Wolf, 1989; Wolf & Pistone, 1991). Varona, a school district just outside Milwaukee, uses portfolio assessments with students, teachers, and administrators alike (Pelavin Associates & CCSSO, 1991). Other examples of districts that have embraced performance assessments include South Brunswick, New Jersey; Frederick County, Maryland; Fort Worth, Texas; and Prince William County, Virginia.

Hansen and Hathaway (1991) attempted a systematic survey of assessments at many levels and sent out 433 questionnaires to school districts across the United States. They received only 110 responses, despite a follow-up mailing. Short of mailing questionnaires with reply-paid responses out to all U.S. school districts, a comprehensive account of district assessment practices does not, at present, seem attainable.

Schools.   Although schools may perceive themselves as powerless to do much in the face of state and district mandates, developing and implementing performance assessments at the school level may be easier than at the district or state levels, simply because it is easier to organize change on a small scale. For example, the notable graduation examinations based on performance assessments are at the school level—the Rite of Passage Experience (ROPE) at Walden III in Racine, Wisconsin, and the graduation portfolio at Central Park East Secondary School in New York City. Both schools are members of the Coalition of Essential Schools, which, as mentioned earlier, advocates exhibitions as replacements for norm-referenced multiple-choice tests (Sizer, 1992).

Many schools utilize portfolio assessments for writing, and some use them for mathematics and other subject areas as well. The use of teacher-designed observations or records of literacy development also is becoming popular at the elementary school level. The California Learning Record, for example, is an assessment developed for both informal and formal record keeping concerning early childhood development in literacy and mathematical ability. It is an adaptation of the Primary Language Record (PLR), which was developed by the Center for Language in Primary Education (CLPE) in London, England. Forms of the California Learning Record are being used in California, and a similar adaptation of the PLR is being promoted by the New York City Assessment Network (NYAN) in New York City schools.

In sum, although states cast a wider assessment net and enjoy more visibility in the reform arena, quieter attempts at reform by districts and schools are generating fundamental changes in education at the most basic level.

RELATIONSHIP OF ASSESSMENT REFORM TO SYSTEMIC AND ORGANIZATIONAL CHANGE

Proponents of assessment reform frequently view performance assessments as a lever for educational reform. In Smith and O'Day's (1990) words: "A major reform in the assessment system … is critical to education. Assessment instruments are not just passive components of the educational system; substantial experience indicates that, under the right conditions, they can influence as well as assess teaching" (p. 253). Proponents also assert that if performance assessment is effectively implemented at the school, district, or state level, it can change curriculum as well as teachers', students', and the community's attitudes toward education. An innovative and far-sighted leadership and a friendly political climate appear to play pivotal roles in the effective implementation of new forms of assessment. Next, we discuss the relationship between assessment reform and other critical components of education reform.

Curriculum and Assessment

That assessments must be integrated with curriculum and instruction is one of the basic premises of assessment reform. What is new in current assessment endeavors is the focus on equally new curriculum and broadly defined valued student outcomes. The stress on cross-disciplinary knowledge, conceptually sophisticated thinking, good writing abilities, application of mathematical and scientific concepts, and social competencies has necessitated overhauling curricular and instructional frameworks as well. To an extent, overhauling writing and math curriculum and assessments has proven to be the easiest reform to undertake at all levels of educational organization. Performance-based writing assessments especially represent assessment reform at its most basic.

Reform of math assessments has been aided by the guidelines provided by the National Council of Teachers of Mathematics in the *Curriculum and Evaluation Standards for School Mathematics* (1989). Reforms in other areas have become easier to implement and more widespread as curriculum guidelines have become available. The National Science Foundation and American Association for the Advancement of Science (AAAS), for example, have sponsored projects that address issues of science curriculum.

States have by and large embraced the movement toward the adoption of new curriculum frameworks or content standards. States' initiatives in this area are receiving important support from the federal government through Goals 2000 grants. Such standards portend revisions of the current assessment systems used in these content areas.

Professional Development

Professional development is crucial to reform, because teachers are the deciding factor in the success of performance assessments in affecting desired student outcomes. In fact, the importance of professional development in assessment reform or any other reform effort cannot be overemphasized (Little, 1993). For performance assessments to be effective (especially assessments based on the premises of current assessment reform), teachers' expectations of their students and of their own teaching methods must change. Teachers must be able to develop their students' ability to construct answers, think critically, and move beyond focusing only on factual knowledge. Currently, for some summative purposes, many teachers are asked to prepare their students for the administration of norm-referenced multiple-choice tests bought from test publishers. They also are being asked to develop their students' abilities to perform well on performance-based assessments. The conflict between these two systems is probably reflected in teachers' pedagogical practices.

Performance assessment therefore demands teachers' participation in assessment development, implementation, and scoring. Teachers must become knowledgeable about assessment design, scoring, and new pedagogical techniques. The benefits of teacher involvement in developing performance assessment is illustrated by the New Standards Project (NSP). The relative success of NSP in developing interesting assessment tasks and associated scoring rubrics can be attributed to its endeavors to build professional capacity at the local level. Teachers themselves develop assessment tasks and scoring rubrics and conduct pilot tests in their classrooms. Teachers then send their tasks to an NSP committee (and receive payment if their tasks are adopted for use by the NSP).

Teams of teachers from participating states and districts attend NSP assessment task and scoring rubric development conferences, as well as sessions in curriculum development and portfolio design. After a prescribed number of training sessions, these teachers are designated as Senior Leaders, and they, in turn, offer professional development in the same areas to other teachers in their districts and states. Vermont, Oregon, Kentucky, and Maryland, among others, are also paying increasing attention to issues of professional development, largely through train-the-trainer professional development models similar to that of the NSP.

Professional development activities are not cheap. All such activities are resource intensive when compared to those associated with traditional systems of testing. Therefore, commitment on the part of leadership to provide money, teacher release time, and materials is essential to successful implementation of performance assessments.

Community Support

In addition to teacher and leadership support, community support is critical throughout the entire reform process, whether or not the assessment system is the chosen mode of change. Without a sense of ownership on the parts of teachers, administrators, students, parents, the community, and other stakeholders, the systemwide changes required to effectively implement performance assessments will not occur. Vermont, for example, engaged in a large-scale consensus process before beginning its statewide portfolio assessments. As a result, its initiative has largely been supported by most stakeholders. On the other hand, Littleton, Colorado, had to rescind its reforms due to community opposition. The community was not kept well informed, and the reforms were enacted too swiftly. In the end, community members felt that vague, nonacademic outcomes were replacing content, and that technically unsound assessments would be used to determine something as important as high-school graduation (Bradley, 1994).

TECHNICAL ISSUES

Because assessment reform can no longer be considered a passing fad, performance assessments must pass technical scrutiny if they are to become an accepted means of judging student performance. Validity, reliability, and generalizability have been the perennial issues with all measurement instruments and remain so with performance assessments. The three major issues are briefly discussed next.

Validity

A central question regarding performance assessments concerns what we term *pedagogical validity*. If the primary goals of performance-based assessments are to be more closely connected to the curriculum and to provide information to the teacher for instructional purposes, then how satisfactorily they are able to fulfill these goals is a central validity concern. A one-to-one mapping of assessment tasks to curricular areas is perhaps the most important piece in the assessment validity puzzle.

Wiley and Haertel (1992) asserted that the connection between the goals of measurement, embodied in curriculum frameworks, and tasks meant to assess progress toward those goals must be quite close: "If no valid system exists for mapping tasks into the frameworks, the curricular coverage of the assessment cannot be evaluated....The link between [sic] task selection, task analysis, task scoring, and curricular goals has to be well understood and relatively tight in order for the system to work" (p. 15). Wiley and Haertel stressed that analyses must be performed to ensure the match between curricular goals and assessment tasks.

Wiley and Haertel also sketched the types of analyses that must be carried out, and concluded by underlining the importance of achieving what they termed *evidential validity*. They contended that the basic reason for rejecting machine-scorable multiple-choice tests is their lack of validity, given that they elicit memorized facts and algorithms, whereas society demands increasingly complex thinking skills. This concept of evidential validity can be extended to include the idea of assessments as diagnostic tools for students' educational needs.

Systematic evidence that performance assessments provide the means for obtaining diagnostic information to improve instruction, and the process of teaching and learning in general, is just beginning to accrue. Studies such as *Whose Work Is It? A Question for the Validity of Large Scale Portfolio Assessment* (Gearhart, Herman, Baker, & Whittaker, 1993) indicate that, in fact, the use of portfolios has pedagogical value in terms of the level of instructional support teachers provide to their students. Similarly, other, smaller studies indicate essentially salutary effects of performance assessments on instructional practices (e.g., Borko, Flory, & Cumbo, 1993; Falk & Darling-Hammond, 1993; Smith et al., 1994).

Consequential validity is another issue within the larger performance assessment validity issue. Linn, Baker, and Dunbar (1991) included the concept under *expanded validity*, which they saw as a major adjustment needed in technical theory to accommodate performance assessments:

> Serious validation of alternative assessments needs to include evidence regarding the intended and unintended consequences, the degree to which performance on specific assessment tasks transfers, ... the fairness of the assessments ... the cognitive complexity of the processes students employ in solving assessment problems, ... the meaningfulness of the problems for students and teachers ... [and] a basis for judging both the content quality and the comprehensiveness of

the content coverage needs to be provided. Finally, the cost of the assessment must be justified. (p. 20)

The fairness issue is of particular concern if assessments are used for student certification and for sorting. There must be some assurance that minority populations (who traditionally have been screened out of institutions or programs that would provide them with social and economic opportunities) not be inadvertently negatively affected by assessment reform. CRESST is conducting research on the responses of minority students to performance assessments in San Diego City Schools. We suspect that results will not generically apply to any and all performance assessments; much will depend on how assessments are constructed, the types of items they comprise, and the type of curriculum they support.

The approaches to validity discussed here are complementary. In fact, they have merged with respect to performance assessments, because the theoretical and ideological bases for these assessments call for a concurrently authentic and fair psychometric system.

Generalizability and Reliability

Generalizability, including reliability, has surfaced as a major issue that must be resolved if performance assessments are to be used for individual student assessments. In addition to redefining validity, Linn et al. (1991) elaborated on the concept of reliability; they argued for subsuming the traditional criterion of reliability under the transfer and generalizability criterion. Whether performance assessments sample sufficiently from the knowledge domain in question to enable fair and accurate judgments about students' achievement in that domain is a question central to assessment reform. After all, if one of the promises of assessment reform is to enable an understanding of students' educational needs, exactly what an assessment product indicates about a student's achievement status must be reliably understood. In this context, then, multiple examples of student work on multiple performance tasks may be the answer to the problem of generalizability. Intertask reliability, however, has been difficult to attain; studies indicate that performance on one open-ended task is often only weakly related to performance on a related task (Linn, 1993).

Interrater reliability is another important issue facing assessment reform. The complexity of the assessment tasks, the myriad answers they can elicit, and the number of people used to score them—with (possibly) different frames of reference—yield a very high potential for low interrater reliability. Although interrater reliability is attainable through standardization of task administration, the establishment of explicit scoring criteria, and scorer training, such procedures impose certain practical constraints on the use of these assessments: "The investment of dollars, time, and energy required to assure that performance assessment actually improves student performance are [*sic*] high. Although many costs are associated with initial development work, many relate to the sustaining structures and processes which will assure that assessments continue to have a positive impact on teaching and learning" (California Assessment Collaborative; 1993, p. 110).

Hardy's (1996) and Monk's (1996) articles contain edifying discussions on how to conceptualize costs and benefits associated with developing and implementing performance assessment systems.

RESEARCH DESIGN

We employed a qualitative, case-study methodology to investigate the development and implementation of performance assessments and their impacts at the school level. We designed a modified time-series approach for gathering data, which enabled us to obtain both cross-sectional and longitudinal data. Cross-sectional data allowed us to make comparative remarks about assessments and school contexts. The longitudinal data allowed us to document the effects of and changes in performance assessments over time within sites.

We selected 16 sites (the definition of *site* for this study encompasses both a performance assessment and a single school at which it is being used), which a team of two researchers visited a single time during a 2-day site visit. We then selected a subset of 7 sites, to which the team returned for a second visit (therefore, longitudinal data were collected for only 7 of the 16 sites).

The overarching objective of our site-selection process was to identify, insofar as possible, a set of school sites that exhibited the range of experiences American schools are having with the development and implementation of performance assessments. For the purposes of our study, we defined a case study site as a single school where a performance assessment was being implemented. The focus of our research was on the assessment and its implementation in the local context. To select the sites, we delineated two sets of criteria—those pertaining to performance assessments and those pertaining to schools.

The first phase of our data analysis consisted of writing case studies of our sites. Data from all sources—documents, interviews, and observations—were synthesized in the case-study report. One member of each site-visit team wrote the case study, and the second member reviewed it for accuracy. Next, the case study was sent to the appropriate officials and school personnel for review and comments. Based on their feedback, we revised the case study writeups.

The second phase of our data analysis focused on extracting and reorganizing information from our case-study writeups into a cross-case comparative format. Based on the case-study data and the theoretical, empirical, and policy papers we collected, we developed a categorization system for each of our major variables—performance assessments, facilitators and barriers, and teaching and learning processes and outcomes. Next, we organized the data from each case study into the categorization system. After the categorization exercise, we identified both common patterns and unique features in our data in order to:

- Develop a taxonomy of performance assessments.
- Illustrate and discuss the facilitators and barriers in assessment reform at different levels of educational organization.
- Identify and discuss the concept of *teacher appropriation* of performance assessments as a prerequisite to meaningful changes in teaching practice.
- Catalog and describe the perceived impact of different performance assessments on teaching and learning at sample schools.

Our approach to data analysis was primarily inductive, and our findings are offered as informed hypotheses that merit further investigation. (A more detailed discussion of the research design appears in Appendix A.)

CONCLUSION

In recent years, advocates of performance assessment have linked reformed assessment strategies with needed reforms in curriculum and instruction. Because assessment reform calls for a deviation from traditional assessment strategies in more ways than one, it presents several challenges to the established organizational structure of education.

First, the challenge is simultaneously to engineer other reforms that support and enhance the use of performance assessments. Second, the challenge is to develop assessment systems that are technically sound and pedagogically useful. Third, the challenge is to involve all stakeholders so that their informed consent provides the momentum for assessment (and associated) reforms. Judgments regarding the efficacy of performance assessment in fulfilling its promises must be based on data from the many educational systems now in the process of reform. Only when these reforms result in enhanced student outcomes will the challenge of assessment reform be met.

In the following chapters, we discuss the findings from our cross-case analyses of 16 schools and school systems involved in reforming student assessment systems. We conclude by summarizing our findings with regard to status of assessment reform and by outlining the research and policy implications emanating from those findings.

2

Characteristics of Performance Assessments

INTRODUCTION TO CROSS-CASE ANALYSES

This chapter and the three that follow it look across the sample of assessments and schools included in this study to address our three overarching research questions:

- What are the characteristics of performance assessments in practice?
- What are the facilitators and barriers in assessment reform?
- What kind of impacts do performance assessments have on teaching and learning?

Our 16 case studies (summarized in Appendix B) generated rich data that allow us not only to provide preliminary answers to the research questions, but also to formulate informed hypotheses about the practicality and usefulness of performance assessments. These hypotheses, in turn, may provide a framework for making policy decisions and for testing the usefulness and practicality of assessment reforms in a variety of educational contexts. In other words, our approach is inductive: Through the analyses, we are able to draw some generalizations about the nature and outcomes of assessment reform, but these generalizations themselves must be tested in future research.

The cross-case analysis is divided into four chapters: Characteristics of Performance Assessments (this chapter), Facilitators and Barriers in Assessment Reform (chap. 3), Teacher Appropriation of Performance Assessments (chap. 4), and Impact of Performance Assessments on Teaching and Learning (chap. 5). Before we embark on the analysis, however, we must summarize our conceptualization of the relationships among performance assessments and assessment systems and identify the elements within the assessment system on which the analyses focus; and define some terms that are employed throughout the cross-case analyses and the concluding chapter of the report.

A Simple Schemata of Assessments

Throughout the cross-case analyses, we employ several terms associated with assessments: *assessment tasks, scoring methods, performance assessments*, and *performance assessment systems*. Figure 2.1 illustrates the simple scheme through which we conceptualize performance assessments and assessment systems and organize the analyses. As illustrated, we conceptualize performance assessments as composed of assessment tasks and scoring methods. Multiple performance assessments may be linked systematically to create a performance assessment system. A performance assessment system, however, may be only one component of a comprehensive assessment system, which would include both a performance assessment system and a variety of non-performance-based assessments, including, for instance, standardized, norm-referenced multiple-choice tests.

Therefore, Fig. 2.1 identifies the two major assessment units considered in our analysis:

- *The performance assessment*, which is comprised of one or more assessment tasks and one or more scoring methods.
- *The performance assessment system*, which typically includes more than one performance assessment and is used for student graduation, certification, or system-wide instructional or accountability purposes. The term *system* subsumes the relationships among the performance assessments and the purposes, administration and scoring procedures, and other relevant features that are external to the performance assessment itself

The distinctions between performance assessments and performance assessment systems are explicated in more detail later in this chapter. For the most part, however, we do not examine performance assessment systems within the context of comprehensive assessment systems.

Conventions of Terminology in the Cross-Case Analyses

Throughout the four chapters of cross-case analysis, we employ the terms *assessment* and *performance assessment* interchangeably, except in cases where use of the word *assessment* is clearly intended to encompass both performance- and non-performance-based assessment techniques. *Assessment system* and *performance assessment system* are used interchangeably in a similar fashion. Finally,

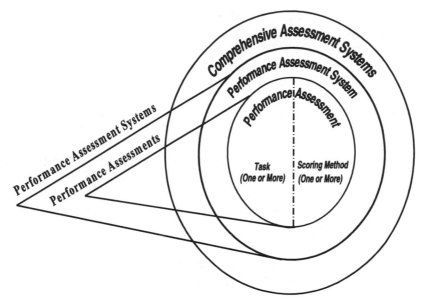

FIG. 2.1. The focus of this study.

in some of the 16 cases included in this analysis, the assessment is, in essence, synonymous with the assessment system, and in those cases use of the term *assessment system* refers to the assessment itself.

ORGANIZATION OF THE CHAPTER

This chapter:

- Describes briefly the purposes and technical characteristics of the performance assessments and performance assessment systems included in this study.
- Develops a taxonomy of performance assessments and performance assessment systems and, insofar as possible, categorizes those performance assessments and performance assessment systems included in this study within this taxonomic system.
- Discusses the educational implications of the characteristics of the performance assessments and performance assessment systems.

To accomplish these purposes, we first summarize the features of the 16 performance assessment systems included in this study. We then group and analyze the characteristics of performance assessments according to three broad categories:

- Purposes of performance assessment systems and subject areas assessed.
- Formats of performance assessments and performance assessment systems.
- Summary reviews and perceived technical properties of performance assessment systems.

Although the purposes, formats, and technical characteristics of performance assessments are considered separately, it is important to recognize that they are interrelated and that the relationships among the three features determine the usefulness and value of assessments and of assessment systems within different educational contexts.

SUMMARY OF PERFORMANCE ASSESSMENT SYSTEM CHARACTERISTICS

Figure 2.2 contains a summary of each of the performance assessment systems included in this study. The figure presents an overview of the factual information pertaining to the assessments illustrated in the case study summaries in Appendix B. It highlights the following features of the performance assessments and performance assessment systems:

- The stated purposes of the assessments.
- The format (i.e., types of assessment tasks and types of scoring instruments—rubrics in current assessment terminology) of the assessments.
- The subject area(s) targeted by the assessments.
- The grade levels at which the assessments are formally implemented.
- The status of implementation of the performance assessments (i.e., whether they are in the developmental, pilot, or full implementation stage).
- The future plans envisioned for the assessment or assessment system; and
- Comments regarding other salient factors that may affect assessment reform at the local level (particularly other assessment requirements or other related reform efforts).

Because the characteristics of assessments in practice are greatly influenced by the level of educational authority at which they were initiated—state department of education, district office, or school—we structure the presentation of the key characteristics of performance assessments according to the level of initiation of the assessments.

STATE-LEVEL SYSTEMS

ARIZONA: Arizona Student Assessment Program's Performance Assessments

Purposes	Measure student progress toward the attainment of state "essential skills"
Format	
Tasks:	Thematic on-demand performance tasks
Rubrics:	Specific
Areas	Reading, writing, mathematics
Grades	3, 8, 12
Status	Full-scale implementation
Future	Science and social studies will be added to the assessments. The state also hopes to award student certificates based on students' performance on these assessments.

Comment:

    The Arizona school included in this study is located in a district that administers its own criterion-referenced tests in all subject areas and at all grade levels. The district also administers its own performance assessments in social studies, foreign languages, English, science, dance, visual arts, and theater arts.

KENTUCKY: Kentucky Instructional Results Information System (KIRIS) — Performance Assessments

Purposes	School accountability Influence instruction and curriculum Monitor student progress toward the attainment of KERA "academic expectations"
Format	
Tasks:	Portfolios and on-demand performance tasks
Rubrics:	Generic for portfolios and specific for performance tasks
Areas	Mathematics and language arts for portfolios Arts & humanities, mathematics, science, social studies, practical living, vocational studies for performance events
Grades	4, 8, 11, 12
Status	Full-scale implementation
Future	In 1995-96, the legislature will decide whether to administer the assessments to 11th or to 12th graders.

Comment:

    The KIRIS system also has a multiple-choice and open-ended component in social studies, mathematics, reading, science, practical living, arts, and humanities.

FIG. 2.2. Summary of assessment reform.

MARYLAND: Maryland School Performance Assessment Program (MSPAP)

Purposes	Monitor student progress toward the attainment of the Maryland Learning Outcomes
	School accountability
	Influence instruction and curriculum
Format	
Tasks:	On-demand performance tasks
Rubrics:	Specific
Areas	Language arts, mathematics, reading, science, social studies, writing
Grades	3, 5, 8
Status	Full-scale implementation
Future	Continue MSPAP

Comment:

Maryland also administers multiple-choice "Functional Tests" in reading, mathematics, writing, and citizenship in Grades 9 and 11, which are required for graduation. In addition, students in Grades 3, 5, and 8 take the CTBS/4.

The school included in this study is located in a district that administers its own performance-based assessments in language arts, mathematics, social studies, and science at all grade levels.

NEW YORK: Regents Portfolios at Hudson High

Purposes	Serve as waivers for a portion of Regents Examinations
	Influence instruction and curriculum
Format	
Tasks:	Extended performance tasks, portfolios
Rubrics:	Specific
Areas	10th- and 11th-grade English and social studies, 11th-grade English, 9th- and 10th-grade global studies, 9th-grade earth science, 10th-grade biology
Grades	9, 10, 11
Status	Pilot and development
Future	The state is developing a performance-based assessment system that is intended to replace the current Regents Examination system

Comment:

Regents Examinations at these grade levels are used to determine student proficiency in the indicated subject areas, and include a mix of open-ended and multiple-choice questions. Scores on Regents Examinations are used for awarding a Regents Diploma (which is more prestigious than a local school diploma), and they are used by college personnel in making admissions decisions.

FIG. 2.2 (cont'd.)

STATE-LEVEL SYSTEMS, continued

OREGON: Assessments for Certificate of Initial Mastery*

Purposes		Student certification
		Influence instruction and curriculum
Format		
	Tasks:	On-demand performance tasks, extended performance tasks, portfolios
	Rubrics:	Generic
Areas		Several skills and competencies, such as the ability to "apply math and science" and recognize "quantitative relationships"
Grades		3, 5, 8, 10
Status		Pilot and development
Future		Most of the assessment system components are being still developed, but eventually it will consist of on-demand performance tasks and portfolios.

Comment:

     All districts in Oregon are required to administer the Oregon State Assessments, which consist of reading, writing, and mathematics items at Grades 3, 5, 8, and 11. The district included in this study also administers the California Achievement Test (CAT).

VERMONT: Portfolios

Purposes		Provide data on student performance
		Influence instruction
Format		
	Tasks:	Portfolios
	Rubrics:	Generic
	Areas	Language arts and mathematics
Grades		4, 5, 8
Status		Full-scale implementation
Future		The state hopes to extend the portfolio system to other grade levels and other subject areas. Specific plans for the near future include a high school mathematics portfolio, and the addition of history and social science portfolios at the middle and high school levels.

Comment:

     The state also administers a multiple-choice test. The school included in this study is located in a district that also administers the Stanford Achievement Tests in reading and mathematics at Grades 2 through 8.

* The Oregon assessment plan was changed in the Summer of 1995.

FIG. 2.2 (cont'd.)

DISTRICT-LEVEL SYSTEMS

HARRISON SCHOOL DISTRICT 2, CO: Performance-Based Literacy Assessments

Purposes	Monitor student performance
	Teach students to become self-assessors
	School accountability
Format	
Tasks:	Extended and on-demand performance tasks
Rubrics:	Specific (rubrics designed for teachers and students)
Areas	Literacy: reading, writing, speaking
Grades	K–12
Status	Full-scale implementation
Future	Develop and implement science, social science, and math curriculum and performance assessments.

Comment:
>   The statewide assessment program was suspended for the academic years 1993-94 and 1994-95. The district also administers the Iowa Tests of Basic Skills at Grades 3, 5, 6, 8, and 10, and a writing assessment at Grades 1 through 5 and at Grades 8 and 11.

SOUTH BRUNSWICK, NJ: Sixth-Grade Research Performance Assessment

Purposes	Align instruction with curriculum to teach research skills
Format	
Tasks:	Extended performance task and demonstrations
Rubrics:	Generic
Areas	Research topic related to the "American experience" (social studies)
Grades	6
Status	Full-scale implementation
Future	The district is thinking about developing a similar 8th-grade research performance assessment.

PRINCE WILLIAM COUNTY, VA: Applications Assessments

Purposes	Monitor student progress
	Influence instruction
Format	
Tasks:	On-demand performance tasks
Rubrics:	Specific
Areas	Mathematics, science, language arts, social studies
Grades	3, 7, 10
Status	Pilot and development
Future	The district hopes to use the assessments for accountability purposes and to communicate to the public what students know and are capable of doing.

Comment:
>   The district participates in the Virginia State Assessment Program, which consists of a norm-referenced achievement test battery given at Grades 4, 8, and 11. The state also administers the Literacy Passport Test in reading, writing, and mathematics at grade 6 (and at grades 7 through 12 for transfer and nonpassing students). In addition, the district is adopting a Basic Skills Assessment to complement the Applications Assessments.

FIG. 2.2 (cont'd.)

SCHOOL-LEVEL SYSTEMS

NIÑOS BONITOS ELEMENTARY: Language Arts and Math Portfolios

Purpose	Align with curriculum and instruction
	Establish instructional goals for students at every level
Format	
Tasks:	Portfolios and teachers' observations
Rubrics:	Generic
Areas	Language arts and mathematics
Grades	Pre-K–6
Status	Full-scale implementation
Future	Change other areas of the curriculum, including science

Comment:
    The school also administers the statewide Abbreviated Stanford Achievement Test (ASAT). In addition, it is participating in the New Standards Project.

PARK ELEMENTARY: Primary Learning Record

Purposes	Monitor and record student progress and intellectual development
	Influence instruction and curriculum
	Communicate each student's development to the next teacher
Format	
Tasks:	Unstructured
Rubrics:	Not applicable (teachers' observations)
Areas	Language arts and other subject areas
Grades	Pre-K–6
Status	Implementation by individual teachers
Future	Continue using the Primary Learning Record

THOREAU HIGH: Rite of Passage Experience

Purposes	Graduation requirement
	Provide the opportunity to learn
Format	
Tasks:	Portfolios, extended performance tasks, and demonstrations
Rubrics:	None
Areas	Most subject areas
Grades	12
Status	Full-scale implementation
Future	Continue the Rite of Passage Experience

FIG. 2.2 (cont'd.)

NATIONAL-LEVEL SYSTEMS

COOPER MIDDLE (Santa Fe, NM):
Coalition Of Essential Schools Influenced Assessments

Purposes	Influence curriculum and instruction
	Monitor student progress
Format	
Tasks:	Portfolios, extended performance tasks, demonstrations
Rubrics:	Specific
Areas	All, including integrated subject areas
Grades	7, 8
Status	Full-scale implementation and development
Future	Change the report card to match the assessments and continually evaluate the validity of the assessments

Comment:
> The district in which this school is located also requires all students to take the Iowa Test of Basic Skills (ITBS) in reading, mathematics, social studies, and science. In addition, the state of New Mexico requires writing portfolios for Grades 4 and 6.

NEW STANDARDS PROJECT (NSP)

Purposes	Influence instruction and curriculum
	Align assessment with new content and performance standards
Format	
Tasks:	Extended performance tasks, performance events, portfolios
Rubrics:	Generic and specific
Areas	English language arts and mathematics
Grades	4, 8, 10
Status	Pilot and development
Future	Establish an assessment system based on matrix-sampled tasks and student portfolios in English language arts, mathematics, applied learning, and science

Comment:
> Two NSP participant schools, Ann Chester Elementary and Noakes Elementary, were included in this study. Their versions of the NSP-influenced assessments are summarized next.

ANN CHESTER ELEMENTARY, Fort Worth, TX: NSP Participant

Purposes	Influence instruction and curriculum
	Monitor student performance
Format	
Tasks:	Extended performance tasks and portfolios
Rubrics:	Generic and specific
Areas	All
Grades	K-5
Status	Full-scale implementation and development
Future	Continue using performance assessments, and also utilize NSP standards

Comment:
> Ann Chester is located in a district that has developed and instituted the Applied Learning Program, which places emphasis on performance assessments. in addition, the state administers the Texas Assessment of Academic Skills (TAAS), a criterion-referenced multiple-choice test, at Grades 3 through 11.

FIG. 2.2 (cont'd.)

NATIONAL-LEVEL SYSTEMS, continued

NOAKES ELEMENTARY, Anton, IA: NSP Participant

Purposes	Influence instruction and curriculum
	Monitor student performance
Format	
Tasks:	Portfolios
Rubrics:	Generic and specific
Areas	Teacher determined
Grades	K–6
Status	Full-scale implementation and development
Future	Continue district help in establishing and using NSP-modeled assessments

Comment:
    The district in which Noakes is located administers the Iowa Test of Basic Skills in Grades 3 through 8.

SOMMERVILLE HIGH (Suburban Maryland): College Board's Pacesetter Mathematics

Purposes	Modify instruction and curriculum
	Better prepare minority and disadvantaged youth in high school mathematics
Format	
Tasks:	On-demand and extended tasks, journals, portfolios
Rubrics:	Specific
Areas	Mathematics (precalculus)
Grade	12
Status	Full-scale implementation with 50 participant schools as of 1994-1995
Future	Continue using Pacesetter Mathematics

FIG. 2.2 (cont'd.)

PURPOSES OF PERFORMANCE ASSESSMENT SYSTEMS AND SUBJECT AREAS ASSESSED

The sampled performance assessments and performance assessment systems are used for multiple purposes and in several subject areas. To a large extent, the purposes depend on the performance assessment system's level of initiation, the degree to which it is integrated into the educational system, and, in some cases, its stage of development.

Figure 2.3 tabulates the stated purposes of the assessments and assessment systems included in this study according to the level of initiation of the assessment or system. The purposes were articulated by the educators involved in the development and implementation of the assessments or assessment systems.

Nóte that multiple purposes are stated for some of the assessments and assessment systems. For example, the purposes of Kentucky's performance assessment system include informing and influencing instruction, monitoring

PURPOSES

Inform and influence instruction and curriculum —
12 assessments or assessment systems:

State (5):   Kentucky, Maryland, New York, Oregon, and Vermont
District (1):   Prince William County
School (2):   Niños Bonitos Elementary and Park Elementary
National (4):   Coalition of Essential Schools: Cooper Middle
                New Standards Project: Ann Chester Elementary and Noakes Elementary
                Pacesetter: Sommerville High

Monitor student progress — 11 assessments or assessment systems:

State (4):   Arizona, Kentucky, Maryland, and Vermont
District (2):   Prince William County and Harrison School District 2
School (2):   Niños Bonitos Elementary and Park Elementary
National (3):   Coalition of Essential Schools: Cooper Middle
                New Standards Project: Ann Chester Elementary and Noakes Elementary

Accountability — 3 assessments or assessment systems:

State (2):   Kentucky and Maryland
District (1):   Harrison School District 2

Align assessment with instruction and curriculum —
3 assessments or assessment systems:

District (1):   South Brunswick
National (2):   New Standards Project: Ann Chester Elementary and Noakes Elementary

Certify student achievement (graduation requirement) —
2 assessments or assessment systems:

State (1):   New York
School (1):   Thoreau High

FIG. 2.3. Stated purposes of performance assessments and performance assessment systems, by level of initiation.

student progress, and school accountability. These stated purposes are not mutually exclusive. For example, accountability assumes that student achievement can be adequately judged and monitored through the use of the performance assessment system. Furthermore, in practice, influencing instruction and aligning instructional practices with curriculum are not completely distinct functions, because both entail integrating assessment and instruction within the same pedagogical framework.

Most educational systems in our sample view informing and influencing instruction and curriculum as one of the most important purposes of performance assessments. In most cases, the initiators and supporters of performance assessments claim that the assessments influence and inform instruction, because they:

- Help teachers and other educators conduct a comprehensive evaluation of students' achievement, including students' strengths and weaknesses (a rationale quite similar to the stated purpose of monitoring student performance).
- Support instruction and curriculum aimed at teaching for understanding, by providing good pedagogical templates.

- Help teachers and other educators better assess students' understanding of procedural knowledge, which is not so easily judged through traditional assessment methods.

Such explanations of the value of performance assessments as a tool to influence instruction and curriculum resonate with the assumptions that underlie the assessment reform movement.

Because, as has been noted, the purposes of assessments and assessment systems often vary according to the level of initiation of the assessment, we now turn to discuss the purposes underlying assessment reform at each level of initiation, as experienced by educators and assessment reformers involved with the 16 performance assessment systems included in this study.

Purposes of National-Level Assessments

The three national-level efforts to develop (or to help develop) performance assessments included in this study are the Coalition of Essential Schools (CES), the New Standards Project (NSP), and the College Board's Pacesetter Mathematics Program (Pacesetter). The purposes of the first two networks are to induce changes in curriculum and instruction by helping participant schools develop their own performance assessment systems. Hence, based on the assessment philosophy and guidelines of these two organizations, participant schools are developing their own performance assessments and performance assessment systems. By contrast, the purpose of the College Board's Pacesetter Mathematics Program is more specific: Pacesetter Math is designed to provide a rigorous course in high-school mathematics for students who have completed coursework in Algebra 2. The College Board calls the math program a *capstone* course in high-school mathematics. Also, although Pacesetter programs may be appropriate for use with a wide range of students, the College Board emphasizes using the programs to enroll minority and disadvantaged students in academically challenging courses. Districts and schools participating in the program implement the Pacesetter's mathematics course that integrates curriculum, instruction, and assessment.

The methods the three organizations employ to leverage changes in assessment systems and the support they provide to their member schools (and member districts and states as well) are quite different. The Coalition of Essential Schools (CES) provides general guidelines, research information, and many examples of the kinds of assessments schools may use to bring about desired changes in educational structures and pedagogy. On the other hand, NSP and Pacesetter provide specific guidelines for designing and using scoring rubrics and assessment tasks, and they organize assessment scoring activities and professional development sessions for their participants. In the case of

Pacesetter, these activities clearly affect teachers' assessment practices, but the emphasis on assessment is subordinate to the overall program. NSP, however, has broader goals in terms of influencing assessment reform than do either CES or Pacesetter. Because one of NSP's stated objectives is to develop a standard, national assessment system, NSP is placing a premium on the technical properties, such as reliability and validity, of assessments, and on systematic professional development.

Reflective of the differences in the three organizations' approaches to assessment development, the four schools in our study that participate in the national reform efforts develop and use different types of assessments. Cooper Middle School (the CES participant) has a unique assessment system, tailored completely to its own environment. Cooper teachers devise their own assessment tasks and scoring rubrics with little, if any, standardization. In contrast, the two NSP member schools have participated in pilots of the NSP assessments and have used some of the NSP scoring rubrics and content area guidelines to develop their own assessments. Teachers at the Pacesetter participant school have tailored their in-class assessments to complement the Pacesetter Program, using the program's units and developing their own assessments.

Purposes of State-Level Assessments

Six of the 16 performance assessment systems included in our study are implemented at the state level. The stated purposes and uses of state-initiated performance assessments reflect, at least in part, the stage of development of the assessment systems.

Maryland's and Kentucky's performance assessment systems (the two most advanced state-initiated systems), are the most ambitious in their stated purposes. These two performance assessment systems are intended to monitor student progress toward the attainment of state-articulated outcomes, and to serve system accountability purposes. Similarly, Arizona's performance assessment system was introduced several years ago and was being used to monitor student performance. The Arizona Department of Education had intended to use the system for both accountability and certification purposes; however, the system was suspended in 1995 due to technical difficulties.

Although Vermont is fully implementing its portfolio system, school accountability is not one of the system's stated purposes. Nonetheless, schools are encouraged to report results of the assessments to the public, which, in effect, functions as a public accountability mechanism, even though no rewards or sanctions are associated with the assessment results.

The other two state-initiated systems—New York's and Oregon's—are still in the research and development phase. In many respects, both systems can be classified as local-level efforts, because much of the development work is progressing at individual schools throughout the states. New York has granted waivers to local high schools to develop performance assessments as partial fulfillment of the Regents Examination. New York's initiative is a small-scale development project that receives little support from the state level, and not all New York high schools are required to participate in developing the system. It is, at the same time, high stakes, because students' performance on Regents waiver course performance assessments are combined with their scores on the standard Regents Examinations. (Students' scores on Regents Examinations are used for awarding the Regents Diploma; they also are used by New York colleges to make admissions decisions.)

The Oregon Department of Education, in contrast, is supporting the development of a performance assessment system through grants to school districts across the state[1]. The assessment system, in its developmental stage, is low stakes. In the long run, however, Oregon plans to use the fully articulated assessment system for student certification and system accountability purposes. However, the specification of the assessment system—how performance assessments will be combined with standardized, multiple-choice tests—remains under debate, making adherence to the original timeline for the institutionalization of the assessment system tenuous.

It is important to note that these six state-initiated or state-supported performance assessment systems are at radically different stages of development and implementation, and no system is fully formulated. The purposes of these assessments are evolving as the assessment systems develop and change—and as data concerning their usefulness and effectiveness become available.

In all, however, these six state-level sample cases support Herman's (1992) assertion that states continue to put their faith in assessments as the model of accountability. States find that traditional multiple-choice assessments, not the general model of accountability, are problematic.

Purposes of District-Level Assessments

Three district-initiated performance assessment systems are included in our study. The stated purposes of these three systems illustrate the reasons districts may have for introducing performance assessments. As illustrated earlier in Fig. 2.3 educators at these three districts identified four of the five purposes of assessment reform. Harrison School District 2's Performance-Based Literacy Assessments are intended to monitor student performance and to hold schools accountable for student achievement. South Brunswick's Sixth-Grade Research Performance Assessment is intended to help align instruction with curriculum. Finally, the purposes of Prince William County's Applications Assessments are

---

[1] The Oregon assessment plan was substantially changed in the summer of 1995. The information presented in this chapter covers academic years 1993–1994 and 1994–1995.

to monitor student progress and to influence instruction. The district plans to use the assessments for accountability purposes. As with the sampled state assessment systems, district-level systems defy comparison because of their differential stages of development.

Purposes of School-Level Assessments

In our sample, school-level systems are the most closely connected to the idea of using assessments to inform instructional practices and to diagnose student strengths and weaknesses. In all cases, teachers tailor the homegrown assessments to the educational needs of their particular students in their particular schools. Thus, school-level systems are typically not static, stand-alone aspects of education, but instead are integrated into the school's pedagogical practices. Accordingly, they constantly evolve and change, based on teachers' evaluations of the assessments' pedagogical utility.

However, it must be noted that four out of the seven school-level assessments included in this study are being developed and implemented at the elementary school level[2]. One high school implementing a performance assessment system obtained waivers from districtwide testing requirements. The one middle school implementing its own performance assessments has not received waivers. As a result, the middle school is experiencing difficulties in maintaining a balance between traditional pedagogical methods and performance-based methods. The students at this school are required to take the Iowa Test of Basic Skills (ITBS), and, thus, teachers feel obliged to prepare them for this test using traditional teaching strategies.

The pattern in our data suggests the possibility that elementary schools may experience the least difficulty in instituting performance assessment systems, because they are less likely to operate in environments that require teachers to teach and assess in traditional ways. It is possible that middle schools and high schools experience more external testing pressures, limiting those schools' capacity to develop and implement innovative assessment systems, even for pedagogical purposes.

---

[2]Note that the four schools participating in national-level assessment reform efforts are included in this discussion as well (as, indeed, they are through much of this report). The seven schools are generally discussed together because the national reform efforts typically require extensive local-level effort and do not dictate the form performance assessments are to take at the school level. However, the assessments developed and implemented by Sommerville High teachers are so closely aligned with the Pacesetter syllabus and guidelines that, in many cases, we do not discuss Sommerville's assessments separately from those of Pacesetter. National reform participant schools are separated from the other school-level efforts only when there is a clear distinction to be made between those school-level efforts that are guided by national efforts and those that are not (e.g., the professional development opportunities provided to teachers vary according to national reform effort participation or nonparticipation).

Subject Areas Assessed

The subject areas most frequently targeted for assessment are language arts (including reading and writing), and mathematics. Social studies and science also are included in some performance assessment systems included in our study. Figure 2.4 shows the frequency of subject areas assessed by assessments and performance assessment systems initiated at different levels of educational authority.

In language arts—the content area most targeted for assessment—the assessment emphasis is typically on different genres of writing. Although previous definitions of "good" writing did not assume purpose or audience (Mitchell, 1992), advocates of reform in the teaching and assessment of writing believe that "good writing" is not *good* under all circumstances. That is, there is not one template for good writing but many, because the ability to write does not automatically transfer from one genre to another; different circumstances require different styles and forms of writing.

Following this logic, assessment reform in writing is based on the ideas that proficiencies in different types of writing skills must be developed through teaching and assessing different genres of writing, and that writing must be tailored to particular purposes and particular audiences. These genres can include, but are not limited to: reporting information; reviewing, evaluating, or critiquing books, plays, and events; writing autobiographical incidents; explaining or developing solutions to a problem; speculating about cause and effect; business writing; reflective writing; and creative writing (after Mitchell, 1992).

Subject Areas

Most subject areas — 4 assessments or assessment systems:

School (3):   Thoreau High, Ann Chester Elementary, and Noakes Elementary
National (1):   Coalition of Essential Schools: Cooper Middle

Language arts — 11 assessments or assessment systems:

State (5):   Arizona, Kentucky, Maryland, New York, and Vermont
District (2):   Harrison School District 2 and Prince William County
School (2):   Niños Bonitos Elementary and Park Elementary
National (2):   New Standards Project: Ann Chester Elementary and Noakes Elementary

Mathematics — 9 assessments or assessment systems:

State (5):   Arizona, Kentucky, Maryland, Oregon, and Vermont
District (1):   Prince William County
School (1):   Niños Bonitos Elementary
National (2):   New Standards Project: Ann Chester Elementary and Noakes Elementary

Science — 5 assessments or assessment systems:

State (4):   Kentucky, Maryland, New York, and Oregon
District (1):   Prince William County

Social studies — 5 assessments or assessment systems:

State (3):   Kentucky, Maryland, and New York
District (2):   South Brunswick and Prince William County

Practical living/vocational — 1 assessment system:

State (1):   Kentucky

FIG 2.4. Subject areas targeted for assessment, by level of initiation.

An example of one performance assessment that focuses on several genres of writing is Kentucky's language arts portfolios. For their language arts portfolios, Kentucky's eighth-grade students are required to write:

- A personal narrative.
- A piece of writing that, among other alternatives, defends a position or solves a problem.
- A short story, poem, play, or script, or other piece of original fiction.
- A personal selection of one additional, original piece of writing.

Harrison School District 2 provides another example. The district's performance-based writing assessments are keyed to one of the district's significant student outcomes: Students will communicate in writing to multiple audiences for the purposes of informing, persuading, organizing, and providing enjoyment.

Assessment reform in mathematics is based on the assumption that the evaluation of mathematical knowledge must go beyond the assessment of memorized algorithms and mathematical facts to include the evaluation of students': understanding of mathematical concepts and ability to apply such concepts to complex problems, proficiency in mathematical communication, acceptance of different solutions to the same mathematical problem, acceptance of different methods of arriving at the same conclusion, and knowledge of and ability to explain the processes used to arrive at mathematical solutions. (The National Council of Teachers of Mathematics guidelines, which reflect these principles, are used widely to inform curriculum and assessment reform in mathematics.) Assessment reform in mathematics is attempting to frame mathematics as a tool for solving problems, not as an abstract subject reserved for academically advanced students. For example, for their mathematics portfolios, Vermont's eighth graders must include three categories of mathematics problems (puzzles, investigations, and applications), and they must describe the decision-making processes they used in solving the problems.

Finally, the focus of assessment reform in other subject areas similarly aims to shift the emphasis from an exclusive evaluation of students' knowledge of facts to include an assessment of knowledge and understanding of procedures and methods.

FORMATS OF PERFORMANCE ASSESSMENTS
AND PERFORMANCE ASSESSMENT SYSTEMS

Performance assessments vary tremendously in the forms they take and the types of demands they make of students and teachers. Indeed, the assessments at the 16 sites included in this study reveal that the only characteristics shared by all performance assessments are the pedagogical assumptions on which they are based and the fact that they require students, in some fashion or another, to construct responses to tasks.

The format or structure of performance assessments can have important ramifications for the power of assessment systems as a tool to leverage changes in teaching and learning. In this section, we use the performance assessments in our sample to develop and illustrate a framework for understanding and classifying the format of performance assessments and performance assessment systems.

Figure 2.5 illustrates our conceptualization of the relationships among the components of performance assessment systems and the factors that influence their power as a tool of education reform. The exhibit illustrates that (a) one or more *assessment tasks* and one or more *scoring methods* are linked to create a *performance assessment*; (b) multiple *performance assessments* can be linked to create a *performance assessment system*; and (c) the relationship of performance assessments to teaching and learning may be characterized across several dimensions, including the extent to which they are integrated with instruction,

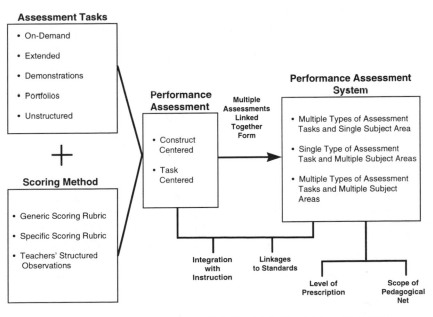

FIG. 2.5. A sample-based conceptual framework of performance assessments.

their linkage to performance and content standards, their level of prescription, and the scope of the pedagogical net they cast[3].

The taxonomic scheme we develop regarding the format of assessment tasks, scoring methods, performance assessments, and performance assessment systems builds on a successively broadening framework; the characteristics of tasks and scoring methods determine the characteristics of a performance assessment, and the characteristics of the performance assessments that comprise the performance assessment system affect the characteristics of that performance assessment system.

The analysis in this section is broken into the following subsections:

- *Assessment tasks*, which include on-demand tasks, extended tasks, demonstrations, and portfolios, and can vary in the time, skill, social, meta-cognitive, and other demands they make of students.
- *Scoring methods*, which include generic rubrics, specific rubrics, teachers' structured observations, and other methods.
- *Performance assessments*, which tend to be either "task centered" or "construct centered" (these terms are defined in the discussion); in this section we also investigate variation in how assessments are intended to be integrated with instruction and how well they are linked with content and performance standards.
- *Performance Assessment Systems*, which vary according to their "level of prescription" and the "scope of the pedagogical net" they cast (again, these terms are defined in the discussion).

Assessment Tasks

The first component of a performance assessment is the task that the student must attempt to complete. Tasks range from short, on-demand tasks to research projects that culminate in exhibitions of student work. Five categories of tasks include the following:

- *On-Demand tasks*, or events, that require students to construct responses to prompts or problems within a short period of time. The prompt problem is supplied to the student by the teacher or the examiner.
- *Extended tasks* that last longer than on-demand tasks. These tasks usually are undertaken by students on an assigned topic or a topic of their own choice; students are given time to think about and research the topic, and then to demonstrate mastery of that topic.

---

[3]Two of these dimensions—integration with instruction and linkages to standards—are linked in the exhibit to both the performance assessment and the performance assessment system, to emphasize again that, in our sample, some performance assessments are synonymous with performance assessment systems. However, later, we discuss the dimensions where they are best understood conceptually.

- *Demonstrations* that take the form of student presentations of their work. Also referred to as *exhibitions*, these can take the form of oral or written presentations.
- *Portfolios* that consist of collections of a student's work and developmental products, which may include drafts of assignments. (Strictly speaking, portfolios are not tasks in themselves; they are composed of different types of tasks. Generally, however, the student must systematically choose and compile a number of different tasks into a folder. Hence, building a portfolio can be classified as an assessment task, because it is something a student must do.)
- *Other* tasks that comprise essentially any activity a student might undertake on his or her own. Such tasks are observed, recorded, and evaluated by the teacher; they are used principally with young children.

Each of these kinds of tasks requires students to be actively engaged in responding to the task. To varying degrees, students must define the parameters of the task, seek information to complete the task, and, in some cases, explain the processes by which they arrived at the answers.

Table 2.1 summarizes the types of tasks used in the assessment systems studied at each of the 16 sites included in our study. The exhibit illustrates that on-demand tasks tend to be used by states for accountability purposes. Most states also have a goal of requiring students to compile comprehensive portfolios that illustrate student performance over the course of the academic year. Among state-level performance assessment systems, Kentucky's and Vermont's already require student portfolios. New York's pilot high-school performance assessment system is based on portfolios, and Oregon's original plan for its assessment reform was to require portfolios (but the likelihood of that plan being implemented is now unclear).

Among districts, Prince William County's Applications Assessments consist only of on-demand tasks, Harrison School District 2's Performance-Based Literacy Assessments consist of on-demand and extended tasks, and South Brunswick's Research Performance Assessment is based on extended tasks and demonstrations. School-initiated assessments, in contrast, consist either of extended tasks, a combination of demonstrations and on-demand tasks, and/or portfolios. Schools involved in national-level assessment reform efforts tend to select among the assessment tasks recommended by the national group—for instance, teachers at Ann Chester and Noakes Elementary Schools use portfolios as recommended by NSP. Teachers at two of the elementary schools in our sample also observe their students' involvement in classroom activities in order to plan lessons and to meet individual students' needs.

TABLE 2.1

Sites by Types of Assessment Tasks and by Level of Initiation*

On Demand Tasks	Extended Tasks	Demonstrations	Portfolio	Other
STATE				
Arizona Kentucky Maryland Oregon	New York Oregon		Kentucky New York Oregon Vermont	
DISTRICT				
Harrison School District 2 Prince William County	Harrison School District 2 South Brunswick	South Brunswick		
SCHOOL				
Sommerville High	Thoreau High Cooper Middle Sommerville High Ann Chester Elementary	Thoreau High Cooper Middle	Niños Bonitos Elementary Park Elementary Ann Chester Elementary Noakes Elementary Thoreau High	Park Elementary Niños Bonitos Elementary
NATIONAL				
New Standards Project Pacesetter (College Board)	New Standards Project Pacesetter		New Standards Project Pacesetter	

*Note that the four schools participating in national reform efforts are represented in the school section, illustrating the assessments in use at the schools, while the reform efforts themselves are identified in the national section, illustrating the types of assessment tasks the national organizations design and promote.

36

Dimensions of Task Specification

Individual tasks within each of the broad task categories can be specified along several dimensions, and the combination of those different dimensions determines how a student must respond to the task. In other words, the task dimensions determine the response structure of the task. Hence, represented within each task type is a variety of student response structures (Messick, 1994). In turn, these different response structures yield different types of information about the student's performance.

Table 2.2 summarizes the following dimensions along which the tasks in our sample vary[4]: time demands, applied problem-solving skill demands, metacognitive demands, social competencies (i.e., group problem solving), and student control. Although the five dimensions are not mutually exclusive, each merits a definition and illustration through examples.

The five task dimensions are defined and illustrated as follows:

Time Demands.   This refers to the amount of time allotted to a student to complete the task. The time allocated to complete the task can vary from a few weeks to less than an hour. For example, on-demand tasks typically require much less time than do extended tasks. Preparation time for demonstrations can be quite long, but demonstrations themselves require little time to execute. Nonetheless, even within broad task categories, time demands can exhibit considerable variation.

Cooper Middle School's research assignment, an essay on the intersection of medicine and science, is an example of an extended task that requires several days to complete. Students are asked to research the topic, present sufficient information in their reports to address the topic, and include in their reports visual aids, such as graphs and charts. In contrast, Arizona's, Kentucky's, Maryland's, and Prince William County's on-demand tasks last only a few hours. In each case, students are asked to write an essay or to conduct an experiment without leaving the examination room.

Applied Problem-Solving Skills Demands.   This refers to the degree to which tasks elicit cognitive skills, such as the ability to apply procedural knowledge to complete a complex, multi-step "applied problem-solving" task or the ability to apply factual knowledge to procedures.

Crandall High School's "Residential Zone" is an example of an applied problem-solving task. This 1-week project requires students to plan a residen-

---

[4]An in-depth analysis of precisely where each task for each of the sampled performance assessments or performance assessment systems falls along the dimensions outlined in their subsection is not possible. It was beyond the scope of this study to collect the massive quantities of data required for conducting such an analysis. Hence, only representative tasks are classified in the table. The sampled tasks do not necessarily characterize the entire performance assessment system to which they belong.

TABLE 2.2

Dimensions of Task Specification by Level of Initiation and by Site

	State level						District level				School level*					National level	
	AZ	KY	MD	NY	OR	VT	PWC	HSD2	SB	CM	PE	NB	TH	AC	NE	NSP	PS
Time demands	+	+++	+	+++	+	+++	+	+	+	+++	n/a	+++	+++	+++	+++	+	+++
Applied problem-solving skill demands	X	X	X	X	X	X	X	X	X	X	n/a	X	X	X	X	X	X
Metacognitive demands	X	X	X	X	X	X				X	n/a	X	X	X		X	X
Social competencies (group problem solving)		X	X	X	X			X		X	n/a	X		X	X	X	X
Student control	L	H/M	L	H/M	M	H/M	L	M	H/M	H/M	n/a	All	M	M	M	All	M/L

*Sommerville is not included in this section, as Sommerville teachers design and implement assessments that are closely aligned with the Pacesetter syllabus and guidelines.

Cell key:
+ = Tasks requiring a single, discreet period of time to complete
+ + = Tasks requiring a few hours to a few days to complete
+ + + = Tasks requiring several days to a semester to complete
X = Demand is present
L = Little control
M = Moderate control
H = High control
All = Tasks at varying levels of student control
n/a = Not applicable

Site key:
PWC = Prince William County
HSD2 = Harrison School District 2
SB = South Brunswick
CM = Cooper Middle
PE = Park Elementary
NB = Ninos Bonitos Elementary
TH = Thoreau High
AC = Ann Chester Elementary
NE = Noakes Elementary
NSP = New Standards Project
PS = Pacesetter

tial zone with a view to maximizing profits for the real-estate developer. For this task, students must work within certain constraints, such as zoning regulations for residential plot size and street widths (thus establishing the task's "applied, real-world" scenario). Students are evaluated on their applied mathematical skills, such as conceptual understanding, use of effective procedures and strategies, interpretation of information, and communication of reasoning and results.

Metacognitive Demands.   This refers to the awareness students must exhibit of their own thinking and problem-solving skills. The task may require students to explain their thinking or the procedures they used in solving a problem. Tasks that attempt to capture such complex skills also are intended to invite student engagement and to motivate student involvement in the process of assessment.

Maryland's on-demand tasks require students to respond to a series of questions that lead to a solution or a decision, accompanied by an explanation or rationale for the student's responses. Kentucky's on-demand tasks ask students to work together in groups to solve problems, but they require students to construct individual responses that describe the process their group followed to solve the problem and the reasoning behind the conclusions they drew. Students also are asked to discuss in their responses whether or not they agreed or disagreed with their group's conclusions, and why.

Social Competencies.   This refers to the interpersonal skills students must use to complete a task. A task may require a student to work with other students in a group to complete all phases of the task, or he or she may be required to collaborate with others on only one aspect of the task. (If a student must collaborate with a team in order to complete a task, the inferences one could draw regarding the student's performance may be quite different from the inferences one would draw had he or she attempted the task by himself or herself.)

Kentucky's and Maryland's on-demand tasks sometimes require students to work in small groups to understand the task and to collect data prior to recording responses independently. For instance, one Kentucky task involves groups of four students working together to test which of several instruments available to them is a more effective tool for separating oil from water in a simulated oil spill. As described previously, students are then asked to construct individual responses that discuss the processes their group followed and the reasoning behind their conclusions. In all such group activities, setting up or performing the task is a group activity, but the final student responses are independent.

The task of constructing a portfolio also can, in some cases, require some elements of group problem solving. For example, at Maple Leaf Middle School in Vermont, the language arts teacher requires her students to critique and confer with one another about the writing samples that are to be included in their writing portfolios, blurring the line between independent work and group work.

Student Control.   This refers to the degree of judgment a student must exercise in defining and completing the task. The response structure of the assessment tasks can range from being very tight, allowing students little leeway in defining the parameters of the task (i.e., topic, resources, length of procedures, products) to very loose, requiring students to formulate the task themselves. The more directive the task, the less control the student has in the types of "correct responses" he or she can give and in the types of procedures he or she can devise to complete the task.

South Brunswick's Sixth-Grade Research Performance Assessment is an example of a system in which students exercise a fair amount of control over the assessment task. Students must decide on a topic related to the "American Experience," use several sources of information to write their research papers, and determine the length of their papers. The structure of Thoreau's Rite of Passage Experience also is quite loose. Students must write essays and demonstrate their proficiency in a number of subject areas. However, students themselves, within a specified structure, choose the topics for their essays, sources of information they use in their essays, and the design of their demonstrations. At times, students choose to combine two or three topics into one demonstration.

In contrast, the structure of the Maryland School Performance Assessment Program's on-demand eighth-grade "Birth Dates" mathematics task is tight, allowing students little control for specifying the task. For this task, students are given information on the percentage of people born in each month of the year. Based on this information, they are asked to respond to a series of subtasks, such as constructing a graph for the birthday data and calculating how many students in the school are likely to share the student's birthday month (given a certain number of students in the school). Hence, students exercise very little control over either the topic or the length of their response.

Relationships Among the Dimensions of Assessment Tasks.   The five dimensions of assessment tasks—time demands, applied problem-solving skill demands, metacognitive demands, social competencies, and student control—are not entirely independent. For example, if the task is intended for evaluating a student's competency in mathematical operations, the student control and social competencies aspects of the task may have to be limited. Time demands, too, can limit the amount of control a student has in constructing responses to an assessment task. Hence, one task dimension may necessarily limit other task dimensions. Therefore, the specification of these dimensions depends, in part, on the intended purpose of the task.

Scoring Methods

One part of the assessment is the task. The second part is the scoring method. The scoring or evaluation instrument or method is used to judge the quality of the student's performance on the task. In many cases, these scoring methods are called *scoring rubrics*. Scoring rubrics are a pivotal feature of assessment reform, because they both specify the knowledge and competencies for which student work must be evaluated and delineate the criteria for determining the quality of student work. Through the combination of the task specification (e.g., on-demand tasks that elicit social competencies and portfolios that elicit metacognitive skills) and the scoring method, states, districts, and schools have attempted to articulate and communicate the skills and competencies that are important to teach and to assess.

Four broad types of scoring or evaluation methods evidenced in the performance assessments included in this study are:

- Generic scoring rubrics that articulate general skills and competencies to be scored and the criteria for judging the quality of student work with respect to those skills and competencies. Generic rubrics can be applied to several different tasks that are intended to elicit the skills and competencies articulated in the scoring rubric.
- Specific scoring rubrics that are tailored to specific tasks and articulate the skills and competencies elicited by those tasks. Specific scoring rubrics can be used for judging student performance only on specific tasks.
- Teachers' structured observations that gauge student classroom behavior. Teachers structure and analyze their naturalistic observations of their students in order to plan lessons and to diagnose individual students' needs. This method is generally used with young children.
- Other methods, including checklists of the components student work should include or unarticulated criteria.

At the state level, specific scoring rubrics are used in the Arizona, Kentucky, and Maryland performance assessment systems with on-demand tasks. Teachers at the New York portfolio pilot site also have developed specific scoring rubrics for extended tasks. Kentucky, Oregon, and Vermont, on the other hand, use generic scoring rubrics to guide teachers in developing and scoring tasks that are included in portfolios. (Note that the Kentucky system uses specific rubrics with one type of assessment task and generic rubrics with another type of task.)

The use of generic scoring rubrics has posed some problems in the implementation of Kentucky's and Vermont's portfolio assessments. Teachers who are responsible for constructing tasks for inclusion in the portfolios have not always been able to develop tasks that conform to and capture the skills and competencies articulated in the generic rubrics. Consequently, the two states have experienced difficulties in standardizing their portfolio assessments and in drawing inferences about the performance assessment results. For example, in some cases in the 1993–1994 school year, Vermont teachers did not design mathematics tasks that were challenging enough for their students; consequently, students' skills and competencies were not adequately elicited by such tasks[5].

The skills and competencies articulated in the two states' generic scoring rubrics in mathematics and language arts are shown in Table 2.3 (for purpose of comparison, Oregon's generic rubric for math and science is included in the exhibit as well). As is illustrated, the generic rubrics are similar in many respects. All three state-level mathematics rubrics stress conceptual understanding, effective problem-solving procedures, and effective mathematical communication strategies. The Kentucky and Vermont language arts scoring rubrics stress purpose, organization, effective development of ideas, and effective and correct language usage.

At the district level, Harrison School District 2 utilizes specific rubrics with extended and on-demand tasks, and Prince William County utilizes them with on-demand tasks. In contrast, generic scoring rubrics are used in South Brunswick with the Sixth-Grade Research Performance Assessment. The difference in choice of rubric type in these three cases is clearly driven by the features of the assessment tasks employed, because the South Brunswick performance assessment allows students to select their own topics to conduct a series of writing and presentation tasks (only a generic rubric could be used in this scenario), whereas the other two districts identify the tasks to which students respond more tightly and can write rubrics specific to those tasks.

School-initiated performance assessments, whether supported by national assessment reforms or not, use a mix of specific and generic scoring rubrics. At these schools, specific rubrics serve a dual function of guiding students in their assignments and helping teachers in determining student grades. On the other hand, generic rubrics help teachers design different tasks that tap into broad content knowledge and critical thinking domains. Because most of the rubrics in school-initiated systems are developed at the local level, teachers understand what skills and competencies are to be evaluated using the rubric. Hence, rubric–task alignment appears to have posed fewer problems at these schools than it did at some schools working with the Kentucky and Vermont performance assessment systems (as described previously).

---

[5]Vermont Department of Education (1995).

TABLE 2.3

Skills and Competencies Articulated by Generic Rubrics Used in Kentucky,
Vermont, and Oregon

	Kentucky	*Vermont*	*Oregon**
Mathematics	Problem-solving Mathematical reasoning Mathematical communication, including language and representation Understanding and connecting loose concepts Use of different types of problems and tools in portfolios	Communication, including: • Language • Representation • Presentation Problem-solving, including: • Understanding the problem • Strategies used in solving the problem • Decision-making process • Connections of solution to another situation	Conceptual understanding of the problem Use of effective processes, procedures, and strategies Analysis and interpretation of information to reach reasonable results/ conclusions Communication of reasoning processes and strategies used
Language Arts	Purpose/audience Idea development/support Organization Sentence construction Effective language usage Correct language usage	Purpose Organization of ideas/information Details in ideas and information Grammar/usage/mech-anics	

*"Apply Math and Science" rubric.

The implementation of two performance assessments included in this study
involves no formal scoring method. The Primary Learning Record is a qualitative method of observing, recording, and analyzing student progress and intellectual development. Certain questions guide teachers' observations of their
students' classroom behaviors, but the evaluation itself includes no method for
quantifying these observations. Thoreau High School's Rite of Passage Experience (ROPE) also has no formalized scoring method associated with it.
Students receive grades on ROPE and its components, but teachers use their
own criteria and standards to judge student performance.

In sum, scoring methods used to judge student performance on tasks range
from generic scoring rubrics (which are applicable to any number of tasks in a
given domain) to specific scoring rubrics (which are applicable only to one or
a few tasks) to implicit, unarticulated scoring criteria. The performance assessments in our sample include a variety of scoring methods, ranging from those
that are quite detailed and clear in the criteria they explicate for judging the

quality of student work, to others that are no more than checklists of the elements—"existence proofs"—that must be present in student work. The data collected in this study suggest that generic rubrics, in particular, can function as highly sophisticated instruments of education reform, because, if they are well constructed, they articulate the general skills and competencies that the state or other education agency believes are important to assess, and, therefore, to teach.

Performance Assessments

Together, the assessment task and the scoring method comprise the perform-ance assessment. (The performance assessment could consist of a single task and a scoring method, or it could consist of multiple tasks and one or multiple scoring methods.) Following Messick's (1994) conceptualization (and modify-ing it somewhat), performance assessments can be divided into two rough categories:

- *Task-centered* performance assessments that are primarily intended to tap into and evaluate specific skills and competencies.
- *Construct-centered* performance assessments that are intended to tap into and sample from a domain of skills and competencies.

Task-centered performance assessments tend to consist of tasks that allow little student control, and specific scoring rubrics for judging student perform-ance on the assessment tasks. On the other hand, construct-centered perform-ance assessments consist of tasks that may allow a fair amount of student control; they often utilize a generic scoring rubric (or some other, nonspecific criteria) for judging student performance.

The two types of assessments have different pedagogical uses and implica-tions. For example, task-centered performance assessments may be easier to use and to score (because all scoring rubrics are specific), but they may not necessarily convey to students the principles behind the tasks. The reverse is true for construct-centered assessments: They may not be as easy to score, but, because the tasks are intended to sample skills and competencies within a given domain, and because the generic scoring rubric articulates the general skills and competencies of interest within the domain, they help to create common understandings among students and teachers of what is important to teach, learn, and assess.

The assessment systems we sampled in Arizona, Maryland, Harrison School District 2, and Prince William County consist of task-centered performance assessments. On the other hand, Vermont's portfolios and Oregon's perform-ance assessments are primarily construct-centered assessments, as is Park

Elementary's Primary Learning Record. Other sites' assessment systems utilize both task-centered and construct-centered assessments. At the state level, Kentucky's performance assessment system is a prime example of a system that includes both types of assessments.

Pedagogical Dimensions of Performance Assessments

Both types of performance assessments—task-centered and construct-centered—can vary in terms of two dimensions that have implications for their pedagogical usefulness: the extent to which they are integrated into instruction, and whether or not (and how closely) they are linked to content and performance standards.

These two dimensions—integration with instruction and linkages to standards—are discussed next. Table 2.4 summarizes the presence and absence of the two dimensions with respect to the performance assessments in our sample[6]. Examples of how these dimensions play out in performance assessments follow.

Integration Into Instruction. Assessments are differentially integrated into instruction; some are used as an instructional tool as well as an evaluation tool, whereas others are intended solely for student evaluation and are not integrated into the classroom activities or assignments.

Harrison School District 2's Performance-Based Curriculum (PBC) Literacy Assessments are an example of assessments that are well integrated with instruction. The classroom teacher prepares his or her students for the assessment by explaining the goals of the performance assessment task. The teacher also explains how to use the scoring rubric designed specifically to aid the student in completing the task. The teacher may, at the end of the task, ask students to perform peer evaluations of one another's work. The assessment—comprised of both the task and the evaluation—is intended to be an integral feature of classroom instructional activities. Students are given the scoring rubrics to guide their own work and to gauge their performance. The teacher assesses student performance at the completion of the task.

Park Elementary's Primary Learning Record provides another example of an assessment technique that has been thoroughly integrated into daily teaching practices. Teachers regularly take notes on students' in-class speaking, reading, and listening behaviors, and analyze them later to plan future instructional activities.

Arizona's, Kentucky's, Maryland's, and Prince William County's on-demand tasks are part of performance assessments that are not integrated into the classroom. Students have no prior knowledge of what tasks to expect, and scoring occurs outside the purview of the teacher and the student.

---

[6]This table is not necessarily descriptive of all performance assessments in the sampled education agencies' assessment systems.

TABLE 2.4

Pedagogical Dimensions, by Level of Initiation and by Site

	State level						District level					School level				National level	
	AZ	KY	MD	NY	OR	VT	PWC	HSD2	SB	CM	PE	NB	TH	AC	NE	NSP	PS
Integration with instruction		X		X	X	X		X		X	X	X	X	X	X		X
Linkage to content standards	X	X	X	X			?	X	X	X		X	X			X	X
Linkage to performance standards	?	?	X	X			X	X	X	?		X				X	X

Cell key:
X = present
? = unclear
Site key:
PWC = Prince William County
HSD2 = Harrison School District 2
SB = South Brunswick

CM = Cooper Middle
PE = Park Elementary
NB = Ninos Bonitos Elementary
TH = Thoreau High
AC = Ann Chester Elementary
NE = Noakes Elementary
NSP = New Standards Project
PS = Pacesetter

Linkages to Standards.   Assessments also differ in how closely they are aligned with content and performance standards. Some assessments have been designed to be closely linked with the state, district, or school curricular guidelines, whereas others are still in the process of being linked.

Maryland's performance assessments are designed to reflect the state's content and performance standards. Each task and associated scoring method is intended to assess students' attainment of Maryland Learning Outcomes in subject areas such as language arts, mathematics, and science. Each assessment task is accompanied by its own scoring rubric, which specifies the criteria for judging student work on that particular task. Hence, both content standards (through the task the student must complete) and performance standards (through the specific rubric that accompanies each task) are clear to the assessor.

In contrast, Vermont's portfolio assessments are not closely aligned with content and performance standards. Vermont's curricular framework, the Common Core Curriculum, was still being drafted when the language arts and mathematics portfolio assessment requirements were institutionalized, and, hence, the assessment tasks are not necessarily keyed to one specific curricular framework. In addition, the scoring rubrics articulate general skills, competencies, and criteria for evaluating the quality of student performance; they are not tailored to tasks at specific grade levels. Thus, teachers must determine the quality of student performance based on some internalized framework of what constitutes quality student performance at different grade levels.

In summary, the two basic types of performance assessments—task-centered and construct-centered—can be characterized by the extent to which they are integrated with instruction and how well they are linked to content and performance standards. We hypothesize that these assessment dimensions affect the pedagogical usefulness and technical rigor of the assessments: How well the assessment fulfills its intended pedagogical purposes depends on the extent to which it is integrated with instruction, and the technical robustness of the assessment depends on its linkages to content and performance standards.

Performance Assessment Systems

Taken together, the combination of a *task* and a *scoring method* forms a *performance assessment*. A *performance assessment system*, in turn, consists of several (in some cases, only one) performance assessments that are assembled and administered to serve one or more specific, systemwide educational purposes. Associated with the assessments is a set of administration and scoring procedures. Our sample includes performance assessment systems that incorporate performance assessments in one of three ways:

- Performance assessments that use a single type of task (e.g., on-demand tasks) and are administered in more than one subject area.

- Performance assessments that use multiple types of tasks (e.g., on-demand tasks and portfolios) and are administered in a single subject area.
- Performance assessments that use multiple types of tasks and are administered in multiple (integrated or unintegrated) subject areas.

Table 2.5 displays our rough categorization of the assessment systems in our sample, according to these criteria.

Regardless of their composition, performance assessment systems can be classified along two major dimensions: their level of prescription, and the scope of the pedagogical net they cast. The first dimension is a subset of the second; thus, the two are not mutually exclusive. However, they do offer distinct ways of thinking about performance assessment systems, especially from a policy perspective. Next, we describe the two dimensions and classify the performance assessment systems in our sample along those dimensions.

Level of Prescription

Level of prescription refers to the degree of control the teacher has over task specifications, scoring methods and procedures, and assessment implementation procedures and timelines. The tighter the level of prescription, the less control the teacher has with regard to the tasks comprising the performance assessment system; the scoring procedures; and when, where, and how the assessment is to be administered. The reverse is true for a loosely prescribed system.

The performance assessment systems focused on in this study run along a continuum of the level of prescription. Figure 2.6 shows this continuum, from loosely to moderately to tightly prescribed assessment systems, and where performance assessment systems in our sample fall across it.

The pattern of our data suggests that performance assessment systems initiated at the state level for the purpose of system accountability tend to be quite tightly prescribed. When accountability is one of the purposes of the system, states (and some districts) may prefer a tightly or moderately tightly

TABLE 2.5

Sites, by Composition of Sampled Performance Assessment Systems

Single Type of Task, Multiple Subject Areas	Multiple Types of Tasks, Single Subject Area	Multiple Types of Tasks, Multiple Subject Areas
Arizona	South Brunswick	Kentucky
Maryland	Harrison School District 2	Oregon
Vermont	Sommerville High	New York
Prince William County	Pacesetter	Niños Bonitos Elementary
Park Elementary		Thoreau High
Noakes Elementary		Cooper Middle
		Ann Chester Elementary
		New Standards Project

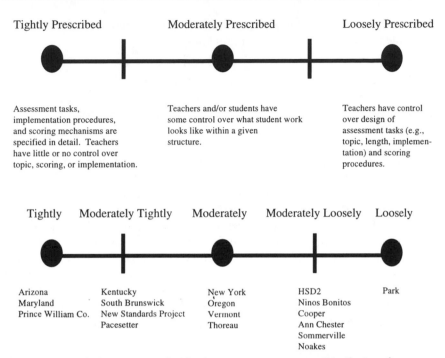

FIG 2.6. Level of prescription of performance assessment systems: Distribution of cases.

prescribed performance assessment system, because these levels of prescription ensure a certain amount of standardization in the development and implementation of assessments. In contrast, assessments developed at the school level for pedagogical purposes tend to be more loosely prescribed (although several states have developed, or, in some cases, fostered the development of, what can be considered to be "moderately prescribed" performance assessment systems).

Next, examples of performance assessment systems that are tightly, moderately, and loosely prescribed are illustrated.

A Tightly Prescribed Performance Assessment System. Maryland's School Performance Assessment Program tests all third-, fifth-, and eighth-grade students in reading, writing, language usage, mathematics, science, and social studies. The tasks, which teachers administer to students as directed by an "Examiner's Guide," last for 9 hours spread over 5 days. Assessment tasks ask students to respond to prompts intended to reveal their process and content thinking. The tasks are developed by a group of Maryland teachers, pilot tested in an out-of-state district, and scored with rubrics by another group of Maryland teachers. The state's assessments are secured. Teachers in this scenario have very little control over the task specifications, scoring methods or procedures, or implementation procedures and timelines.

A Moderately Prescribed Performance Assessment System.   Vermont, in contrast, offers an example of a state-initiated assessment that we would classify as only moderately prescribed. The Vermont portfolio assessment system:

- Requires that all eighth-grade students prepare portfolios in mathematics and writing, all fourth-grade students prepare portfolios in mathematics, and all fifth-grade students prepare portfolios in writing.
- Specifies the types of tasks and the number of tasks to be included in the portfolio, but leaves precise task specifications and the choice of tasks for inclusion in the portfolio up to the student and his or her teacher.
- Provides generic rubrics for math and writing tasks for teachers to use in scoring portfolios. (Teachers score their own students' portfolios, which are then rescored by other teachers in the district to ascertain interrater reliability; about 30% of portfolios are then scored again at the state level, again to confirm the reliability of cross-site scoring procedures.)

Under this assessment system, students prepare work in response to tasks constructed by their teachers. From these assignments, the student and teacher then select pieces for inclusion in the portfolio, according to the state-specified guidelines. Thus, a structure exists, but teachers have the flexibility to design assessment tasks for use in their classrooms and to determine when to assign the assessment tasks. Teachers then score the portfolio assessments by applying state-established generic rubrics to their students' completed work.

A Loosely Prescribed Performance Assessment System.   Finally, a loosely prescribed performance assessment system is being used at the elementary school in New York City included in the study. The Primary Learning Record (PLeR) is an assessment technique, based on a method developed by educators in England and used by teachers to help structure and analyze their observations of students. Analysis of individual observations allows teachers to diagnose children's learning styles, to monitor their progress, and to plan appropriate instructional and curricular strategies. Teachers at the New York City elementary school use the PLeR voluntarily; about half of the school's teachers have chosen to use the PLeR. Furthermore, teachers do not use the PLeR uniformly. For example, some teachers record most of their observations during the school day, whereas others make mental notes of observations that they then transfer to paper after school. Some teachers use the PLeR with only a few students, whereas others use it with all students in their classrooms, and some teachers make sure they obtain observations on every child each week, whereas others are less strict with themselves in this respect. The PLeR, as it is used at this elementary school and other New York City schools, is a record of children's activities maintained by and for the child's teacher. Completed PLeR forms are not handed in to any supervisor.

Summary. Differences across performance assessments in the level of prescription—that is, how loosely or tightly prescribed performance assessments are—can have a dramatic impact on the pedagogical usefulness of the assessment system, at least in the short term. The more tightly prescribed the performance assessment system is, the less room teachers have to use the assessment in their classrooms in ways that make sense to them pedagogically. Conversely, performance assessment systems that are more loosely prescribed allow teachers the room to adapt assessment tools for use in their classrooms. This thesis is further developed in chapter 4.

Scope of Pedagogical Net

A second way in which assessment systems can be characterized is by the pedagogical net they cast.

Scope of pedagogical net refers to the extent to which a performance assessment system collects data on student performance, requires student involvement, samples from different domains of skills and competencies, and requires teacher involvement.

A performance assessment system that casts a wide pedagogical net:

- Collects data on student performance at several points in time.
- Includes tasks that require extended student involvement and elicit a wide variety of skills and competencies.
- Consists of a mix of task- and construct-centered assessments.
- Is moderately to loosely prescribed.

Based on our data, we hypothesize that such performance assessment systems help reform teaching and learning in profound ways, because they have the features—ongoing student and teacher involvement in performance assessments—that are necessary preconditions for developing common assumptions about teaching and learning and, therefore, for bringing about pedagogical changes.

In contrast, a performance assessment system that collects data on student performance at only one (or at a few) point(s) in time; includes tasks that require only limited student involvement; contains assessments that sample only from a limited number of skills and competencies and that are only task-centered; and does not require much teacher involvement in task design, administration, and scoring can be thought of as casting a narrow pedagogical net. A performance assessment system that casts a narrow pedagogical net, places a premium on standardized implementation and scoring procedures, and requires little day-to-day teacher and student input might best be characterized as casting a "measurement net."

The idea of "pedagogical net" differs from the idea of "level of prescription" in that an assessment system can be loosely prescribed (i.e., it may allow a large degree of teacher control over design and implementation), but it still might cast a narrow pedagogical net because it requires little extended student and teacher involvement and does not focus on a wide range of skills and competency demands. Similarly, a system that is moderately prescribed may cast a wide pedagogical net, but the scope of the pedagogical net would depend on how extensively the assessment is used within the classroom and the types of tasks that comprise the assessment system.

At the state level, Kentucky's and Vermont's performance assessment systems cast the widest pedagogical nets, whereas Arizona's and Maryland's cast narrow ones. For example, one component of Kentucky's performance assessment system is a portfolio that requires extended teacher and student involvement with assessments on a regular basis. Kentucky fourth- and eighth-grade students must compile language arts and mathematics portfolios over the course of the academic year. The language arts portfolio requires students to include tasks that reflect different genres and styles of writing, and the mathematics portfolio requires them to include tasks that represent different types of mathematical skills. Therefore, over the course of the year, teachers must devise, assign, and score tasks that represent the full range of portfolio requirements.[7]

In contrast to Kentucky's portfolio assessment system, Maryland's and Arizona's performance assessment systems cast narrower nets. They consist of on-demand tasks that are administered only once during the year, providing little room for extensive student and teacher involvement.

At the district level, Prince William County's Applications Assessments cast a narrow pedagogical net, whereas the other two district-level performance assessment systems cast wider nets, even though both address only specific content or competency areas. At the school level, by design, almost all performance assessment systems and assessments are intended to cast a wide pedagogical net, because most are developed and used by teachers for pedagogical purposes.

---

[7]The Kentucky performance assessment system also includes on-demand tasks that are administered once a year, enabling the state to assess skills and competencies that might not have been assessed through portfolios. Kentucky teachers we interviewed have begun to expand their repertoire of assessments by designing assessments modeled on these on-demand tasks.

TECHNICAL FEATURES

A third major characteristic of performance assessments and performance assessment systems is their technical features. Experts in the field of testing are actively debating the different technical features that performance assessments must possess to fulfill their purposes. The technical features enumerated for performance assessments include not only the traditional technical criteria of content validity and reliability (interrater, internal, and test-retest), but also consequential validity, equity, and generalizability (from scores on individual performance tasks to student achievement and capabilities; Linn, 1993). Furthermore, the notion of content validity criteria has been expanded to include content quality and meaningfulness of performance assessment systems (Herman, 1992; Khattri & Sweet, 1996). We briefly discuss these criteria as they apply to the performance assessments systems in our sample.

For the performance assessment systems included in this study, the answer to the question of how valid and reliable the assessments are in assessing student learning—and how well they are accomplishing their intended purposes—is largely dependent on both the status (i.e., developmental, pilot, implementation) of the performance assessment system and the purposes for which it is implemented. Procedures to determine and ensure the technical robustness of the assessment systems have been established in some cases and not in others, depending on the stage of implementation and the purposes of the performance assessment system. However, it is beyond the scope of this study to evaluate the *validity* and *reliability* of the assessment systems in the sample for the following two reasons:

- The assessment tasks and scoring methods that comprise a performance assessment system are continually changing. Consequently, it is difficult to comment on whether or not a system is valid and reliable. Validity and reliability depend on the quality of the assessment tasks, scoring, and administration procedures associated with the system.
- We did not collect data to the extent that would be necessary to determine a performance assessment system's validity and reliability at any given point in time, because this was beyond the intended scope of our study.

Therefore, we limit our discussion here to: the issues pertaining to establishing the technical robustness of performance assessment systems; and the types of procedures states, districts, and schools in our sample have instituted to establish and monitor the technical quality of their systems. Table 2.6 summarizes the formal evaluation procedures that sites have established for use with their performance assessment systems. In addition, the table provides information about the development of assessment tasks and scoring methods and about who is involved in scoring the assessments.

TABLE 2.6

Sites Having Adopted Various Procedures to Establish Validity and Reliability of Performance Assessment Systems, by Level of Initiation and by Site

	State Level						District Level			National Level	
	AZ	KY	MD	NY	OR	VT	PWC	HSD2	NB	NSP	PS
Validation Procedures											
Content validity	X	X	X		?	?	X	X	X	X	X
Consequential validity		X		?	?	X	X			X	X
Development of Assessment Tasks											
Teachers, onsite		X		X	X	X			X	X	
Offsite		X	X		X		X	X		X	X
Contract with external agency	X	X	X				X	X			
Interrater Reliability Procedures	X	X	X		X	X	X		X	X	X
Development of Scoring Rubrics											
Teachers, onsite				X				X		X	
Offsite		X	X		X	X		X	X	X	X
Contract with external agency	X	X	X				X		X		X
Scoring Procedures											
Teachers, onsite		X		X	X	X	X	X	X	X	X
Offsite	X	X			X	X		X		X	X
Offsite, with teachers	X		X								X

TABLE 2.6 (cont'd.)

| | School Level | | | | | |
	CM	PE	NB	TH	AC	NE
Interrater Reliability						
Procedures		*	x	R		
Validation Procedures						
Content validity		*				
Consequential validity						
Other						

*The assessment in use at Park Elementary has been evaluated in California. However, the validity at Park Elementary (or in New York City) has not been determined.

R = The raters come to an agreement on what score to assign to the students, but this moderation technique is not tied to any external criteria.

Cell Key:
x = present
? = unclear

Site Key:
HSD2 = Harrison School District 2
PWC = Prince William County
SB = South Brunswick
CM = Cooper Middle
PE = Park Elementary
NB = Niños Bonitos Elementary
TH = Thoreau High
AC = Ann Chester Elementary
NE = Noakes Elementary
NSP = New Standards Project
PS = Pacesetter

Validity

Messick (1994) suggested that the major validity question that must be answered for each performance assessment system pertains to the purposes of the assessment and to the substantive domains of interest that the assessment purports to capture. He further suggested that major threats to the validity criteria are construct underrepresentation and construct-irrelevant representation in any given assessment or assessment system. Therefore, he argued, a unified view of assessment validity is necessary, because most of the validity criteria are linked and, therefore, are difficult to disentangle. In agreement with this view, we discuss the validation procedures established for the sampled performance assessments under distinct aspects of the validity criteria—with the understanding that the discussed criteria are not stand-alone aspects of validity; they are linked with each other in predictable ways.

Content validity, assessment meaningfulness, consequential validity, generalizability, and fairness all can be subsumed under traditional criteria of validity. These validity criteria are discussed next.

Content Validity. The sites in our sample use a variety of procedures for ensuring the content validity of their performance assessment systems. Such procedures include, but are not limited to:

- Arriving at a consensus about which domains of competencies and knowledge—content area knowledge, social skills, problem-solving strategies, and multi-disciplinary understanding—are worth assessing.
- Choosing the appropriate assessment format.
- Connecting the assessment tasks to the domains to be assessed.
- Pilot testing and reviewing the assessment tasks and scoring rubrics.

In arriving at a consensus regarding which domains of competencies and knowledge are worth teaching and assessing, states, districts, and schools in our sample have utilized various sources of information and expert help. At the state level, for example, Arizona, Maryland, Vermont, and Oregon have based their mathematics assessment tasks and scoring rubrics on the National Council of Teachers of Mathematics (NCTM) standards for curriculum and evaluation. (New York State's extant mathematics curricular frameworks also are based on the NCTM standards.) Kentucky, Maryland, and Oregon have utilized the American Association for the Advancement of Science guidelines for formulating their curricular frameworks and associated assessment tasks. States also have involved expert teacher committees in reviewing the assessments. In addition, sites at all three levels have sought help from experts in education and testing to formulate their assessment systems.

The sites have tapped outside sources of information to guide the development of their performance assessment systems. Information and expert help used to conceptualize and develop the assessment tasks and scoring rubrics range from local-level teacher involvement to contracts with an external agency. At the state level, testing companies have supplied the expertise to conceptualize, develop, and pilot test the performance assessment systems. At the district level, Prince William County's assessments are developed, pilot tested, and reviewed by a testing company. South Brunswick involves the Educational Testing Service only in evaluating the assessment system, and Harrison School District 2's assessments are locally developed and scored. At the school level, professional groups in education, such as the Coalition of Essential Schools and the New Standards Project, provide information to schools in developing and using their school-based assessment systems.

The national organization, the New Standards Project, is unique in many respects in the developmental work it has undertaken to ensure the technical robustness of its assessment system. It is developing content and performance standards for various subject areas and infusing these standards into its assessment framework. The Coalition of Essential Schools provides the vision and examples of the assessments schools could use, but expects the member schools to develop their own systems based on what they consider to be educationally important for their students. Pacesetter has relied on the NCTM and the Mathematical Association of America standards to develop its mathematics curriculum and assessments.

Arizona, Kentucky, Maryland, and Vermont have established systematic procedures to determine the content validity of their assessments[8]. Oregon and New York are still in the very early phases of development and, therefore, have not yet established rigorous validation procedures. Harrison School District 2 and Prince William County also have instituted pilot-testing and review processes to determine the content validity of their assessment systems, whereas South Brunswick has instituted an annual review of the scoring rubrics and procedures established for the Sixth-Grade Research Performance Assessment. However, it is not possible for us to comment on the extent to which these procedures are effective in boosting construct-relevant variance and minimizing construct-irrelevant variance.

For the assessment systems developed at the school level, validation procedures are not necessarily undertaken in a systematic fashion. Most validation procedures at the school level consist of reviews of face validity of the assessment tasks and scoring rubrics and methods. In the case of Niños Bonitos Elementary, such reviews have been systematized through regular staff meetings and the establishment of clear, agreed-on scoring criteria. In other cases,

---

[8]Please see the full case studies for details regarding these procedures. The case studies appear in, Khattri, Reeve, Traylor, Adamson, & Levin (1995).

teachers use "what works" (i.e., a trial- and- error method), taking that criteria as evidence of the assessments' content validity. In any case, school-level assessments are likely to be closely tied to the curriculum that teachers use in their classrooms, because they are integrated with instruction on a more regular basis.

Meaningfulness. The meaningfulness criterion of assessments extends beyond the content validity of the assessment. Content validity studies are insufficient for determining the meaningfulness of tasks—it is not enough to observe that an assessment item taps into a particular subject area. The meaningfulness criterion refers to the properties that an assessment task must possess in order to motivate students to truly engage in completing the task.

One of the principles of assessment reform is that the assessment tasks that are contextualized in applied or real-world problems will be more meaningful to the student. Thus, several performance assessment systems in our sample contain assessments that are contextualized mathematical and science problems. Whether or not such contexualization works to enhance the meaningfulness of assessment tasks and, therefore, student learning is at present poorly understood. The issue pertains to what types of tasks can be considered to be "meaningful" in a given school environment for a given child. This issue is currently being debated within schools and, indeed, between parents and teachers.

The issue of meaningfulness has not been studied systematically in any of the systems in our sample. Meaningfulness of assessment tasks has been presumed, but not directly evaluated. Thus, Messick's remark (1994) that the terms *authentic* or *direct* assessments "have all the earmarks of a validity claim but with little or no evidential grounding" (p. 14) is applicable to our sample. At least one study (of the California Learning Assessment System mathematics performance assessments) shows that students find open-ended assessment tasks more interesting and challenging than multiple-choice tasks, but they do not necessarily like such challenges (Herman, Klein, Heath, & Wakai, 1994).

Consequential Validity. Consequential validity pertains to whether or not an intervention such as an assessment system achieves its intended purposes. The consequential validity of the sample performance assessment systems is not clear. Most state-, district-, and school-initiated performance assessment systems purport to influence and improve pedagogical practices, and that is the only aspect of consequential validity some sites have attempted to establish.

Studies of Vermont's (Koretz et al., 1993) and Kentucky's (Kentucky Institute for Education Research, 1995) systems show that teachers' instructional practices in those states have been influenced by the assessment systems.

Evaluation of data gathered from teachers in those states indicate that teachers are asking their students to write more and do more collaborative work. Other state-, district-, and national-level systems have not yet systematically evaluated this consequential validity criterion.

At the school level, assessment tasks are used for their pedagogical value; that is, they are used primarily as a teaching tool and as a tool for assessing student performance. In this respect, their *pedagogical validity* is supposedly quite high. For example, the assessments used at Cooper, Ann Chester, Niños Bonitos, and Park Elementary are embedded within daily classroom practices. Teachers design and use assessments to monitor student progress and to modify their curriculum and instruction.

Generalizability. *Generalizability* refers to the inferences one can draw from task-specific performance to the universe of tasks that are associated with the knowledge or skill domain of interest; that is, to what degree is a student's performance on one or a few assessments representative of his or her performance on other, similar assessments or, more importantly, on similar real world tasks? In our sample, only Maryland has systematically evaluated the generalizability of some MSPAP tasks. Thus, based on assessment scores, appropriate inferences regarding student achievement and school and district performance are quite limited.

Fairness. In our sample, to date, Maryland is the only state that has systematically evaluated the fairness of each task in its performance assessment system. Tasks that function differently for different student groups are flagged to inform the development of subsequent tasks. District-level and school-level assessments in our sample have not systematically generated and evaluated such data. In part, they have not done so because of the limited resources available at these levels to conduct such analyses.

Reliability

Interrater reliability procedures are well established for the state- and district-level systems, but not for the school-level systems—where they are not deemed to be very important. The outstanding issue is still that of intertask reliability.

At this phase of assessment development, because of the legacy of the multiple-choice tests, the emphasis on obtaining reliable scoring is quite strong. Among states, the Arizona, Kentucky, Maryland, Oregon, and Vermont performance assessment systems require some form of calibration or moderation activities to ensure reliable scoring of the assessments. Interrater reliability estimates for Vermont portfolios increased between the 1991–1992 and 1993–1994 school years. For Kentucky, interrater agreement increased between the 1992–1993 and 1993–1994 school years.

Among districts, Prince William County employs a testing company to score its assessments, and South Brunswick uses a moderation procedure with its scorers. At the school level, scoring reliability is not generally determined through any systematic procedure (or is expressly ignored in favor of individualizing standards).

The issues related to intertask reliability have not been fully addressed. Studies indicate that performance on one task is often weakly related to performance on another, seemingly related task (Linn, 1993). Experience with licensure examinations in law and medicine show that intertask reliability can be increased only by increasing considerably the number of tasks administered (Linn, 1993). However, among sites included in our study, no intertask reliability studies were available.

Summary

The validity and reliability aspects discussed in this chapter are interrelated. If scoring is inaccurate and the content of the assessments does not adequately and accurately assess what is intended to be assessed, then the ability to draw meaningful inferences from the data these assessments generate is jeopardized. Furthermore, given the emphasis on problem solving and applications in assessment tasks, construct irrelevant variance is especially important to identify in order to draw valid inferences about student performance. Changes from year to year (not necessarily in the overall format of performance assessment systems, but in the actual tasks that form the assessment instrument) preclude evaluating whether or not these performance assessment systems are reliable and valid. What is important to note, at this stage, are the types of procedures that have been instituted to ensure the reliability and validity of the assessments that comprise the performance assessment system. Performance assessment systems' validity and reliability will be better measured in the future as more data become available.

CONCLUSION

The performance assessment systems sampled for this study show that the term *performance assessment* is used to describe a very wide range of student testing instruments and systems. The characteristics of performance assessments show variations in terms of their purposes, formats, and the procedures used to ensure their technical robustness.

Performance assessments are being used for a variety of purposes—ranging from monitoring student progress to holding schools accountable for student outcomes—but the implicit purpose of each of the performance assessment systems sampled for this study is to leverage pedagogical changes at the local level. The stated purposes of performance assessment systems differ, however, according to their level of initiation: School-initiated performance assessments are intended primarily for pedagogical purposes, whereas districts and states also tend to include accountability functions in their stated purposes. The format of the performance assessments in practice also varies greatly, depending on how the assessment tasks and scoring methods are specified. In addition, performance assessment systems show a great variety in how they are to be implemented and used by teachers at the school level. Some are tightly pre-scribed, leaving little room for teacher adaptation, whereas others are very loosely prescribed, giving teachers much leeway in how to adapt the system to their classrooms. Performance assessment systems can also be characterized by the scope of the pedagogical net they cast. Some cast a wide pedagogical net for instructional purposes, enabling teachers and students to be involved with the system on a regular basis and in a variety of assessed areas. Others cast narrower nets, not requiring extended student and teacher involvement or a wide array of assessment tasks or scoring procedures.

The types of technical characteristics performance assessment systems must possess is still under debate. Nonetheless, the states and districts included in this study have instituted procedures to ensure their performance assessment systems' reliability and validity. Although in some cases the results with regard to scoring reliability have been encouraging, evidence regarding the systems' validity is rather slim.

In sum, the samples from our study suggest that performance assessments cannot be classified in one mammoth category; the only commonality among them is the fact that they are non-multiple-choice and are based on the assumption that they are pedagogically useful. Hence, from policy and research perspectives, a number of factors require consideration before an assessment system is implemented or evaluated. Such considerations include a clear state-ment of purposes, coordination between performance assessment systems and purposes, and the establishment of procedures to continually evaluate the technical robustness and meaningfulness of assessment systems. Under-standing the issues involved in assessment design and implementation also should enable educators to understand the issues involved in interpreting assessment scores and drawing inferences about student performance.

3

Facilitators and Barriers in Assessment Reform

As described in the preceding chapter, assessment reform is taking place at multiple levels—national, state, district, and school—with the goal of meeting several purposes:

- Monitoring student progress.
- Holding schools and teachers accountable for student performance.
- Certifying student achievement and skills.
- Aligning curriculum, instruction, and assessment.
- Influencing instructional practices.

These purposes are not mutually exclusive, and any one performance assessment system may be intended to target several purposes at once.

Data collected during our study reveal that several factors function as facilitators or as barriers in the assessment reform process and, thus, as facilitators of or barriers to achieving the stated purposes of performance assessment systems. For example, if a state develops and implements an assessment system for the purpose of certifying student achievement, then a reliable scoring procedure is a facilitator for the intended use of the system. However, if there are technical problems (e.g., low interrater reliability) with the system, then those problems serve as a barrier to using the system to certify student achievement; no system that is technically unsound can be justifiably used for certifying student capabilities.

Our analysis of facilitators and barriers in assessment reform is complicated by the fact that many performance assessment systems—particularly those established at the state level—are intended to achieve multiple purposes, and factors that facilitate the achievement of one purpose may serve as a barrier to the achievement of a second, equally desirable purpose. For instance, a high degree of standardization and technical perfection (i.e., reliability and validity) may facilitate the gathering of reliable student data for monitoring student progress, but the rigidity of the system may serve as a barrier to adapting the system to inform and guide everyday instructional practices.

FACILITATORS AND BARRIERS: ACHIEVING THE STATED PURPOSES OF ASSESSMENT REFORM

This chapter examines the facilitators and barriers in assessment reform vis-à-vis the purposes of assessment reform. The facilitators and barriers in achieving the first four purposes listed earlier are considered in the analysis:

- *Monitor student progress.* Perhaps the most obvious purpose of any assessment system, monitoring student progress toward desired outcomes is an important feature of most assessments developed at any level of initiation.
- *Accountability.* Performance assessments can also be intended to hold schools and teachers accountable for student achievement, either formally through a system of rewards and sanctions, or informally through such mechanisms as reporting school and district performance averages in the media.
- *Certify student achievement.* Some assessment systems aim to certify student skills and capabilities. Satisfactory performance on these assessments may be required for graduation.
- *Align curriculum, instruction, and assessment.* Some national education reform efforts and school-level efforts have focused specifically on achieving better alignment of curriculum, instruction, and assessment; this objective is sometimes an implicit goal of state-initiated performance assessment systems as well.

The final stated purpose of performance assessment systems—to influence instructional practices—is left for consideration in subsequent chapters of this report. Although the first four listed purposes of assessment reform can be conceived of and met outside of the classroom, this last purpose—as well as the ultimate objective of assessment reform, improved student learning—cannot. For this reason, the facilitators and barriers in bringing about instructional change are taken up separately in chapter 4, and the observed impacts of assessment reform on teaching and learning are explicated in chapter 5.

Finally, the analysis in this chapter is organized by the level of initiation of the assessment: state, school and national (considered together because the schools in this study participating in national reform efforts do so because of their own school-level purposes for assessment reform), and district. The analysis is divided according to the level of initiation of the performance assessment because, although some facilitators and barriers in reform are the same at the different levels of initiation, they tend to vary across the different levels in their manifestation and in their impact.

Limitations of the Analysis

The analysis is constrained by several limitations that should be noted at the outset. The first, and perhaps most important, limitation stems from the school-site-level emphasis of the study. Although information was collected about the extent of success in achieving the stated purposes of assessment systems, this information tends to be more detailed for school- and district-initiated assessments than for state-initiated assessments: Information about progress toward attaining state objectives tended to come from documents and general (as opposed to detailed and probing) interviews. Therefore, detailed information pertaining to achievement of purposes may be more complete and reliable for assessments initiated by schools and districts than for those initiated by states.

A second limitation is inherent in the timing and time frame of our study. Because even performance assessments that are being fully implemented are still relatively new, the current study can identify only those barriers and facilitators that have emerged during the early and intermediate stages of assessment development and implementation. Facilitators and potential barriers to sustained reform and to achieving all stated purposes must be identified through further studies.

Third, barriers imposed by the financial costs associated with developing and implementing performance assessment systems can be substantial. However, data concerning this particular barrier at the 16 sites were not uniformly available, and those cost data that were available encompassed different aspects (e.g., costs of assessment development, costs of professional development activities, costs of scoring) of performance assessment systems. This unevenness in data makes it difficult to identify common themes across sites.

Finally, an important caveat must be reiterated at this juncture. Our analyses of facilitators and barriers in the implementation of assessment systems initiated at the state and district levels are based, in part, on documents provided by and interviews with state and district officials, and on the experiences, opinions, and perceptions of individuals associated with a single school within the district or state developing or using the assessment. Although information from state- and district-level documents and from state and district officials is true of the state and district as a whole, the experiences and perceptions of individuals at the school level cannot be taken to be representative of the experiences and perceptions of their counterparts in other schools within the state or district. Still, by comparing data across sites, we are able to identify themes and to formulate understandings of potential facilitators and barriers in assessment reform, even though we cannot generalize the reactions of individuals at a single school to their peers across schools and districts. In other words, this study is not an evaluation of the *status* of reforms in any one state, district, or school; it is focused instead on gaining an understanding of cross-site issues that arise in developing and in implementing performance assessment systems.

FACILITATORS AND BARRIERS: STATE-INITIATED ASSESSMENTS

The six state-initiated performance assessments included in this study—Arizona, Kentucky, Maryland, New York, Oregon, and Vermont—aim to achieve, in some combination, all four purposes under consideration in this section: monitoring student progress; holding schools and districts accountable for student performance; aligning curriculum, instruction, and assessment (this is not an explicitly stated purpose of any of the six state assessment reform initiatives, but it is an *implicit* purpose of several of them); and certifying student achievement. We identified the following facilitators and barriers (depending on their presence or absence) to achieving or making progress toward these purposes:

- Utilization of outside sources of information to guide development.
- Technical soundness (actual and perceived) of the assessment system.
- Coordination with associated reforms.
- Public perceptions of the fairness of the assessment and its consequences.
- Adequacy of the timeline and the politics of reform.
- Professional development provided to teachers.

Table 3.1 summarizes the role played by each of these factors in facilitating or obstructing assessment reform in each state-initiated performance assessment system. In the following discussion, each factor is considered in terms of its impact on attainment of the stated purposes of performance assessments. Note, however, that the impact of each facilitator and barrier can be relatively strong or weak, depending on whether or not other facilitators or barriers are present. In other words, the impacts of these factors, as they serve to facilitate or impede assessment reform, are interdependent. In addition, certain factors serve as facilitators (or barriers) to the achievement of all purposes of assessment reform, whereas certain factors may affect only one or some of the stated purposes.

TABLE 3.1

Factors Facilitating or Obstructing Assessment Reform: State-Initiated Reforms

Factor	Serves as a Facilitator	Serves as a Barrier	Neutral effect (or not Applicable)
Outside sources of information	Arizona Kentucky Maryland Oregon Vermont		New York
Technical soundness of assessment (actual or perceived)	Maryland New York*	Arizona Oregon[+]	Kentucky Vermont (in both cases there are perceived problems but they are outweighed by perceptions of utility)
Perceptions of fairness (to students and schools) of assessment and consequences	New York Vermont	Arizona Kentucky Maryland Oregon	
Coordination with associated reforms or assessments	Kentucky Maryland Vermont	Arizona[•] Oregon	New York
Timeline of reform	New York	Arizona Oregon	Kentucky Maryland Vermont
Professional development	Kentucky Oregon Vermont		Arizona Maryland New York

Note: * New York's assessment is a pilot without much standardization; therefore, it in many ways resembles a local reform effort.

[+]Perceptions of poor technical quality have served as a barrier at the high school level, but not necessarily at the other sites within the district included in the study sample.

[•]Arizona's performance assessment system is aligned with the state's Essential Skills. However, the inconsistency across years in the skills tapped by the assessments led to the accusation that the assessments were invalid and the subsequent derailing of the system.

Utilization of Outside Sources of Information and Expert Help

Outside sources of information and expert help have facilitated the development and implementation of assessment systems (regardless of the purposes of the assessment systems). States have frequently found the legwork previously done by others to be useful in their conceptualization and development of performance-based assessments. In addition, the utilization of expert help in developing and scoring assessments or in evaluating assessment systems has enhanced states' capacity to develop, implement, and track the quality of their assessment systems.

All states in our sample have drawn on extant information resources in both conceptualizing and designing their performance assessments. The usefulness of doing so is clear: Extant information eliminates the need to "reinvent the wheel" at every juncture. For example, four out of the five states—Arizona, Maryland, Oregon, and Vermont—that are assessing mathematics outcomes turned to the National Council of Teachers of Mathematics (NCTM) for assistance in formulating their mathematics curriculum frameworks and in designing assessments in mathematics. Officials and teachers in these states consider NCTM's standards to be among the forefront of standards documents published by professional educators' associations, and these states wanted to benefit from the work already conducted by NCTM.

Similarly, three of the four states—Kentucky, Maryland, and Oregon—using performance assessments in science used the American Association for the Advancement of Science (AAAS) guidelines to conceptualize and design their science performance assessments. In the fourth state, New York, the extant science curriculum framework draws on the AAAS guidelines, but teachers at our New York site did not necessarily utilize new sources of information to determine the content of their assessments.

In addition to utilizing information from professional organizations, several states have contracted with experts in education and measurement to help with the development, evaluation, and scoring of assessments. Arizona contracted with a private test developer, Riverside Publishing Company, to design its performance assessments, thereby easing the development process. Kentucky, Maryland, Oregon, and Vermont hired consultants to help teams of educators and policymakers develop their assessment systems, including developing tasks, scoring rubrics, and standards of performance. Both Arizona and Kentucky continue to contract with testing and measurement firms to score the assessment tasks.

New York's experimentation with waivers allowing schools to develop performance-based assessments to substitute for portions of the Regents Examinations clearly emerges as the outsider in this group of six state-initiated assessments. At this point in time, the New York Department of Education works with schools to ensure that these performance assessments are sufficiently rigorous to serve as substitutes to the Regents, but schools pursuing these waivers are otherwise left to their own devices to seek assistance in the conceptualization, development, and implementation of the assessments. In this regard, New York's initiative behaves as a small, local-level reform rather than a massive state-level change in the state's assessment system.

In sum, the existence of standards and guidelines developed by professional associations has facilitated states' efforts to develop new curriculum and assessment frameworks. The new frameworks, in turn, have provided the basis for designing and developing performance assessments that are consonant with up-to-date understanding of the subject matter. Furthermore, states also have enhanced their ability to develop and design large-scale assessments by seeking help in designing and scoring assessments from testing and in measurement companies and from experts in education and measurement.

Technical Soundness of the Assessment

Another important facilitator (in its presence) and barrier (in its absence) of the state's ability to achieve the intended purposes of assessment reform is the technical soundness of the assessment system. This factor is clearly important to a state's ability to achieve at least three of the four purposes under consideration. Technical soundness of an assessment is crucial to a state's endeavor to:

- Monitor student progress toward desired outcomes.
- Hold schools accountable for student achievement.
- Certify student achievement.

The interdependence of these three purposes is clear: that for which schools are held accountable and those skills for which student mastery is certified clearly must be monitored in some way. Because the technical soundness of assessment systems is discussed in chapter 2, we touch on it only briefly here, focusing specifically on the implications of the public's perceptions (the public both inside and outside the education system) of the technical aspects of performance assessment systems.

The importance of technical soundness is twofold. First, in the absence of construct validity and scoring reliability, student progress toward desired outcomes is not adequately measured. Data generated from the use of these assessments cannot legitimately be used for holding schools accountable or for certifying students. Second, if the state does not establish the assessment system's construct validity and interrater reliability, public confidence in the assessment may deteriorate, thereby derailing the assessment reform process.

In essence, the first of these issues is the problem educators perceive with standardized, norm-referenced, multiple-choice tests: Performance assessments are believed to be a more valid method for assessing the types of skills and competencies that educators want students to learn and demonstrate. Whether or not performance assessments are, indeed, valid and reliable must be determined, and it must be determined with each administration of the assessment. Kentucky and Maryland are using their systems for high-stakes purposes (holding schools accountable for their students' performance) and have instituted measures to ensure the validity of their assessment systems. Oregon and Vermont are at an earlier developmental stage and have not yet established the validity of their systems, although Vermont has instituted measures to improve its scoring reliability. Arizona, on the other hand, instituted validity measures but had its performance assessment system rejected due the perception (and apparent reality) that it was a technically unsound system.

The second issue is that of convincing the stakeholders that a compromise must be made (at least to date and certainly for the foreseeable future) in turning to performance assessments. Stakeholders must believe that (a) *all performance assessment systems* face the barrier posed by sub-perfect interrater reliability, but that interrater differences in scoring can be minimized; and (b) the assessments reveal valuable information about student learning despite problems in standardizing scoring. (Issues of equity, which proponents of performance assessment must also address, are discussed later in this chapter.)

The state-initiated assessment system most hampered by perceived problems with the assessment's technical quality is the Arizona Student Assessment Program (ASAP), which has been hindered in its efforts to monitor student progress toward attainment of the state's Essential Skills because of perceived technical problems with the assessment instruments. Teachers interviewed for this study suggested that the performance assessment contained several technical problems. Specifically, teachers said:

1. The tasks were not valid measures of student abilities.
2. Designing the assessment to audit only a subset of the Essential Skills, a subset that would change yearly, led to incomparable results across years.
3. Standards of satisfactory performance on the assessment had not been established.
4. Interrater reliability in scoring tasks was inadequate.

In response to such objections, the state superintendent suspended the program indefinitely in January 1995.

In contrast to ASAP, other state-initiated systems—including those in Maryland, Kentucky, and Vermont—are considered by teachers and other education constituents to be relatively sound technically, and they have encountered less opposition. Although the performance assessments in these states have been controversial in the past and have attracted some challenges to their technical soundness (particularly in Kentucky and Vermont, where interrater reliability has posed a problem), these states have, to date, successfully addressed concerns by instituting professional development sessions to improve interrater reliability and to convince teachers of the utility of the assessment system. This greater demonstration—and public perception—of validity, reliability, and utility has, so far, led to the continued implementation and acceptance of Kentucky's and Vermont's assessment systems. In addition, Kentucky's public relations campaign during the 1994–1995 academic year has led to greater public acceptance of the system.

It should be noted that the perception of the utility of performance assessments in Kentucky and Vermont—teachers participating in this study find that the use of portfolios has benefitted their classroom practice—can be a counterbalance to the problems associated with interrater reliability. In Kentucky and Vermont, where teachers find value in the state's performance assessment, teachers are more accepting of technical problems than are teachers in Arizona, who find little to value in ASAP (again, in the cases of the three schools participating in this study).

The performance assessments being developed in Oregon and New York are still in the developmental phase. The procedures to ensure the technical soundness of the assessments have, therefore, not yet been fully instituted. However, teachers in Oregon in particular expressed concerns about the content validity of the assessment tasks the state intends to adopt. These concerns are driven by the fact that the state initiated the development of assessment tasks before revising curriculum guidelines to better support the newly articulated student outcomes. Thus, teachers were being asked to develop tasks coordinated with a curriculum that did not yet exist. The anxiety about the technical soundness of the assessment system was particularly acute in Oregon because the assessment system eventually was to be used to certify student achievement[1].

In the case of New York, each school is piloting its own portfolio. Hence, those teachers (as well as others associated with the school) who are developing the assessments believe the assessments to be valid and do not appear to be concerned about interrater reliability.

Coordination with Associated Reforms

Ensuring the compatibility of assessment reform with other related reforms can serve as a potential facilitator in assessment reform. This factor is particularly important when the objective (explicit or implicit) is to align curriculum, instruction, and assessment. It also is important when the objective of the assessment system is to hold schools accountable for student performance.

In theory, coordinated curriculum and assessment reforms should facilitate the implementation of both. At this point in time, coordinated efforts to introduce curriculum guidelines have been most successful in those states in which the efforts clearly reinforce each other and are visible at the local level. They have been less successful when the timing of the reforms has not been in sync or when there has been a lack of linkages with content or performance standards.

The reform efforts of two states in our sample illustrate how coordination of initiatives can facilitate reform: In both Maryland and Kentucky, coordination of performance assessments with associated reforms has served as a facilitator of assessment reform. The Kentucky Education Reform Act of 1990

---

[1]As stated earlier, Oregon's plan was substantially revised in late summer 1995.

established six broad learning goals and a set of academic expectations for all students, and the assessment system is based on these academic expectations. This integration of reforms has, arguably, facilitated the state's introduction of its accountability measures: Because school administrators and teachers know where the state is going, their acceptance of KIRIS is enhanced. Similarly, "Maryland Learning Outcomes" are the bedrock of the assessment system in Maryland. These two states use the results of their assessment systems for accountability purposes, because the assessment system is integrated with a set of articulated outcomes. Coordination of reforms, however, is not in and of itself a facilitator. Teachers' and other constituents' acceptance of other aspects of the reform efforts is an equally important criterion.

Two counterexamples show the tenuousness of coordinated reforms. In Oregon, the state introduced Foundation Skills and Core Applications for Living to guide both curriculum and assessment for the state's Certificate of Initial Mastery. However, the articulation of the skills and applications and the initial progress toward developing performance assessments met with opposition in the state legislature, because the legislature wanted more rigorous content standards infused into the two reforms. Similarly, in Arizona, performance assessments were introduced to audit students' progress toward the state's newly adopted Essential Skills, representing a coordination between elements of reform. However, the technical problems with ASAP rendered moot any advantage of coordinating the reforms.

Actual or Perceived Fairness of the Assessment System

Actual fairness (as determined by objective criteria) and public perceptions of the fairness or lack of fairness of the assessment can also serve as facilitators or barriers in initiating and sustaining assessment reform and, hence, meeting its purposes. (Clearly, the issue of fairness is closely related to perceived technical soundness of the assessment system.) The fairness factor has two dimensions:

- Fairness of assessment systems whose purpose is to hold schools and teachers accountable for student performance.
- Fairness of treatment of individual students in assessment situations (including inclusion of students with disabilities and accommodations made for them and methods of certifying student achievement).

Fairness of Accountability Mechanisms. When accountability systems are "high stakes," the fairness of those mechanisms will come under close scrutiny. Based on some criteria, critics will examine the system to judge whether or not the system deals fairly with schools in the system. In addition, public perceptions of fairness may be based on criteria that are not the same as those employed by objective evaluators or by the education authority itself, but which may nonetheless pose roadblocks in the implementation of performance assessments for accountability purposes.

Two states in our sample—Kentucky and Maryland—have built into their performance-based assessment systems high-stakes accountability mechanisms. Both states have established performance goals for which schools should strive, although Kentucky's goals are for gain scores and differ across schools, whereas Maryland's standards are uniform across all schools. The two accountability systems are summarized in Fig. 3.1.

To date, the Kentucky system (arguably the "fairer" of the two systems because school performance is measured according to gain—not absolute—scores) has drawn more criticism than has Maryland's. However, the state has taken a proactive approach toward identifying any weaknesses in the system. An evaluation of the system commissioned by the Kentucky Institute for Education Research suggested:

> The accountability index is influenced by factors beyond a school's control, but these are not taken into account when the index is interpreted....Among the factors not considered are adequacy of resources, changes in the economic climate of a community, and changes in student mobility....There is concern, but as yet limited evidence, about whether the administration of rewards and sanctions is fair to schools with large numbers of economically disadvantaged students, high turnover rates, or a very small number of students[2].

Kentucky	Maryland
Schools are rewarded or sanctioned based on point differentials between their "biennium accountability index" and the "biennium point threshold" set for each school by KDE. Thresholds were established using 1991–1992 baseline scores that reflect the percentage of the school's students scoring in the proficient range. To avoid sanctions, schools were expected to achieve, over a 2-year period, an average improvement of 18% of the difference between their baseline score and 100. Baseline scores and improvement thresholds are recalculated each biennium. (Note that accountability indices are calculated using four KIRIS components, of which we have examined only two; the other two components are not performance assessments.)	The state has adopted the following school performance standard: For a given school to achieve satisfactory performance in a particular content area/grade level, 70% of students must achieve satisfactory performance. Furthermore, to achieve excellent performance, a school must meet the satisfactory performance criteria and 25% of students must achieve excellent performance. All schools are expected to reach the satisfactory standards by the year 2000. Sanctions have been imposed on five Baltimore schools to date; sanctions will only be used in the future with schools falling far below the satisfactory level.

FIG. 3.1. Accountability systems in Kentucky and Maryland.

---

[2]Evaluation Center, Western Michigan University for the Kentucky Institute for Education Research (1995).

By taking steps to identify potential problems, the Kentucky Department of Education may move to remedy problems and to explain its actions adequately to the public. The ultimate success of these actions remains to be seen. However, parents interviewed for this study said that, although they harbor concerns about the equity of the accountability system, they believe that some such system is necessary.

Maryland's accountability system also has drawn some criticism. District administrators interviewed for this study believe that it is premature to use the MSPAP for accountability purposes, because "The state has yet to pull off a test that is fully comparable one year to the next." (Note that the issue of "fairness" here affects all schools in the state equally.) However, overall complaints about Maryland's intended use of MSPAP for accountability purposes seem to have been few. In both cases, the fairness of the systems for accountability purposes has come under criticism, but in neither case has the barrier been strong enough to derail the assessment system or to dissuade the state from refining the system and continuing to use it for accountability purposes.

Fairness to Students. Perceptions of fairness to individual students also serve as a facilitator or barrier in adequately monitoring student progress and accountability in particular, and other purposes in general. This may be the case especially when certification of student skills is an objective of the assessment, but it is also an important factor in achieving the support of parents for a new assessment, regardless of the purposes of the assessment.

This issue was salient in Maryland and in Kentucky. In Maryland, teachers participating in this study said that the MSPAP presented too great a challenge for students with learning disabilities, and that too many of these students experienced frustration and failure during the assessment. Similarly, in Kentucky, all students regardless of disability are included in the KIRIS, and the work of disabled students is scored according to the same criteria as the work of their nondisabled peers. Teachers suggested that not only was this situation unfair to students, but that the undifferentiated standards led some teachers virtually to do some assignments for their students with disabilities.

In addition to inadequately monitoring student performance, if the assessments do not take into consideration special needs of students, both teachers and parents can raise opposition to assessments if they believe that those assessments treat some students unfairly. In particular, the inclusion of students with disabilities and the accommodations made (or not made) for their participation can lead to dissatisfaction on the part of parents and teachers. Such sentiments were evident at the schools we visited in Maryland, Kentucky, and Vermont. Again, in none of these three cases has this potential barrier been strong enough to derail the assessment reform process.

The Adequacy and Politicization of the Timeline for Reform

The adequacy of the amount of time allowed for development, introduction, and institutionalization of assessment reform can have a dramatic impact on a state's ability to sustain its reform efforts and to meet its various objectives. In particular, sufficient time must be allowed for developing, piloting, and refining assessments and for collecting baseline data if a state is to monitor student progress accurately.

The pressure to produce results is typically intensified when the introduction of the performance assessment takes place in the political realm. Furthermore, changing political climates can threaten the reform.

Three of the six state-initiated performance assessments included in this study resulted from an act of the legislature—those in Arizona, Kentucky, and Oregon. In the case of Oregon, the state department of education, district officials, and teachers worked toward the stated goals of an act of legislation only to have those goals dramatically revised a couple of years later. In 1991, the Oregon legislature enacted the Oregon Educational Act for the 21st Century, mandating, among other reforms, a system of student certification. Four years later, however, the legislature revisited the Act, eliminating the Certificate of Initial Mastery outcomes and replacing them with content standards.

Such vacillations in the elements of a reform effort leave teachers, administrators, and district and state officials with a dilemma regarding how much time and effort they should invest in the reforms. At the schools in Oregon, Arizona, and Kentucky participating in this study, the political uncertainty underlying the performance assessments resulted in teachers' skepticism about the longevity of the new assessments and desired student outcomes. The Oregon high school that had participated in the state's assessment reform effort withdrew from the pilot assessment development project. Teachers at the Arizona school said they would not invest substantial effort on ASAP until it was clear the assessment was "here to stay," and a school board member in the district visited in Kentucky noted that the number of representatives in the Kentucky legislature who supported KIRIS was dwindling and that KIRIS could be dramatically altered or even abolished in the not-too-distant future. In such atmospheres, teachers and administrators we interviewed were cautious about investing their time and effort to support the state's objectives, because those objectives may soon change or be eliminated.

New York's, Vermont's, and Maryland's timelines for reform are, as yet, unthreatened by politicization of their reform efforts. In the case of New York and Vermont, the assessment systems are voluntary. Furthermore, additional components are only gradually being added to the assessment system. In addition, in the case of New York, the reform efforts are primarily local, leaving little room for large-scale disenchantment. In the case of Maryland, the system is mandatory and is being implemented statewide. However, Maryland's investment in public relations, in avoiding sensitive topics, and in involving teachers and local district educators in formulating the system has paid large dividends in terms of the lack of outright public opposition.

Professional Development

Professional development clearly is a critical component of a state's efforts to introduce assessment reform. Our findings indicate that teachers' understanding of the assessment—its purposes, format, pedagogical underpinnings, scoring procedures, and consequences—and their ability to work with the assessment are crucial to progress toward attaining the state's purposes for the assessment system.

Professional development is perhaps most crucial to those assessments that have among their purposes the goal of influencing classroom curriculum and instruction. As has been noted, findings regarding facilitators and barriers in assessment reform with respect to this purpose are discussed in chapter 4, and for this reason the discussion of professional development as a facilitator of reform is cursory in this chapter. In general terms, however, it should be stressed that the professional development provided to teachers typically serves to acclimate them to the new assessment environment, thereby increasing the likelihood that they will sympathize with (or at least understand) the state's other objectives and decreasing the likelihood that they will actively oppose the new assessment.

In the five states introducing performance assessment systems statewide, teachers identified, at a minimum, value in the professional development they received with respect to the mechanics and logistics of the new assessment. Furthermore, teachers in Kentucky and Vermont identified additional, more general value to professional development activities concerning the assessment.

Kentucky's and Vermont's continual refinement and provision of professional development marked a clear shift in the attitudes of the teachers we interviewed in these two states. From one year to the next, teachers said that they had become more comfortable with and more proficient in the use of performance assessments. They also stated that they improved their skills in scoring portfolios during these professional development sessions. By providing professional development opportunities that led teachers to improve their skills in working with portfolios, these two states were also, at least in theory and over time, furthering the technical quality of their assessments in terms of the interrater reliability achieved.

FACILITATORS AND BARRIERS: SCHOOL-INITIATED ASSESSMENTS[3]

School-initiated performance assessments are typically developed to meet four purposes, in some combination:

- To provide feedback to teachers on their instructional techniques and curriculum.
- To monitor student progress and to measure student achievement (traditional or non-traditional methods of grading and reporting on student progress are subsumed under this purpose).
- To obtain diagnostic information about student modes of learning (a purpose that falls under the broader rubric of the first two purposes).
- To align or integrate curriculum, instruction, and assessment.

Our findings suggest that, at the school level, these four purposes are fairly compatible with each other; that is, it is possible to use a single assessment reform to meet all of them. Several factors, however, contribute toward a school's ability to meet these purposes. These factors include:

- Waivers from district testing or reporting requirements.
- Availability of information and resources to support development and implementation of the assessment.
- Availability of time and existence of supporting organizational structures.

Each factor, as it serves as a facilitator or a barrier, is considered next.

Waivers

Waivers can serve as a facilitator of assessment reform by freeing schools from external mandates that are either incompatible with the reform or that compete too much with the reform for limited teacher time. In our sample, three of the four elementary schools involved in nationally or school-initiated, school-adopted assessment reform received waivers from district-mandated report card systems. The one school-initiated high school system in our study has obtained a waiver from district assessment requirements. Waivers obtained by the seven schools that are involved in school- or national-level assessment systems are reviewed in Table 3.2. In addition to the waivers obtained by schools

---

[3]Because district-initiated assessments encounter some of the same facilitators and barriers experienced by states or by schools, those performance assessment systems are considered after an analysis of the facilitators and barriers that face schools initiating performance assessment systems.

TABLE 3.2

Waivers Obtained by Schools

Waiver from District Testing Requirements	Waiver from District Report Card Requirements	No Waivers
Thoreau High	Park Elementary	Cooper Middle
	Niños Bonitos Elementary	Noakes Elementary (no
	Ann Chester Elementary	school waivers from district)
		Sommerville High

from district requirements, the Anton, Iowa school district, of which Noakes Elementary School is a part, applied for and received a 5-year waiver from state requirements to "report measures of student progress" at the time the district elected to participate in the New Standards Project.

These two types of waivers allow teachers to formulate their curricular materials, performance standards, and assessment systems more logically than they believe they could in the absence of the waivers; in turn, they are better able to achieve the purposes stated for school-initiated assessment reforms. Teachers using narrative report cards (as is the case at all three schools with waivers from district reporting requirements) testified to the lack of a link between performance-based assessment and traditional report cards. Teachers at other schools without these waivers expressed the same reaction. For instance, teachers at Thoreau would like to use narrative report cards (and, indeed, briefly experimented with them at one point) but say that the university system in the state was unwilling to work with narrative reports. (Thoreau is one of two high schools among these seven schools. Using narrative reports in lieu of traditional report cards may pose unique problems at the high school level, because colleges and universities seek comparable data about students across schools.) Teachers at Sommerville (the other high school) also identified an incompatibility in assessing students' performance in an alternative way but reporting it in a traditional way.

The problem with not obtaining waivers from testing or reporting requirements is highlighted by Cooper Middle School. Teachers involved in developing and implementing Cooper's extensive performance assessment system testified to the difficulties inherent in teaching their students skills for taking the Iowa Test of Basic Skills (ITBS) while also preparing them for the types of assessments they normally conduct in their classrooms. (The content coverage and the types of skills required for the two types of testing systems are different.) In addition, students spoke about the difficulties in understanding the presentation of their grades by certain subject areas when much of the teaching and learning that goes on in their classrooms is thematic.

Availability of Information and Resources

The most important information resource available to four of the seven participant schools comes through their participation in national-level education reform efforts: Ann Chester and Noakes in NSP, Cooper in CES, and Sommerville in Pacesetter. However, it is important to note that the other three school-level reforms studied here (Niños Bonitos, Thoreau, and Park) also draw on the work of NSP and CES to some extent in developing their performance assessments (Niños Bonitos works with NSP, Park with CES, and Thoreau with both). Teachers at all seven schools are accustomed to seeking information from outside sources and using what they find useful to guide their reform efforts.

Teachers at Ann Chester, Noakes, Cooper, and Sommerville have all participated in the national conferences, symposia, and institutes offered by the national-level reform effort in which each school participates. The impact these professional development opportunities have had on teachers' abilities to construct and use assessment tasks are explored in chapter 4.

The extent to which participation in national reform efforts has fostered each school's ability to change or alter assessments varies across the four schools. At Noakes and Ann Chester, for example, participation in NSP is an integral piece of the school's reform efforts. At Noakes, teachers' adoption of NSP tenets and methods is central to reform; at Ann Chester, NSP is compatible with and supports a district-initiated reform effort, the Applied Learning Program, which focuses on capacity building at the local level.

Similarly, at Sommerville High School, the Pacesetter mathematics program has a dramatic impact on how math is taught to enrolled students, but there is little spillover of the curriculum, instructional methods, and assessment practices from Pacesetter into the school's other math courses. However, this lack of schoolwide impact is not at odds with the school's goal for Pacesetter: to teach math better to a particular group of students.

Cooper Middle School also benefits from the information resources it gains through its participation in the Coalition of Essential Schools, which provides information to support the school's goal of more fully integrating curriculum, instruction, and assessment. For example, Cooper's Rite of Passage Experience and Planning Backwards are based on the Coalition principles. However, the professional training support that Cooper obtains is far less extensive than the support received by the three other national reform effort participants included in this study.

Cooper teachers articulated the need for much more professional development and support on an ongoing basis. The stress generated by the lack of professional support was evident in the decision of Cooper teachers to go back to teaching mathematics in a traditional way, because they felt that they had insufficient mastery in teaching mathematics through thematic units (as they had been doing).

Teachers without ready networks to turn to have also found outside sources of information to be useful as they develop and implement their performance-based assessments. Teachers at Niños Bonitos Elementary School described the difference between developing their school's language arts learning outcomes and portfolio assessment in the late 1980s with developing their mathematics outcomes and portfolio assessment several years later. When they went to work on the language arts assessment, they found no models to guide them. Although they obtained some assistance (from outside experts, including Dennie Wolf and Grant Wiggins) in developing the portfolio assessment, teachers basically worked alone to develop the school's language arts learning outcomes, scoring rubrics, and assessments. In contrast, when they turned to mathematics a few years later, teachers had the resources of the NCTM standards and content areas. They also were able to tap the experiences of colleagues in other schools, because the school was no longer alone in its shift toward performance-based assessment. Niños Bonitos is now refining its assessments and content standards based on the work conducted by the New Standards Project. In addition, the school participates in the National Alliance for Restructuring Education and has access to the expertise and models of educational reform of that organization.

Teachers at Thoreau High School, which pioneered its Rite of Passage Experience (ROPE) more than 20 years ago, "went it alone" for years. (Thoreau's principal tells the story of the school's application to be an associate member of the newly founded CES. The application described the school's Rite of Passage Experience and the philosophy underlying the school, both of which resonated perfectly with the principles on which CES was founded. The principal received a phone call from a dumbfounded Ted Sizer, who asked, "Who are you guys and how did you do all this?") They now participate (in small ways, according to teachers and the principal) in both CES and NSP. However, these teachers are accustomed to doing ROPE their way and remain convinced that they know how to do it best. They say they adopt ideas from CES, NSP, and other efforts they read about, but they are not interested in "swallowing hook, line, and sinker" something new. Teachers at Park Elementary School, also a long-time leader of child-centered education reform, are similarly accustomed to working within their group to identify appropriate methods of integrating assessment with instruction, turning to outside resources as they find them to be useful. For example, the New York City Assessment Network provides the individualized support and guidance Park teachers need in order to adapt the Primary Learning Record to their particular classroom situations.

In each of these seven cases, informal and semi-formal support networks and professional development sessions have facilitated schools' efforts to develop assessment systems.

Time and Organizational Structures

Perhaps the most difficult barrier to confront assessment reform initiated at the school level is finding the time for teachers to design, experiment with, and refine the reform itself. If any single obstacle to assessment reform was mentioned at every site participating in this study (both at the seven sites with school-initiated assessments and at the nine schools involved in district- and state-initiated assessments), it was the factor of *insufficient time*.

In contrast to state-initiated assessment reforms, however, schools do enjoy the luxury of undemanding timelines for introducing the reforms: Although it may be difficult for teachers to find enough time to devote to designing the reform, they are typically not under pressure to introduce it by any specific date. Teachers at Niños Bonitos took 4 years to develop their language arts learning outcomes and portfolio assessment; teachers at Park "dabbled" in using the PLR and joined other teachers who were using it voluntarily if and when they decided the tool would be valuable to the teaching and learning that goes on in their classrooms; and teachers at Thoreau make adjustments to ROPE as they deem necessary, but remain content with the current version until they have time to make changes. In this sense, loose timelines for reform clearly serve as facilitators of reform, or revisions to reforms, taking place over the long run.

However, finding time—both to design and to use—performance-based assessments remains a sizable barrier to assessment reform. In the words of an educator supporting the implementation of the Primary Learning Record at Park Elementary, "Time must be legislated into the school day [or week] to allow teachers to talk to one another, to share their experiences, and to work together to understand what's going on in the classroom." Some schools have addressed such issues by modifying school schedules to provide teachers with more time (through release time or joint planning time) to think about and to develop assessment tasks and rubrics, as well as to plan instruction.

The resource of "time" has been provided on an ongoing basis in some form or another at five of the seven sites involved in school-initiated or national-initiated assessment reform. Common planning time (sometimes in the context of team teaching and sometimes in the context of teacher-initiated "study groups") has been introduced at Cooper, Park, Ann Chester, Sommerville, and Niños Bonitos. In addition, release time—to attend conferences and scoring sessions, or to develop assessment tasks and rubrics—has also been provided by schools to teachers at Sommerville, Niños Bonitos, and Ann Chester. Although teachers lament that they still lack the time to carry out reforms well, they do value the time that is allotted to help them better learn to use performance-based assessments.

At Noakes, teachers participate in districtwide professional development sessions every other Wednesday. However, teachers also invest a fair amount of their own time; as one teacher said, "It [performance assessments] puts stress on our free time, after school time, and weekends." At Thoreau, on the other hand, the assessments are so thoroughly institutionalized that no new schedules or structures have been developed to support the adaption of these assessments. New teachers are inducted into the school's education philosophy and approach by pairing them with veteran Thoreau teachers.

FACILITATORS AND BARRIERS: DISTRICT-INITIATED ASSESSMENTS

The three district-initiated assessments included in this study are so distinct from one another in terms of purposes of the assessments, format, scoring procedures, and the subject areas assessed that it is not possible to identify a set of common facilitators and barriers that pertain to district-initiated assessments. Rather, each of the three assessment reform efforts initiated at the district level shares some characteristics with assessment systems introduced at either the state or the school level. Therefore, in this section, we:

- Describe facilitators and barriers experienced at each of these three sites.
- Show how those facilitators and barriers encountered by districts do and do not resemble the facilitators and barriers of state- and school-initiated assessment reforms.

Each of the three district-initiated performance assessment systems is considered separately.

Prince William County: Applications Assessments

As noted in chapter 2, the Prince William County Public Schools' Applications Assessments were in the pilot and initial implementation phase at the time of this writing. The purposes of the assessments are to monitor student progress and to influence instruction. The major barrier thus far to both of these objectives is that the district's curriculum frameworks are not yet fully revised. Although all reforms are being guided by the district's Quality Management Plan and the six Standards of Quality, the concrete curriculum goals have not as yet been finalized. Furthermore, most teachers at the middle school included in this study were not aware of the substance of the new curriculum frameworks.

A second factor that might work against the goals of the assessment system is the lack of professional development in how to use the assessments for instructional purposes in the classroom. Putting assessment reform before revisions to curriculum frameworks has left teachers wondering about the future of the assessment and about just what they should be emphasizing in their classrooms. However, it must be emphasized that assessment development and administration is in the early stages in Prince William County. Hence, the potential barriers in this early stage may very well be hurdled down the road.

South Brunswick: Sixth-Grade Research Performance Assessment

The South Brunswick Township Public Schools' Sixth-Grade Research Performance Assessment is intended to assess sixth graders' research skills and to align instruction with curriculum to teach research skills. The district's specification of the research skills that sixth graders should master, coupled with the perception that the schools were not graduating students with adequate research skills, served as a facilitator of the development of the assessment. In addition, technical help from the nearby Educational Testing Service facilitated the design of the assessment.

A potential barrier to the continual success of the assessments is that the assessment may be unfair to students with disabilities, because procedures for implementation and the scoring criteria are identical for all students, and no special arrangements are made for students with disabilities. Nonetheless, because of the low-stakes nature of the assessments, this potential barrier has not served to change the assessment purposes or the assessment format. As a result, district teachers fine-tune the assessments on an annual basis and continue to experiment with the scoring and implementation procedures of the assessment.

Harrison School District 2: Performance-Based Literacy Assessments

Harrison School District 2's Performance-based Literacy Assessments are intended to monitor student performance, to teach students to become self-assessors, and to serve accountability purposes. The impetus for reforming the district's language arts curriculum derived from the state's requirement that every district in the state develop standards-based education in reading and writing by the 1994–1995 academic year. (The state's requirement in other areas has a longer timeline.)

Given the state mandate, the district developed a detailed language arts curriculum that provided the basis for designing the aligned assessment system. Each assessment is keyed to one of the district's 13 significant student outcomes appropriate for the developmental level of students at different grade levels. In addition, the district involved every language arts teacher in the process of reforming the curriculum and also sought the help of experts in performance assessment in designing the coordinated system. Next, the district provided teachers with professional support (a peer coach model within schools) and development (through an "Assessment Academy") as well as assessment tasks to use in their classrooms.

In order to meet the purpose of teaching students to become self-assessors, the district devised scoring rubrics specifically for student use, and in order to meet the accountability purpose, the district devised scoring rubrics for teachers. Teachers use their scoring rubrics to assess student work and to report student scores to the district, and students use their scoring rubrics to assess themselves. The district, however, reports aggregate scores back to schools and does not use the results for high-stakes purposes.

The combination of aligned reforms, professional development, and use of assessment results for feedback purposes has resulted in a relatively smooth reform process. In addition, the state requirement for locally determined, standards-based education provided the essential framework for the reform to be initiated.

The two barriers to effective implementation of the performance assessments teachers most often noted, however, were the lack of time and the lack of effective instructional models. An additional barrier both district and school administrators noted was that the parent community is not ready for narrative report cards because they continue to expect traditional grading. However, because the district is taking a long-term view of the reform process, this barrier is not a salient one for the Harrison education community.

CONCLUSION

Our study findings indicate that several factors function either as facilitators or barriers in the assessment reform process, depending on their presence or absence. These facilitators and barriers either enhance or restrict a state's, school's, or district's capacity to design, develop, and implement assessment systems to meet certain purposes.

To reiterate, the factors that serve as facilitators or barriers at the state level are:

- Utilization of outside sources of information to guide development.
- The actual and perceived technical soundness of the assessment.
- Public perceptions of the fairness of the assessment and its consequences.
- Coordination with associated reforms.
- Reasonableness of the timeline and the politics of reform.
- Professional development provided to teachers.

These factors, however, do not function independently. Our study indicates that the potency of any one factor depends, in part, on the presence and strength of other factors. For example, even if an assessment system is designed and based on content standards, the perception that it is unfair may undermine its credibility (e.g., Arizona's performance assessment system). Thus, the system may not be used for accountability purposes.

At the school level, the factors that serve as facilitators and barriers in assessment reform are:

- Waivers from district testing or reporting requirements.
- Availability of information and resources to support development and implementation of the assessment.
- Availability of time and existence of supporting organizational structures.

The presence of these factors serves as a facilitator in assessment reform, whereas the absence of these same factors serves as a barrier. Assessment at the school level is intended primarily for monitoring student progress and for improving pedagogical practices. Hence, when teachers obtain time, support, and freedom from certain regulations that are antithetical to assessment reform, they are much better able to design systems that are tailored to meet their own classroom needs.

Our sample of district-level assessment initiatives indicates that the kinds of facilitators and barriers that districts experience can be similar to those that states face (although on a smaller scale), or similar to those that schools face. In large part, the existence or absence of various facilitators and barriers is reflective of the district's purposes in introducing assessment reform.

In the next chapter, we extend further our analysis of the facilitators and barriers in assessment reform by focusing on the factors that support or impede the purposes of assessment reform at the school and classroom levels. Specifically, we explore the factors that affect teachers' abilities to use performance assessment technologies to guide meaningful changes in their teaching practices.

4

Teacher Appropriation of Performance Assessments

Where the previous chapter focused primarily on facilitators and barriers in assessment reform outside the classroom, this chapter looks at facilitators and barriers in assessment reform at the classroom level. The ultimate objective of any educational reform is to improve student outcomes. Based on the findings and inferences we can draw from our data, we suggest that: for learning to improve, instruction must change; for meaningful instructional change to result from assessment reform, teachers must "appropriate" assessment technologies; and teacher appropriation of assessment technologies is fostered or impeded by a variety of factors, including:

- Teachers' level of involvement in the design and implementation of the assessment system.
- The level of prescription of the assessment system, including assessment tasks and implementation procedures.
- The type and extent of professional development provided to teachers with respect to the assessment and its intended objectives.
- The presence or absence of other, complementary or competing, education reforms and assessment systems.
- School organizational structures that support or hinder teacher use of the assessment.

Figure 4.1 illustrates the posited relationship among student learning, pedagogical change, teacher appropriation of assessment technologies, and facilitators and barriers in that appropriation.

As is clear from the analysis that follows, each of these factors can serve either as a facilitator of or a barrier to reform, depending on its presence or

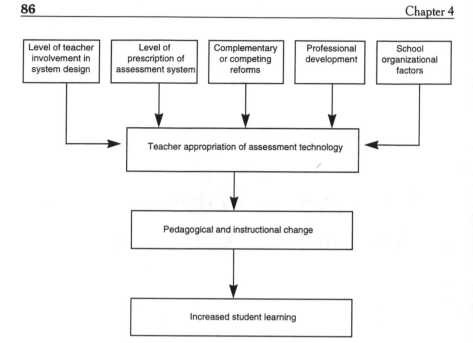

FIG 4.1. Factors affecting changes in teaching and learning.

absence and its manifestation. Furthermore, because variation in these factors often parallels the level of initiation of an assessment, the level of initiation can be used as an organizing factor in analyzing the effects of these facilitators and barriers. For example, teachers' involvement in developing and implementing state-initiated performance assessments tends to be more limited than it is in district- and school-initiated assessments. In addition, the extent to which assessments are tightly or loosely prescribed also tends to follow the level of initiation, with states introducing more tightly prescribed systems than do districts and schools. Where assessment system characteristics tend to vary according to the level of initiation, the discussion is organized in terms of state-, district-, and school-level assessments.

Finally, it should be reiterated that this discussion of teachers' appropriation of assessments is based on the information collected at the 16 schools participating in this study. Findings concerning teachers' appropriation of state- and district-initiated assessments cannot be generalized to teachers outside the participant schools. However, we have identified patterns of teachers' experiences with state-, district-, and school-initiated assessments across the sites.

Teacher Appropriation Defined

In this chapter, we investigate and discuss the impact of several characteristics of performance assessments on the extent to which teachers appropriate an assessment technology in their classrooms. By *appropriation* we mean a host of uses teachers may make of and attitudes they may hold toward performance assessment technologies. To summarize, these uses and attitudes include:

- *Uses of the assessment technology.* Does the teacher use the assessment regularly in his or her classroom? Has the teacher modeled his or her own assessments after the new assessment? How often does the teacher use these assessments? Does the teacher use information provided by the assessment to guide instructional strategies?
- *Attitudes toward the assessment.* Does the teacher believe the assessment provides valuable information about:
  - Students' progress and achievement?
  - Students' learning styles?
  - The effectiveness of instructional strategies and curriculum?

Figure 4.2 provides definitions and examples of what, for the purposes of this chapter, we designate high, moderate, and low levels of teacher appropriation of performance assessment technologies.

Level of Initiation and Mediating Factors (Facilitators and Barriers)

Manifestations of facilitators and barriers in teacher appropriation of assessment technologies can, to a great extent, be predicted by the level of initiation of an assessment. In other words, the level of initiation of an assessment is closely associated with the extent to which teachers appropriate assessments. However, this relationship is more satisfactorily explicated by examining the effects of the five factors under consideration, which themselves tend to vary with the level of initiation of an assessment as well. Table 4.1 illustrates the relationship between teacher appropriation and the level of initiation of the assessment. In the balance of this chapter, we explore each of these five factors as they facilitate or impede teacher appropriation at our 16 sites.

LEVEL OF INVOLVEMENT

The first factor that influences teacher appropriation of an assessment is the extent to which teachers are involved in the design and implementation of the assessment system. Teacher involvement can be present or absent at many stages of assessment development and implementation, including: the design of assessments and assessment tasks; the development of scoring rubrics and the establishment of standards of performance; and participation in scoring the assessments. Table 4.2 operationally defines high, moderate, and low levels of involvement in assessment design, standard setting, and scoring. It also sum-

High Level of Appropriation—Teachers use an assessment technology, or their own modified version of it, regularly. Alternatively, especially in the case of assessments developed outside the school building, teachers have modeled some of their in-class assessments on an assessment technology. Teachers value the information the assessment provides about their students' learning or their own teaching, and they use this information in one or more of a variety of ways, such as monitoring student progress and obtaining instructional feedback. These teachers also have typically modified some of their teaching practices to place greater emphasis on the types of skills and competencies emphasized by the assessment.

Example—Teachers at Niños Bonitos Elementary School have developed and fully appropriated a system of performance-based assessment in language arts that is thoroughly integrated with instruction. Teachers develop tasks for assessing students' emerging language skills, and they judge students' achievement on these tasks using generic language arts rubrics tailored to reflect achievement at different stages of English language learning. Children's growth is further monitored through the compilation of a language arts portfolio (which is stored electronically as well as in original paper form). All teachers in the school use the language arts rubrics and portfolios to assess their students' achievement, and they insist that the information they collect is vital to their ability to understand and plan for individual students' learning.

Moderate Level of Appropriation—Teachers may occasionally use a new assessment technology, but they are not yet clear on how it fits into their instructional system. Alternatively, teachers may value the information provided by an assessment introduced from outside the school but still not model their own in-class assessments to resemble the new assessment technology. In general, teachers who have moderately appropriated an assessment are open-minded about its utility but remain uncertain about how they can best use it (sometimes because of a dearth of models available to help teachers learn how to incorporate new instructional and assessment techniques into their classrooms).

Example—Teachers at McGary Elementary School in Colorado Springs, Colorado, have moderately appropriated their district's performance-based literacy assessments. Teachers use the assessment tasks, as they are required to do by the district, and they are beginning to modify their instructional techniques (e.g., providing more cooperative learning activities) in response to their increased understanding of how to assess student achievement. However, teachers are less clear on how they should interpret the information about students' learning generated by the district's assessment tasks, and they apparently are not modeling their own assessments after the district-developed tasks. In sum, teachers are beginning to identify value in the district's assessments but have not yet fully made them a model for classroom assessment practice.

FIG. 4.2. Levels of teacher appropriation of assessment technologies.

Low Level of Appropriation—Teachers do not use an assessment technology, or they use it only when required to do so. They do not value the information generated by the assessment, and they have not modeled their own assessment practices on it or modified their instructional practices to any appreciable degree.

Example—Teachers at Manzanita High School in Arizona have not appropriated the state's system of performance assessment at all. Although they devote 1 to 2 weeks of class time to preparing students for the ASAP, they see this as lost time—time that could be better spent teaching other material. Teachers also say that the information that ASAP provides about their students is not valuable (some also suggest it is misleading), and they do not base their classroom assessment practices on the state's model.

FIG. 4.2 (cont'd.)

marizes the extent of teacher involvement in each of these three areas as experienced at each of the 16 participating schools. Table 4.3 summarizes the coincidence of the levels of teacher involvement and appropriation. Examples of how the extent of teacher involvement in assessment design and implementation can affect teacher appropriation follow.

Design of Assessment Tasks

The level of initiation of an assessment to a great degree determines the extent to which teachers are involved in the development of assessment tasks. School-

TABLE 4.1

Teacher Appropriation of Assessments by Level of Initiation

	High Appropriation	*Moderately High Appropriation*	*Moderate Appropriation*	*Moderately Low Appropriation*	*Low Appropriation*
State		Breckenridge (KY) Hudson (NY) Maple Leaf (VT) Windermere (SB) Sommerville	Crandall (OR)	Walters (MD)	Manzanita (AZ)
District			McGary (HSD2)	Westgate (PWC)	
School	Ann Chester Cooper Niños Bonitos Noakes Park Thoreau				

TABLE 4.2

Extent of Teacher Involvement in the Assessment Design Process

Teacher Involvement in	High Level of Involvement[*]	Moderate Level of Involvement[+]	Low Level of Involvement[•]
Designing assessment tasks	Cooper (school) Noakes (school) Ann Chester (school) Niños Bonitos (school) Thoreau (school) McGary (district) Windermere (district) Crandall (state) Hudson (state)	Sommerville (school) Westgate (district) Breckenridge (state) Maple Leaf (state)	Park (school) Manzanita (state) Walters (state)
Developing scoring rubrics and setting standards of performance	Cooper (school) Park (school) Niños Bonitos (school) Thoreau (school) McGary (district) Hudson (state)	Westgate (district) Crandall (state) Noakes (school) Ann Chester (school) Sommerville (school)	Breckenridge (state) Manzanita (state) Maple Leaf (state) Walters (state)
Participating in scoring	Park (school) Thoreau (school) Niños Bonitos (school) Noakes (school) Ann Chester (school) Cooper (school) McGary (district) Crandall (state) Maple Leaf (state) Breckenridge (state) Hudson (state)	Manzanita (state) Walters (state)	Windermere (district) Westgate (district)

[*]Teachers are responsible for designing or implementing the particular aspect of the assessment, individually or in cooperation with their colleagues.
[+]Teachers are involved in designing or implementing some, but not all, aspects of the assessment; or teachers are turned to for feedback about an assessment designed by others; or teachers are represented in design and implementation, but most teachers are not involved.
[•]Teachers are not involved in designing or implementing the particular aspect of the assessment.

initiated assessments, almost by definition, involve teachers in the development of assessment tasks. What is more, all or most of a school's teachers, not just a few, will be involved in the development process. Teacher appropriation of assessment tasks they develop, use, and score is clearly quite high. For example, teachers at Niños Bonitos, Cooper, and Thoreau all clearly demonstrated their appropriation of their respective assessments. These teachers repeatedly stressed, in particular, their belief in the high instructional and content validity of the assessments they have developed for use with their students. Further-

TABLE 4.3

Teacher Appropriation, by Level of Involvement*

	High Appropriation	Moderately High Appropriation	Moderate Appropriation	Moderately Low Appropriation	Low Appropriation
High Involvement	Ann Chester Cooper Niños Bonitos Noakes Thoreau	Hudson	Crandall McGary		
Moderate Involvement	Park	Breckenridge Maple Leaf Sommerville Windermere		Westgate	
Low Involvement				Walters	Manzanita

* Note: Overall "involvement levels" were determined by assigning each participant school a score of 1, 2, or 3 for each of the three involvement areas—1 for low, 2 for moderate, and 3 for high. Therefore, total involvement scores could range from 3 to 9. For example, teachers at Breckenridge had a moderate level of involvement in design of assessment tasks (2), low involvement in setting standards (1), and high involvement in scoring (3), for a total score of 6 on the involvement scale. Total scores of 3 and 4 are interpreted as "low," 5 to 7 as "moderate," and 8 and 9 as "high" on the overall level of involvement scale.

more, teachers who have developed assessments for use at their schools testify to the value the development process has for teachers. Teachers at Noakes, Niños Bonitos, and Cooper, for example, all stated that the development process has helped them reflect on and articulate the types of skills they want to foster in their students, and to identify and understand the evidence necessary to demonstrate students' acquisition of those skills.

Involving teachers in the development of assessment tasks is a more difficult endeavor for state departments of education designing new assessment systems. Even in states that have included teachers in the development process, only a small fraction of teachers are involved. Thus, teachers are less familiar from the beginning with assessments initiated at the state, and even district, level. Occasionally, this isolation from the development process can induce a markedly negative response from teachers. For example, one teacher commented about the Arizona Student Assessment Program, "I don't understand why they went to the so-called 'experts.' We're the experts. They should have come to the teachers and asked us to develop it."

In contrast, there are some examples of state assessment programs that foster teacher development of assessment tasks. In New York, for instance, the state has allowed schools to petition to replace portions of the Board of Regents Examinations with teacher-developed assessments. Teachers at Hudson High School have developed alternative performance assessments for use in English, social studies, earth science, and biology courses. Students who choose to enroll in these classes take these assessments as a waiver for up to 35% of the Regents Examination in the given subject area. Teacher appropriation of the assessments in this instance is quite high, as evidenced by teachers' voluntary contribution of hours and hours of their own time to what one of them has called their "labor of love."

In between these two cases of high and low teacher involvement in the design of state-level assessments are the experiences of teachers at Breckenridge in Kentucky and Maple Leaf in Vermont. Teachers at these two schools were not involved in either the decision to introduce performance assessments statewide or the process of developing the structure of the assessment systems. (Although both state departments of education did include some teachers in the development process, no teachers at Breckenridge or Maple Leaf were involved.) However, within the two states' portfolio assessment systems as developed, teachers are required to develop assessment tasks that adhere to specified criteria. This involvement in specifying assessment tasks has encouraged teachers to work actively with the states' assessments, resulting in a fairly high level of appropriation of the portfolios required by the systems.

Development of Scoring Rubrics and Establishment of Performance Standards

Closely related to the development of assessment tasks is the establishment of scoring criteria for those tasks (e.g., scoring rubrics) and standards for student performance on assessments. Teacher involvement in setting those criteria and standards can be an important facilitator of appropriation of the assessment. Teachers who are involved in developing scoring rubrics and setting performance standards are more likely, in general, to have confidence that the skills being assessed and the standards to which students are being held are developmentally appropriate. This confidence, in turn, fosters appropriation of the assessment technology.

Teacher involvement in developing scoring rubrics and performance standards at the 16 participant schools falls into three categories. Within the first two of the three categories, the criteria and standards vary in terms of their uniformity (i.e., whether the criteria and standards are applied uniformly to all students' efforts or are allowed to vary across students). The three categories are:

- Teachers are highly involved in establishing scoring criteria and performance standards:
  - Scoring criteria or performance standards do not exist as a uniform set of standards, but rather are a function of teacher judgment and discretion.
  - Scoring criteria or performance standards are uniformly applied to the efforts of all students.

- Teachers are moderately involved in establishing scoring criteria and performance standards: Scoring criteria or performance standards are developed by teachers for some assessment tasks and not for others.
- Teachers are not involved in establishing scoring criteria and performance standards.

In addition, in the second two cases—when teacher involvement is only moderate or low—the clarity of the criteria or standards is sometimes low from the teachers' perspective, thereby inhibiting teacher appropriation. The effects on teacher appropriation of (a) teacher involvement in the establishment of scoring criteria and performance standards, (b) the uniformity or flexibility of application of criteria and standards across students, and (c) the clarity of criteria and standards are explored next.

Teachers are Highly Involved in the Development of Scoring Criteria and Performance Standards.   In cases in which teachers are involved in the development of scoring criteria or performance standards, teachers have demonstrated fairly high levels of appropriation of the assessments. This finding holds for both cases in which criteria and standards are left to teacher judgment and cases in which criteria and standards are applied uniformly to all students' efforts.

Teachers who work with assessments without uniform scoring criteria or performance standards are, by definition, involved in the setting of standards for student performance. For example, at Thoreau, all teachers are involved in the senior-year portfolio and performance event process. Teachers not only have the freedom to design the details of the assessment as they desire, but, additionally, they openly acknowledge (and students know this as well) that their standards of performance are not uniform across students: Teachers expect better performances from their better students, and they hold them to the standards they believe the students are capable of achieving.

In cases, too, where teachers have developed a set of scoring criteria or performance standards to be applied to all students, appropriation of the assessment technologies remains high. For example, at Niños Bonitos Elementary, scoring rubrics developed by some of the school's teachers are used to assess students' English literacy growth; every child within a homogeneously grouped language arts class is assessed according to the same rubric. Teachers at Niños Bonitos are confident of the effectiveness of the approach to teaching and assessing English language literacy they have developed, and all teachers in the school use the system. Similarly, all sixth-grade teachers in the South Brunswick Unified School District meet multiple times during each school year to review the district's Sixth-Grade Research Performance Assessment scoring rubric, which sets both scoring criteria and standards for the assessment.

Although teachers do not score their students' performances themselves, they are centrally involved in developing the standards of performance. These teachers also give testimony to their appropriation of the district's assessment technology, noting that they have introduced their students to many similar research and demonstration assessments over the course of the school year.

Teachers are Moderately Involved in Establishing Scoring Criteria and Performance Standards.

Teachers are Moderately Involved in Establishing Scoring Criteria and Performance Standards.   Teachers at several schools (Noakes, Ann Chester, Westgate, Sommerville, and Crandall) are, in our terms, "moderately" involved in developing scoring criteria and performance standards. In terms of the level of involvement in developing these features of assessment systems, these teachers have typically been involved in developing some part, but not all, of the scoring criteria and performance standards, or have been involved in setting criteria or standards for some assessment tasks but not others within the assessment system. Although teacher appropriation of performance assessments runs from moderate to high at four of these five schools (the exception being Westgate), being further removed from the process of setting scoring criteria and performance standards has served as a barrier to appropriation in at least two of these cases.

Pacesetter teachers at Sommerville are responsible for developing their own criteria and standards for their in-class use of the Pacesetter program, but they are not involved in developing either aspect of the College Board's uniform end-of-the-year performance assessment, administered to all Pacesetter students. These teachers expressed reservations about the appropriateness of some of the standards and the applicability of some of the task-specific rubrics used to score the assessments.

Teachers at Crandall High School, as part of the development work they agreed to undertake for Oregon's performance assessment system, also reviewed and refined the generic scoring rubric that was to be applicable for all math and science tasks developed by teachers throughout the state. Teachers found this task confusing, primarily because the rubric was divorced from actual tasks and, more importantly, from content standards and curriculum frameworks, which remained to be developed by the state. This incompatibility of criteria and standards made it hard for teachers to work with the assessment system as a whole and, consequently, to appropriate it.

For teachers at Noakes and Ann Chester Elementary Schools who used New Standards Project assessment tasks and rubrics with their students (among other assessments), the lack of involvement in development of scoring criteria did not serve as a barrier to appropriation of assessments. This finding is probably attributable to the fact that teachers at those schools chose voluntarily to become involved with NSP. Furthermore, interpretation of the NSP rubrics remained at the discretion of the individual teacher at both schools, fostering appropriation of the assessment (both schools, however, aim to achieve common understandings across teachers of what evidence establishes accomplishment of what performance level, but teachers are actively involved in developing that common understanding).

Finally, some teachers at Westgate Middle School were involved in the establishment of performance standards for the district's Applications Assessments, although not in the development of scoring criteria for assessment tasks. However, this involvement did not remedy teachers' perceptions that some of the assessment tasks and scoring criteria expected levels of performance from students that are developmentally inappropriate. For example, a seventh-grade math teacher said that she planned to teach her students how to work with percents earlier in the year because the topic had been emphasized on the previous year's seventh-grade mathematics assessment. She did not, however, believe it was appropriate to teach her students these new concepts before she had laid a foundation for them, and yet she felt compelled to do so against her better judgment.

Teachers Are Not Involved in Establishing Scoring Criteria and Performance Standards.
In several schools working with state-initiated performance assessments, teachers have not been involved in the development of scoring criteria or the establishment of performance standards, and this lack of involvement tends to serve as a barrier to teacher appropriation of performance assessments.

In the case of teachers at Breckenridge Middle School in Kentucky, teachers believe some of the performance standards to be developmentally inappropriate. As with Westgate teachers who felt the same way about their district's assessment, this skepticism serves as a barrier to teachers' appropriation of the assessment.

In one instance, teachers at Manzanita High School in Arizona were unaware if performance standards exist for the assessment. (Although teachers are familiar with the types of scoring rubrics used, they assert that no overall standards for performance on the ASAP's performance assessment exist.) In this case, teachers expressed skepticism about the value of the assessment and the assessment reform effort. For example, one teacher commented about ASAP, "How can we take this assessment seriously if we haven't even decided yet what a passing score is?" Quite clearly, teachers who find themselves unable to take an assessment seriously cannot possibly be said to have appropriated it.

Participation in Scoring of Assessment Tasks

In general, teachers who are regularly involved in scoring assessments have more opportunity, and perhaps propensity (because in some cases participation in scoring is voluntary), to appropriate assessment mechanisms than do teachers who are not. For example, at Maple Leaf and Breckenridge in Vermont and Kentucky, all teachers of students in the grade levels assessed are involved in scoring portfolios (and at Breckenridge, other teachers help score portfolios as well—e.g., sixth- and seventh-grade math teachers help the eighth-grade math teachers score math portfolios). Regardless of teachers' positive and negative feelings toward other aspects of the assessment systems in those states, teachers comment that participating in scoring not only helps them to understand the assessment system better, but also helps them understand better how to adapt what they do in their classrooms to support and reflect the assessment system.

Similarly, the College Board's Pacesetter mathematics culminating assessment is scored during a single scoring session attended by all teachers participating in the program. Pacesetter teachers at Sommerville High School asserted that their participation in these reading sessions gave them a much better sense of the objectives of the assessment and of how the rubrics were applied to assessment tasks.

In other instances, however, teachers are less involved in the scoring process, and have typically not appropriated the assessment technology. For example, only a few teachers at Walters and Manzanita in Maryland and Arizona have been involved in scoring assessments. Similarly, in Prince William County, Virginia, all assessments are scored outside of the district by a private corporation. Teachers involved with these three assessments feel removed from the scoring process and from the appropriation of the assessment technology that participation might foster.

Summary

To some extent, the level of teacher involvement in developing and implementing assessment systems is little more than a reflection of the level of initiation of the assessment. Necessarily, states and districts cannot include all teachers in these endeavors. However, insofar as a goal of assessment reform is to effect instructional change, it is clear that a low level of involvement in the development and implementation processes does impede the appropriation that will ultimately lead to changes in teaching practice. From comments of teachers at several schools working with state-and district-initiated assessments (e.g., teachers at Breckenridge, Maple Leaf, and Windermere), a hypothesis can be supported that the converse is also true: Teachers who are involved in some part of the development (Windermere) or implementation (Maple Leaf and Breckenridge) process gain knowledge about the assessment, grapple with the nuances of learning involved, and, subsequently, begin to appropriate the new technology.

LEVEL OF PRESCRIPTION OF ASSESSMENT TASKS
AND IMPLEMENTATION PROCEDURES

Differences across performance assessments in the level of prescription—that is, how loosely or tightly prescribed assessment systems are—can have a dramatic impact on teacher appropriation of assessments. In general, the more tightly prescribed an assessment system, the less likely teachers are to appropriate it, and vice versa. To summarize the discussion in chapter 2 of characteristics of high, moderate, and low levels of prescription:

- *Tightly prescribed assessment systems* are characterized by implementation procedures and scoring mechanisms that are specified in detail. Teachers have little or no control over assessment task specification or implementation.
- *Moderately prescribed assessment systems* are characterized by prescribed structures of assessment tasks and implementation procedures within which teachers have some control over what student work looks like (e.g., students must write an expository essay, but teachers may choose the essay's topic, length, and time frame for completion).
- *Loosely prescribed assessment systems* are characterized by substantial teacher control over the design of assessment tasks and assessment system implementation and scoring procedures and timelines.

In general, data collected from the 16 schools participating in this study suggest that the more tightly prescribed the procedures are, the less ability teachers have to appropriate the assessment for use in their classrooms in ways that make sense to them pedagogically. Conversely, assessments that are more loosely prescribed allow teachers the room to adapt assessment tools for use in their classrooms and to integrate the assessments into their regular teaching practices.

Descriptions and examples of tightly, moderately, and loosely prescribed assessments appear in chapter 2. In this section we revisit those examples to examine the effects of level of prescription of assessments on teacher appropriation of the assessment. In general, we find that assessments developed at the state-level tend to be more tightly prescribed and have lower levels of teacher appropriation of assessment technologies, whereas assessments developed at the school level are more loosely prescribed and have higher levels of teacher appropriation (however, several states have developed, or, in some cases, fostered the development of what we call "moderately prescribed" assessments). A summary of the data presented in Fig. 2.6 illustrating how the 16 sites fall out along the level of prescription continuum appears in Table 4.4, and Table

4.5 illustrates the relationships between levels of prescription and appropriation at each of the 16 participant schools.

Effects of a Tightly Prescribed Assessment on Teacher Appropriation

In chapter 2, the Maryland School Performance Assessment Program was described as an example of an assessment with tightly prescribed assessment format and implementation procedures. Teachers in the assessment grades have very little control over assessment tasks, implementation, or scoring procedures; as well, assessment administration occurs during a single, discrete time period determined outside the classroom. What is more, assessment results are

TABLE 4.4
Distribution of Study Sites, by Level of Prescription of Assessments

Tightly Prescribed	Moderately Tightly Prescribed	Moderately Prescribed	Moderately Loosely Prescribed	Loosely Prescribed
Manzanita (state)	Breckenridge (state)	Hudson (state)	Niños Bonitos (school)	Park (school)
Walters (state)	McGary (district)	Crandall (state)	Noakes (school)	
Westgate (district)	Windermere (district)	Maple Leaf (state)	Sommerville (school)	
		Thoreau (school)	Cooper (school)	
			Ann Chester (school)	

TABLE 4.5
Level of Appropriation, by Level of Prescription

	High Appropriation	Moderately High Appropriation	Moderate Appropriation	Moderately Low Appropriation	Low Appropriation
Tightly Prescribed				Walters Westgate	Manzanita
Moderately Tightly Prescribed		Breckenridge Windermere	McGary		
Moderately Prescribed	Thoreau	Hudson Maple Leaf	Crandall		
Moderately Loosely Prescribed	Niños Bonitos Noakes Cooper Ann Chester	Sommerville			
Loosely Prescribed	Park				

made public so long after administration as to be only marginally useful to teachers as they review their own teaching over the long run.

This high level of task and procedural prescription (combined with a low level of teacher involvement in designing the assessment system) has contributed to limited teacher appropriation of the assessment among teachers at Walters Middle School. Because they do not develop tasks, score student responses, or even see results in a timely manner, they do not utilize the assessment technology in any regular way. Teachers' most frequently shared comment about the state's assessment is their complaint about the excessive amount of time required to plan and set up the assessment's experiment component; furthermore, these teachers suggest that the assessment's impact on their classrooms is, at most, marginal.

Effects of a Moderately Prescribed Assessment on Teacher Appropriation

As described in chapter 2, Vermont's portfolio assessment provides a contrast to Maryland's, serving as an example of a moderately prescribed assessment. In the Vermont system, a structure exists, but teachers have the flexibility to design assessment tasks for use in their classrooms, and they score the portfolio assessments by applying state-established rubrics to their students' work. Also, in general, the timelines for completing assessment tasks and scoring the assessment are determined by teachers.

Teacher appropriation of the assessment technology among teachers at Maple Leaf Middle School is more far-reaching than in the case of Walters, illustrated previously. Although teachers have criticisms of the portfolio system (e.g., it places burdens disproportionately on language arts teachers and, to a lesser extent, math teachers; and the system's validity and reliability are uncertain), they also profess to have learned from the system. One Maple Leaf math teacher said he had gained insights into the learning processes of one child with limited math skills. A language arts teacher said that, in response to what she has learned from the portfolio technique, she now places greater emphasis on the thinking and editing aspects of the writing process than on mere mechanical reporting. She also mentioned that by addressing the concept of *voice* in writing she has gained insights into her students' learning; in her words, "It [the portfolio system] has made me a better teacher." However, perhaps the highest testimony to teacher appropriation of the state's portfolio assessment is that teachers not required to work with it are doing so voluntarily. At Maple Leaf, the seventh-grade math teacher started to use a portfolio assessment after the state began to require an eighth-grade mathematics portfolio, and other teachers at the school are "experimenting" with this assessment technique as well.

Effects of a Loosely Prescribed Assessment
on Teacher Appropriation

Teachers at Park Elementary who use the Primary Learning Record (PLeR) have appropriated the assessment technique to a high degree. As was described in chapter 2, these teachers use the PLeR voluntarily, and each teacher decides for himself or herself how to use it most beneficially with students. In a sense, teacher appropriation of this loosely prescribed assessment is absolute: Teachers choose voluntarily to use it, and they themselves determine how they will use it.

OPPORTUNITIES FOR PROFESSIONAL
DEVELOPMENT

Our interviews with teachers at the 16 participant schools reveal that the type and extent of professional development provided to teachers with respect to the performance assessment has an impact on teacher appropriation and assessment reform. For purposes of this discussion, "professional development" is limited to training activities that are formally structured in some way and that involve individuals from outside the school working with teachers. We leave our discussion of other teacher-centered, teacher-directed activities—such as joint planning time or regular meetings among teachers to share and discuss classroom experiences—for our examination of the impact of school organizational factors on teacher appropriation of assessments.

Teachers at the 16 schools participating in this study experienced a range of professional development activities. These activities included:

- Train-the-trainer models.
- Conferences, symposia, and institutes.
- Collaboration with outside experts.

However, teachers at some schools participated in no, or virtually no, formal professional development activities related directly to the performance assessment. Table 4.6 illustrates the *primary vehicle of professional development* experienced by teachers at each of the 16 schools and teachers' comments about the usefulness of these professional development activities. Table 4.7 illustrates the coincidence of the primary form of professional development to teacher appropriation of the assessment technology.

A fairly clear pattern emerges in Table 4.6, suggesting that the predominant model of professional development employed closely follows the level of initiation of the assessment. Specifically, states developing performance assessments favor train-the-trainer models of professional development (such models

TABLE 4.6

Types of Professional Development and Teachers' Comments Concerning Their Helpfulness

School	Primary Mode of Professional Development	Teacher Comments Concerning Helpfulness of Professional Development Activities
	State-initiated assessments	
Manzanita (AZ)	Train-the-trainer	Helpful with respect to logistics of administration but not in other respects
Breckenridge (KY)	Train-the-trainer	Not enough professional development with respect to how to score portfolios, but the scoring sessions themselves provide good professional development
Walters (MD)	Train-the-trainer	Teachers could not remember what professional development they received
Hudson (NY)	None	Not applicable
Crandall (OR)	Conferences, symposia, institutes	The sessions were helpful but the numerous aspects of assessment reform were hard to keep straight
Maple Leaf (VT)	Train-the-trainer	Several sessions are held each year and are helpful, especially with respect to scoring portfolios
	District-initiated assessments	
McGary (CO)	Conferences, symposia, institutes	Teachers are very enthusiastic about the district-run "Assessment Academy"
Westgate (VA)	Train-the-trainer	Helpful with respect to logistics of administration but not in other respects
Windermere (NJ)	Collaboration with outside experts	Helpful for evaluating the system and ensuring reliability of scoring procedures
	National/school-initiated assessments	
Ann Chester (NSP)	Conferences, symposia, institutes	NSP conferences are useful to teachers learning to construct tasks and use rubrics
Noakes (NSP)	Conferences, symposia, institutes	NSP conferences are useful to teachers learning to construct tasks and use rubrics
Cooper (CES)	Conferences, symposia, institutes	The few teachers who have been able to participate in CES conferences have found them to be helpful, but the school cannot afford to have many teachers attend
Sommerville (Pacesetter)	Conferences, symposia, institutes	The College Board's summer and mid-year institutes are useful to teachers, but they find some of the emphases of the activities to be irrelevant to the situation they face at their school
	School-initiated assessments	
Thoreau	None	Not applicable
Park	Collaboration with outside experts	Teachers highly value collaborating with the Center for Collaborative Education
Niños Bonitos	Collaboration with outside experts	Teachers found it very useful to be able to work with outside experts in developing their mathematics assessment; collaboration facilitated development (a few years earlier they developed their language arts portfolio on their own)

TABLE 4.7

Level of Appropriation by Primary Type of Professional Development

	High Appropriation	Moderately High Appropriation	Moderate Appropriation	Moderately Low Appropriation	Low Appropriation
Train-the-trainer		Breckenridge Maple Leaf		Walters Westgate	Manzanita
Conferences, Symposia, Institutes	Noakes Cooper Ann Chester	Sommerville	McGary Crandall		
Expert Consultants	Park Niños Bonitos	Windemere			
None	Thoreau	Hudson			

are likely to be economical), whereas national efforts to support assessment reform (and education reform, in general) emphasize conferences and symposia that bring together teachers from across the country. Schools and districts that participate in these national education reform networks take advantage of the professional development activities they offer insofar as financial resources allow. Schools going it alone tap the expertise of outsiders insofar as they are able to afford their assistance.[1]

In the context of the discussion of professional development opportunities, it is useful to distinguish between school-initiated assessments and assessments initiated at the school level but participating in national education reform efforts. This distinction is important here because of the unique opportunities for professional development offered by the national education reform efforts. (The distinction is less useful where school-initiated assessments resemble each other, regardless of their participation or nonparticipation in national reforms.)

In general, we have found that, although some teachers express ambivalence toward the training they received concerning the new performance assessment, teachers typically find these opportunities to be useful. If nothing more, teachers find it valuable to learn about the purposes, format, and logistics of state- and district-initiated assessments when they are first being introduced. Beyond issues of merely knowing what's coming, however, teachers in many schools found that the structured professional development activities in which they participated helped them appropriate assessments for their own classroom use. Teachers reported improved understanding of how to construct tasks, write and use rubrics, and think about evidence of student learning.

The extent to which each of these models of professional development has contributed to teachers' abilities to use assessments and to their subsequent

---

[1]The paucity of data available on the financial costs of performance assessments (including costs of conducting professional development activities) makes it impossible for us to compare costs across sites.

appropriation of the assessments is explored next. To reiterate, two effects of professional development opportunities contribute specifically to teacher appropriation of new assessments:

- Teachers' understanding of the performance assessment system.
- Teachers' understanding of how to use or modify the assessment for use in the classroom.

Train-the-Trainer Models of Professional Development

The train-the-trainer approach to professional development is used by four states and one district implementing performance-based assessment systems (Arizona, Kentucky, Maryland, Vermont, and Prince William County, Virginia). This model is the traditional model of professional development employed by state departments of education when they introduce reforms. Its advantage is that it is economical, whereas its disadvantage is that it does not necessarily achieve the far-reaching professional development and communication intended.

In each place where this model is being used, the format of professional development is similar. The state (or, in the case of Prince William County, Virginia, the district) conducts a training session for representatives from schools and districts throughout the jurisdiction. Participants are then charged with sharing what they have learned with other teachers in their schools and districts. Next, examples of instances in which this model has contributed little to teacher appropriation of an assessment technology and instances in which it has contributed more toward appropriation are considered.

Limited Impact on Teacher Appropriation.   Teachers at three schools participating in this study suggested that this model may not have the desired effect at the school level. For example, only some teachers at Manzanita High School in Arizona remembered the training they received from their district's representative, and those who did remember it found the training to be useful only with respect to the logistics and mechanics of ASAP: They learned what would be expected of them in terms of administering the assessment, and seeing sample assessments helped them to understand the types of skills they should review with their students prior to the assessment. These teachers said that the professional development did not contribute to their understanding of performance-based assessment, because their district already engaged in extensive performance assessment that was, in these teachers' opinions, more valid and useful for their teaching than was the ASAP. Thus, any contribution toward Manzanita's teachers' appropriation of the ASAP performance assessment is negligible.

Teachers at Westgate Middle School in Prince William County had inconsistent recollections of their participation in any development activities with respect to the district's Applications Assessments. Teachers who participated in the district's development sessions said that the sessions were valuable opportunities for communication between teachers and district administrators, but most teachers who did not participate in the district-run sessions did not remember how they learned about what would be required of them with respect to the assessment. Similarly, teachers at Walters Middle School were unable to recollect which assessment training activities they had participated in had focused on Maryland's performance assessment and which had focused on the district's performance assessment.

In each of these three schools, the scope of professional development opportunities was quite limited in practice, although not necessarily in design: Teachers, at least according to those who recalled the professional development activities at all, participated in single training sessions. Next, two more extensive professional development systems illustrate positive impacts on teacher appropriation of assessment technologies.

Positive Impact on Teacher Appropriation. In some assessment systems, the train-the-trainer model involves more than just a chain of development sessions. In Kentucky and Vermont, teachers designated to serve as the school or district representative assume a role requiring ongoing work and leadership in the assessment reform effort. These teachers have titles such as "network leaders" (Vermont) and "cluster leaders" (Kentucky). Teachers who serve in this capacity are responsible not only for sharing professional development with other teachers in their schools or districts, but also for facilitating administration of the assessments and scoring activities[2].

Teachers at Maple Leaf Middle School testify to the usefulness of the professional development activities they participate in with respect to Vermont's portfolio assessment. The state has developed its professional development system with an eye toward building local level capacity to support the reform effort. Each year Maple Leaf teachers attend three 1-day Network Sessions—professional development activities run by the district's Network Leaders. These sessions focus on issues such as the use of benchmarks and anchor papers. Sessions have also focused on scoring calibration. Teachers at Maple Leaf have expressed their increasing confidence in developing tasks appropriate for inclusion in students' portfolios and their increasing ability to glean and use the information from the portfolio system of assessment.

---

[2]Maryland, too, has a designated "test coordinator" in each school who functions in a capacity similar to that of Vermont's and Kentucky's network and cluster leaders. However, as was described earlier, the impact of MSPAP professional development on teacher appropriation of the assessment at Walters Middle School is quite low.

Changes Over Time in Teacher Response to a Professional Development System: Breckenridge Middle School.   Teachers at Breckenridge Middle School in Kentucky testify to how the professional development opportunities supporting KIRIS have improved over time, thereby improving their own ability to appropriate the state's assessments—and the portfolio assessment in particular. Although these teachers said that the training they received with respect to scoring portfolio assessments was inadequate in the 1993–1994 academic year, they also suggested that it improved between that year and the next: As a result of improved training, they were better prepared to administer and score the portfolio part of KIRIS in 1994–1995 than in 1993–1994. The school's three cluster leaders also all stated that they are confident in their ability to teach their colleagues how to use and score the assessment. Furthermore, teachers identified a wide range of KIRIS-related topics in which they had received training during the 1994–1995 school year, including how to include students with disabilities in KIRIS, how to generate open-ended writing prompts, how to encourage writing across the curriculum, and how to integrate portfolios into daily classroom instruction. Finally, teachers at Breckenridge commented that they are now better able to work regularly with writing prompts and portfolios in their classrooms, suggesting increased appropriation of the state's performance assessment system.

Conferences, Symposia, and Institutes

Conferences, symposia, and the like are the favored model of professional development offered by the three national assessment reform efforts included in this study (the New Standards Project, the Coalition of Essential Schools, and the College Board's Pacesetter Program). In addition, these methods of providing professional development have also been adopted by one state-level assessment system (Oregon) and one district-level system (HSD2).

National Education Reform Networks: Impact of Professional Development Opportunities.   Perhaps the most unique feature of the three national-level reform efforts considered in this study is the opportunity they provide participating teachers to attend conferences, symposia, and institutes with teachers from all over the country who are also participating in the nationwide programs. These professional development opportunities share some features with the train-the-trainer activities, in that both types of professional development involve training over several days provided by outsiders to only a subset of a school's staff. However, comparing remarks about the train-the-trainer opportunities experienced by some teachers with those of teachers who participated in a national reform effort's professional development activities suggests that the latter tend to emphasize "capacity building"—expanding teachers' abilities to works with new assessment techniques—and involve "hands-on" practice with assessment tasks and rubrics. Train-the-trainer activities (with the exception of Vermont), on the other hand, tend more to emphasize the communication of information.

Teachers at Noakes and Ann Chester elementary schools who have participated in the New Standards Projects national conferences described some of the skills they developed at these events. For instance, teachers at these schools attended conferences to learn about benchmarking performance tasks in reading, how to write commentaries for student work, how to use portfolios, and how to develop new performance tasks and write scoring rubrics. Teachers suggested that these experiences were very valuable in helping them learn how to use performance-based assessments (including portfolio assessments) in their classrooms, and their comments give testimony to their appropriation of the types of performance-based assessment activities the New Standards Project is trying to promote.

Similarly, teachers at Sommerville High School participating in the College Board's Pacesetter Program have attended multiple Pacesetter "institutes," both during the summer and in the middle of the school year. Although these teachers suggested that the institutes were not always as accommodating of differences across participating schools as they might be, they still said that they have found the experiences (and these teachers have now attended two summer institutes and two mid-year institutes over a period of 2 years) to be extremely beneficial to them, enabling them to better implement Pacesetter's integrated program of curriculum, instruction, and assessment in their classrooms.

By way of contrast, the professional development opportunities available through the Coalition of Essential Schools have only contributed peripherally to teachers' ability to develop and use performance assessments at Cooper Middle School. Although Cooper teachers do say that their participation in CES has helped them think through and plan education reform at their school, they, quite simply, have not been able to afford to attend CES conferences frequently enough to apply what they may learn to their assessment practices.

Harrison School District 2's "Academy" Model of Professional Development: Impact on Teacher Appropriation of Assessment Technologies.

The case of the district-developed Colorado Springs "Assessment Academy" is an interesting and impressive effort on the part of a school district to make extensive professional development available to all teachers. The district's Academy has trained all district teachers in the district's "performance-based curriculum" in literacy; three development sessions per grade level had been conducted as of spring 1994. The district operates the Academy by drawing mostly on the expertise of its administrators, and also by inviting outside experts to work with teachers. Teachers who have participated in capacity- and skill-building conferences and the like have, in general, responded favorably to them, reporting that these activities have improved their abilities to develop and work with performance-based assessments. According to one teacher, "The district has done a very good job of allowing teachers access to adequate support, such as training and materials"; another teacher concurred, saying, "I haven't had to go outside the district to get the support I need" to meet the assessment requirements of the performance-based curriculum.

Collaboration With Outside Experts and Other Networks

Some local level assessment reform efforts draw on the expertise of outside experts to provide professional development for teachers. For instance, in South Brunswick, New Jersey, teachers worked with an expert in "resource-based instruction," David Loertscher, to revamp their approach to teaching research skills to elementary school students. Similarly, teachers at Niños Bonitos Elementary School in San Diego, California, used grant money to bring in experts in portfolio assessment, including Dennie Wolf and Grant Wiggins, to help teachers develop their new system of assessment. Although any direct impacts of these collaborations on teacher appropriation of new performance assessments are unclear, teachers said that these experiences were positive.

An elaborate local-level collaboration among teachers and other educators to support assessment reform is taking place in New York City. There, the New York City Assessment Network (a consortium of three organizations—the Center for Collaborative Education, the Center for Educational Outcomes, and the Elementary Teachers Network) works with teachers at approximately 62 elementary schools across the city to implement the Primary Learning Record. These three organizations provide a range of professional development activities to participating teachers, including placing "teacher consultants" in the schools to assist in implementation, coordinating "study groups" led by these teacher consultants and other mentor teachers, and providing free continuing education classes at Lehman College for all interested participating teachers. Teachers suggest that the study groups in particular are a crucial element of the network that has helped them to use the PLeR effectively.

INTERACTION WITH OTHER REFORMS
AND OTHER ASSESSMENTS

The successful introduction of new performance-based assessments can be facilitated or hindered by the interaction among the assessment reform and two other factors that inherently must either be compatible or at odds with the assessment reform. These factors are:

- The presence or absence of an effort to coordinate reforms to curriculum frameworks or performance standards with the assessment reform effort.
- The complementary or competing nature of other assessments in use, whether these other assessments are initiated at the state, the district, or the school level.

Table 4.8 illustrates the relationship between the level of teacher appropriation of new assessment technologies and the coordination of assessment reform with other reform efforts, other assessments, both, or neither.

Coordinated Efforts to Reform Curricula or to Establish Standards

The coordination of assessment reform with the introduction of curriculum reform can be an important facilitator of assessment reform; similarly, the articulation of clear standards for content and performance can also serve as a facilitator of assessment reform. When teachers perceive coherence in the entire reform initiative, they are more likely to embrace each piece, including the new performance assessment; when the performance assessment is not clearly related to other reforms, or when these other reforms lag behind assessment reform, teachers remain cautious before they invest effort in coming up to speed on the new assessment. Table 4.9 summarizes the parallel reform efforts in the

TABLE 4.8

Level of Appropriation and Coordination With Other Reforms and Assessments

	High Appropriation	*Moderately High Appropriation*	*Moderate Appropriation*	*Moderately Low Appropriation*	*Low Appropriation*
Coordination with both other reforms and other assessments		Breckenridge Maple Leaf		Westgate	
Coordination only with other reforms	Ann Chester Cooper Niños Bonitos Noakes	Sommerville Windermere	McGary Crandall	Walters	Manzanita
Coordination only with other assessments (explicit coordination)		Hudson			
Neither	Park Thoreau				

TABLE 4.9

Parallel Reform Efforts: Curriculum Guidelines and Performance and Content Standards

	State-Initiated Assessments
Arizona	Essential Skills
Kentucky	6 Learning Goals and 75 Valued Outcomes
Maryland	Learner Behaviors
New York	None
Oregon	Foundation Skills and Core Applications for Living
Vermont	Common Core Framework
	District-Initiated Assessments
Colorado Springs	13 Significant Student Outcomes
Prince William County	Standards of Quality
South Brunswick	Outcome statements for sixth-graders
	School-Initiated Assessments
Cooper	CES Common Principles
Park	None
Niños Bonitos	Designated learning outcomes in language arts and math
Thoreau	None
Ann Chester	District's Applied Learning Program (articulates standards of competent adult performance); NSP content and performance standards
Noakes	NSP content and performance standards
Sommerville	Pacesetter integrated program of curriculum, instruction, and assessment

areas of curriculum guidelines and content or performance standards experienced at each of the 16 participant sites.

In some instances, curriculum and assessment reform have been coordinated efforts, and this coordination has furthered teacher appropriation of performance assessments. For example, teachers at Sommerville High School described how the Pacesetter mathematics program led them to overhaul their teaching practices for their Pacesetter classes. Although early on they modified their instructional practices to be compatible with the program, they realized only slowly that they had to modify classroom assessment practices to support the program's curriculum and instructional techniques.

Another example reveals simultaneously how coordination can facilitate, and lack of coordination can hamper, assessment reform. In Prince William County, Applications Assessments were developed to support implementation of the district's designated Standards of Quality, and coordination between these two reforms served as a facilitator of assessment reform. At the same time, however, the district implemented its Applications Assessments prior to completing its revisions to the district's curriculum—revisions were being made in all subject areas and at all grade levels. Although there is no inherent reason why assessment reform cannot precede curriculum reform and have a coherent system emerge, putting assessment reform first does leave teachers in a temporary quandary. Teachers at Westgate Middle School repeatedly asked, "How can we introduce this test when we haven't even decided on the curriculum yet?" Teachers also suggested that they would wait to see what the revised curriculum looked like before they invested a lot of time in adapting their classroom practices to support the new Applications Assessments. Note, however, that this example illustrates a short-term, and not necessarily a permanent, barrier to teacher appropriation of the new performance assessments.

Similarly, at Crandall High School, the absence of state-delineated content and performance standards left teachers involved in the development of assessment tasks feeling a bit rudderless. The fact that most of Oregon's Foundation Skills ran across subject areas exacerbated the problem, because teachers were unclear about how to connect them to the traditional content areas that continue to define how most high school courses are organized.

Compatibility with Other Assessment Requirements

Teachers also are more likely to appropriate performance assessment technologies that do not compete with other assessment requirements they face. Perhaps the clearest example of the challenge to appropriation that can occur if assessment systems compete comes from Manzanita High School. Teachers there are being asked to accommodate ASAP within the context of an already extensive district assessment program. Because ASAP represents no "added value" from these teachers' perspective (it is, they say, a performance assessment inferior to the one employed by the district), teachers view it as an add-on, not as a reform that can be coordinated with existing assessment requirements or that supplements the information yielded by those efforts in some valuable way.

Both Vermont and Kentucky explicitly designed their performance assessments to be coordinated with other, more traditional and standardized components of an assessment system. In Kentucky, in particular, this coordination of assessments fostered teacher appropriation of the state's portfolios and performance tasks. Regardless of their particular criticisms of KIRIS, teachers at the participant Kentucky school say they believe the assessments—in combination as well as individually—in and of themselves have proven their value in the classroom.

SCHOOL ORGANIZATIONAL STRUCTURES

Certain school organizational structures can also serve as facilitators or barriers in teacher appropriation of new assessment tools. This is particularly true when an assessment is intended to be used regularly, to be integrated with instruction, and when successful use of an assessment requires or is enhanced by coordination among teachers. School organizational facilitators in assessment reform include:

- *Time.* The provision of time for teachers to work with and discuss the assessment can be crucial to the success of an assessment reform effort. This time may be either general or specific in purpose—that is, release time and joint planning time may be provided for teachers to plan for a variety of activities, including performance assessments, or release time or time for participation in study groups may be provided with the explicit purpose of supporting the assessment reform.
- *Leadership.* Strong leadership for assessment reform may be embodied in a single strong leader at the school or district. Alternatively, an entire school may be quite progressive in its educational philosophy, inspiring teachers to actively pursue improved assessment practices.

Both of these two factors can provide a powerful impetus for effecting assessment reform.

Time

Our case studies demonstrate that when time is freed up for teachers to work with assessments—to plan jointly for integrated assessments, to discuss and share experiences with other teachers, or to devote time to assessment-related research and development work—teachers gain valuable institutional support that fosters their appropriation of new assessment methods.

Teachers gain access to time to undertake such activities in one of three ways:

- Time is legislated into the school calendar (e.g., daily, weekly, or biweekly) for teachers to devote to activities outside the classroom during times that might normally be considered class time. The message that the school values the time teachers devote to improving their skills is manifested through this institutionally supported time.
- Time is provided occasionally or intermittently. For example, a small number of release days are provided for teachers who undertake specific responsibilities for assessment development.
- Time is not provided (specific or related to the assessment). Teachers, however, often organize support activities on their own time (after school and on weekends) because they believe these activities to be valuable to their teaching and to their students. Many teachers who do not have access to institutionally provided time commit themselves to spending their own time honing their teaching skills.

Table 4.10 illustrates the relationship between the way in which time is provided to teachers to work with the assessment (regularly, intermittently, or not at all) and the level of teacher appropriation of the assessment. Table 4.11 summarizes the time accommodations made for teachers at each of the 16 participating schools—excepting professional development and scoring activities—specifically intended to accommodate their use of the new assessment (or the assessment and related reforms).

Examples of how teachers use the time provided and their testimony to how valuable institutionalized provision of time is to them are illustrated next; when appropriate, uses of time by teachers who devote their own time to furthering assessment reform (and their own appropriation of the assessment technology) are explicated as well. The uses teachers make of time fall into three broad categories:

- Development of assessment tasks and scoring rubrics.
- Teacher-initiated study and discussion groups.
- Joint planning time.

Time to Develop Tasks and Rubrics and Score Assessments. Teachers working with the most time-intensive assessment systems testify to the importance of release time from regular teaching duties. For some teachers, this time is institutionalized through regular early release of students from class (generally once each week or every other week). Additionally, teachers at several schools have received release time to support their endeavors on behalf of assessment and associated reforms.[3] These teachers all suggest that this time

TABLE 4.10
Level of Appropriation and Legislated Time

	High Appropriation	Moderately High Appropriation	Moderate Appropriation	Moderately Low Appropriation	Low Appropriation
Time is regularly provided	Cooper Niños Bonitos Park Noakes	Sommerville	McGary	Westgate	
Time is occasionally provided		Breckenridge Hudson Maple Leaf	Crandall		
Time is not provided	Ann Chester Thoreau	Windermere		Walters	Manzanita

[3]Note again that release time provided for attendance at specific professional development activities is not included in this discussion of school organizational factors; rather, the current discussion is limited to release time that is provided to support the reform but for which teachers direct their own activities.

TABLE 4.11

Types and Extent of Time Provided Teachers to Work With Performance Assessments

State-Initiated Assessments	
Manzanita	None
Breckenridge	2 release days to compensate for attendance at summer and weekend training sessions
Walters	None
Hudson	2 days paid joint planning time over the summer
Crandall	5 release days for teachers who develop assessment tasks (teachers may opt to be paid for the work instead of taking release days)
Maple Leaf	Release days (in varying quantities) for teachers, both those directly affected by the state's portfolio assessment and for other teachers to experiment with portfolios
District-Initiated Assessments	
McGary	5 release days for the school's two designated "peer coaches"; early release of students each Friday to provide teachers with extra planning time
Westgate	Joint planning periods every other day (an element of team teaching; in theory, integrated assessment is one objective of team teaching)
Windermere	None
School-Initiated Assessments	
Cooper	Joint planning time every day as an element of team teaching (supports integrated assessment)
Park	Weekly meetings of teachers to share experiences with the PLR; voluntary teacher study groups (largely conducted on own time)
Niños Bonitos	Restructured school day provides teachers with extra planning time in the afternoon; release time funded by grant money; students are released early every other Wednesday to give teachers additional planning time
Thoreau	None (teachers devote their own time to revise ROPE and to discuss modes of implementation)
Ann Chester	Teacher-initiated study groups (largely conducted on own time)
Noakes	Students are released early every other Wednesday to give teachers additional planning time
Sommerville	Joint planning time, including one extra planning period each day, for Pacesetter teachers

away from the classroom is crucial to fostering their ability to develop assessment tasks and rubrics and to work with assessment systems.

For example, teachers at Niños Bonitos have used some of their grant money to pay for release time. They use this time to support the implementation of their electronic portfolio assessment and to develop new assessment tasks and rubrics. They have also restructured their school day so that every teacher teaches only one afternoon class, freeing up the rest of the afternoon for planning time.

Teachers at two high schools working on piloting and developing state-initiated performance assessments—Crandall High School in Oregon and Hudson High School in New York—provide contrasting examples of how teachers have reacted to release time or its absence. Teachers at Hudson High School felt a great need for release time but had none available to them (at least, none specifically to support assessment reform). These teachers say they have devoted numerous hours to developing performance assessments to replace segments of the New York Regents Examinations. However, with the exception of some small financial compensation for time spent planning over the summer, these teachers have not received any release time or regularly scheduled joint planning time beyond what all teachers in their school and district receive. Although these teachers are very committed to the work they are doing and believe strongly that their assessments benefit their students, they say that such a labor-intensive assessment system should not be mandated, at least not in the absence of substantial support—in terms of both professional development and time—for teachers.

Teachers at Crandall High School also agreed to develop pilot assessments for Oregon's assessment reform efforts. However, unlike teachers at Hudson, these teachers both participated in structured activities associated with Oregon's assessment reform and also were provided with additional release time (5 days) to devote to their development work. In this case, however, the release time did not contribute to the ultimate appropriation of the assessment system. Although teachers worked hard to develop appropriate assessment tasks and to score them with the state's generic scoring rubric, most of them opted to be compensated financially for this development work rather than accept the release time (teachers had a choice between release time and compensation). Ultimately, in the 1994–1995 school year, Crandall High opted out of the assessment pilot.

Time to Share Experiences and Knowledge. Several schools have institutionalized meetings among teachers that focus not on "business matters" but rather on discussions of experiences teachers are having with students—including how they identified strengths and weaknesses in their students and how they might use or have used assessments effectively to identify students' modes of learning. In addition, in some cases, teachers have initiated their own study groups to support assessment reform.

Two schools in which these meetings take place regularly are Park Elementary and Ann Chester Elementary. At Park, all teachers who use the Primary Learning Record come together once a week to discuss their observations of children's learning and to share ideas about how best to use the assessment technique. Frequently, teachers will spend the time discussing a single child, focusing on evidence from the classroom that illustrates the child's learning style, including strengths and weaknesses, and the types of learning activities that would be well suited to the child. Teachers say that this time together looking in-depth at individual children is invaluable, in part because the in-depth analyses of individual children generally illuminates the learning of several other children at the same time, and in part because of the insights colleagues share with each other. Teachers at Park participate in these conversations both with teachers who use the PLeR (teachers who are at Park and at other schools) and schoolwide but not limited to PLeR users; these latter, schoolwide discussion periods are an institutionalized part of the Park educational program.

Teachers at both Park and Ann Chester have also initiated study groups in which teachers set reading assignments for themselves and discuss the relevance of what they read to their classrooms. Again, teachers say that the time spent in conversation with colleagues is very valuable to their ability to work with performance assessments and other reforms. In both of these two cases, teacher appropriation of new assessments is high, and, in the case of Park in particular, this high level of appropriation seems clearly to be in part an effect of the extensive amount of time teachers spend communicating with one another.

Joint Planning Time. Time designated for teachers to spend planning together can be crucial, especially when assessments are designed to be integrated across subject areas or to tap cross-cutting, rather than subject-area-specific, skills. Most of the seven participant schools working with their own or national assessments have institutionalized joint planning time, sometimes in conjunction with team teaching.

Cooper Middle School provides an example of a school in which assessment reform is dependent on teachers having regular opportunities to come together to plan instructional and assessment activities that will cut across subject areas. The school is organized into "families"—groups of students and teachers who work together for most instruction—and teachers who work together plan integrated activities. Teachers have 45 minutes of common planning time every day, time without which, the teachers say, they could not possibly follow their restructured educational program.

Teachers at Sommerville High School who work with the College Board's Pacesetter program also found that their new approach to teaching mathematics required additional—and joint—planning time. The school's three Pacesetter teachers requested and obtained of their principal one additional planning period each day, a period that they could spend together to plan Pacesetter instruction. These teachers said that this extra time was very important in supporting their ability to adopt the new program of integrated curriculum, instruction, and assessment, which required teachers to dramatically modify their instructional and assessment techniques.

Several other schools have also supported education reform in general and, in some cases, assessment reform specifically, by providing teachers with extra joint planning time. At Noakes, Niños Bonitos, McGary, and Westgate, joint planning time is a regularly scheduled part of the school calendar (e.g., every other day at Westgate, once a week at McGary, and once every other week at Noakes and Niños Bonitos), and many teachers suggest that this time together outside the classroom is critical to planning—and "appropriating"—reforms.

Leadership

Leadership at the school level, and, in some cases, at the district level, can serve as an important facilitator of assessment reform, and of teacher appropriation of new assessments specifically. In addition, several participant schools describe the philosophy of their schools or districts as particularly "reform-minded," a philosophy that often lends administrators and teachers, at the very least, a willingness to experiment with new reforms. Table 4.12 summarizes the type of leadership explicitly identified by teachers at each of the 16 participant schools. Several examples in which leadership at the school level—either from an individual or from a shared philosophy—clearly served as a strong impetus for assessment reform are described next.

Teachers at Niños Bonitos attribute their school's successful restructuring of classroom groupings and the school day, the development of language arts and mathematics scoring rubrics, and schoolwide use of portfolios to the leadership of their principal. A one-time California Principal of the Year, the principal was also selected to be a 1994–1995 U.S. Department of Education Principal in Residence. Quite simply, this woman recognized frustration on the part of staff and students alike with the traditional program the school ran, required teachers to think about the kind of program that would make sense for the school's poor and multilingual population, and led the implementation of that program.

In at least two cases, leadership at the district level has inspired teachers to become active players in assessment reform. Teachers at Windermere Elemen-

TABLE 4.12

Type of Leadership Experienced by Teachers

Strong Individual (School or District)	Strong Atmosphere Supporting Reform	Neither
Niños Bonitos	Cooper	Breckenridge
Windermere	Park	Maple Leaf
McGary	Noakes	Westgate
	Ann Chester	Walters
	Thoreau	Manzanita
	Hudson	Sommerville
	Crandall	

tary School say that the ongoing success of their district's Sixth-Grade Research Performance Assessment is largely attributable to the efforts of the district's Assistant Superintendent for Curriculum and Instruction. In particular, they describe her relentless drive to push the district's sixth-grade teachers to consensus when they revisit the assessment's scoring rubric each year, and they know that nobody works harder at the process than she does. Similarly, district administrators and a school principal in Harrison School District 2 spearheaded the district's literacy performance-based assessment and together developed the district's Assessment Academy. Teachers testify to the usefulness of the work these leaders carried out, commenting that they have not found it necessary to go outside the district to find the support they need to work with the new performance assessment.

Finally, teachers at some schools suggest that their schools tend to be "reform minded" and that this shared philosophy both leads them to dive into reform efforts and to be willing to invest the work necessary to discover whether or not a reform is useful or not. Teachers at both Park Elementary and Thoreau High School have long been innovators in education reform, operating programs for over 20 years that are now, in the 1990s, frequently turned to by other educators seeking models of what schools should look like.

CONCLUSION

In this chapter, we have traced evidence in our data that point to the existence of facilitators and barriers in teacher appropriation of performance assessment technologies. Teacher appropriation of the assessment, we have argued, is a necessary prerequisite to any meaningful pedagogical change that will result in improved teaching and learning.

In sum, findings described in this section suggest that:

- Teachers who are involved in designing and implementing assessment systems are more likely to appropriate them, as a result of the sustained or focused thought that teachers give to the problems of validly assessing what it is students know and can do.
- Teachers who work with assessments that are relatively loosely prescribed—that is, assessments that leave (in all or in part) task specification, implementation and scoring procedures, and timelines to teachers' discretion—are more likely to appropriate the assessment than are teachers who work with more tightly prescribed assessments. Again, the thought teachers devote to assessment design, here coupled with the flexibility to integrate the assessment with other teaching practices, fosters appropriation.

- Professional development opportunities support teacher appropriation of new assessments. However, some models of professional development work better than others. Specifically, collaborations with outside experts and attendance at the conferences, symposia, and institutes run by national education reform efforts more frequently provide information and experiences that teachers value and can translate into classroom practice than do more traditional train-the-trainer models of professional development. More importantly, professional development activities that focus on building teachers' capacity to work with performance-based assessment techniques have more substantial impacts than do activities that focus merely on the mechanics and logistics of assessment administration.
- The compatibility of assessment reform with other facets of education reform or with other assessments serves as a facilitator of teacher appropriation. Teachers working with assessments that are unclearly aligned with efforts to revise curricula will typically bide their time, waiting for the whole system to become clear, before investing effort in appropriating the assessment. Similarly, performance assessments that do not compete with other elements of an assessment system are more likely to be appropriated than are performance assessments that represent no "value added" from teachers' perspective.
- Two school organizational factors—regularly scheduled time for teachers to work with an assessment and leadership—can also serve as powerful facilitators of teacher appropriation of assessments. Both factors communicate to teachers that the assessment reform effort is valued by the school or district and that the work teachers undertake to further that reform is valued as well.

In the next chapter, we turn to the effects that performance assessments—most apparent when teachers have appropriated them for regular use—are having on teaching and learning in the classroom.

5

Impact of Performance Assessments on Teaching and Learning

The previous chapter discussed the factors involved in "teacher appropriation" of assessment technologies. In this chapter, we extend the notion of "teacher appropriation" of assessment technology and discuss what we have learned about *how* teachers appropriate and extend performance assessments to change the pedagogical strategies they employ in their classrooms. We also discuss the impact of performance assessments and changed pedagogical practices on student learning. The discussion presented in this chapter is based primarily on three sources of information—student work; classroom observations; and interviews with students, teachers, parents, and principals. The data are indicative of the potential impact of various types of performance assessment systems on teaching and learning.

ORGANIZATION OF THE CHAPTER

The discussion of the impact of performance assessments on teaching and learning is organized into the following sections: (a) teaching, including curriculum, instruction, and teacher role; (b) learning, including motivation to learn, thinking skills, and writing skills; and (c) barriers to effective classroom use, including lack of time and lack of clearly articulated content and performance standards.

Our data indicate that an important factor in understanding the impact of performance assessment systems on teaching and learning is the *type* of assessment tasks used to influence pedagogy. In this sample, interviewees involved in assessment systems composed of portfolios or extended performance tasks tended to report the most extensive effects on teaching and learning, whereas interviewees involved in implementing only on-demand assessment tasks tended to report the smallest number of effects. Therefore, we discuss the impact of assessments on teaching and learning by the types of assessment tasks being implemented at each site.[1]

Limitations to the Analyses

Certain limitations must be noted with regard to discussing the impact of performance assessments on teaching and learning. First, teachers and students at most sites reported changes in teaching strategies and learning outcomes due to the influence of performance assessments. The absence of such reports at some sites does not necessarily imply the absence of similar teaching strategies and learning outcomes at those sites; it only means that assessments were not appropriated and, therefore, did not drive pedagogical changes. Second, the impact data for the state- and district-initiated systems are valid only for the school site included in this study; the results obtained for a particular school site are not generalizable to other sites developing or implementing the same assessment system. Thus, for example, impact information collected for the Kentucky performance assessment system is true only for Breckenridge Middle School in Kentucky, not for all Kentucky schools. Third, the impact on teaching and learning is not necessarily schoolwide; the impact is primarily on students and teachers involved in the assessment systems included in this study. Fourth, some teachers involved in the assessment system may have profoundly changed only one aspect of their pedagogical practices, whereas other teachers may have tried to alter their pedagogical practices completely but not very successfully. Therefore, in this study, it is not possible to evaluate thoroughly the depth, breadth, and quality of pedagogical changes.

Last, in some cases, the effects of assessment systems on teaching and learning may be minimal because the assessment system is at a very early development stage, or the effects may be washed out due to the presence of other competing assessment systems. The PWC Applications Assessments are in the early implementation phase and, hence, have not been institutionalized at Westgate Middle. In the case of Walters Middle and Manzanita High, the state-level performance assessment systems (composed of on-demand tasks) are administered once a year. However, both of these schools are located in

---

[1]In the previous chapter, we noted that one characteristic of assessment systems—level of prescription—is an important factor in whether or not the assessment system is appropriated for use in the classroom. Loosely to moderately prescribed assessments tend to be more readily appropriated than are tightly prescribed systems. Our data also indicate that loosely to moderately prescribed systems tend to consist of portfolios and extended performance tasks, whereas tightly prescribed systems tend to consist of on-demand performance tasks.

districts that have implemented their own performance assessment systems. Thus, the state-level assessment systems compete with the locally developed assessment systems in influencing the teaching and learning processes at these schools.

The cross-case information contained in this section is intended to provide a framework for understanding the general relationships between assessment systems and classroom outcomes. It is not meant to describe comprehensively the impact of any one assessment system on any one school or school system; a representative sample of schools and teachers utilizing the assessment system would be required for such analyses.

TEACHING

Our discussion of impacts on teaching is divided into the following sections: curriculum, instruction, and teacher role (see Table 5.1).

Curriculum

Our information on the impact of performance assessments on the classroom curriculum is based on interviews with teachers and principals. One limitation to our analyses is that such interview data may not be complete and reliable. Teachers may not have been willing to talk about how much they might have changed the curriculum they implement in their classrooms, because diverging from established guidelines and curricular frameworks may have negative professional consequences for them. Therefore, our information with regard to curricular changes may not be complete.

Keeping this limitation in mind, we still find some interesting patterns in our data. Some sites using portfolio assessments show some significant shifts in the curriculum teachers use in their classrooms, whereas most sites using on-demand assessments exhibit only marginal, if any, impact of assessments on the classroom curriculum.

Curricular Changes.   At four sites using portfolios, teachers reported two types of changes in the curriculum they implement in their classrooms:

* In-depth coverage of curricular topics.
* Curtailment of curricular topic coverage.

Teachers at Hudson High, Maple Leaf Middle, Cooper Middle, and Breckenridge Middle reported that, as a result of appropriating and using portfolios and extended performance tasks, they covered certain curricular topics in more

TABLE 5.1

Impact on Teaching, by Type of Assessment Task and by Site

	Portfolios						Performance Tasks and Portfolios				Extended Performance Tasks		On-Demand Performance Tasks			Teacher Observation
	Hudson High, NY	Maple Leaf Middle, VT	Niños Bonitos Elementary, CA	Cooper Middle, NM	Breckenridge Middle, KY	Crandall High, OR	Ann Chester Elementary (NSP), TX	Thoreau High, WI	Sommerville High (PS), MD	Noakes Elementary (NSP), IA	McGary Elementary, HSD2	Windermere Elementary, SB	Westgate Middle, PWC	Walters Middle, MD	Manzanita High, AZ	Park Elementary (PLeR), NY
Curriculum																
Interdisciplinary teaching (thematic unit)				X		X										
Curtailment of content area coverage	X	X		X	X	X									X	
In-depth teaching of certain aspects of a subject	X	X		X	X											
Instruction																
Research/performance-based projects	X	X		X	X	X	X	X	X	X	X	X				
Stress on writing skills	X	X	X	X	X			X	X	X	X	X	X			
Group work	X	X	X	X	X	X	X		X	X	X					
Use of scoring rubrics with students	X	X		X	X	X	X			X	X	X				
Use of technology for student work		X	X	X	X	X				X						
Teacher role																
Teacher collaboration		X	X	X			X	X	X			X				X
Teacher creativity and initiative	X	X	X	X			X	X	X	X	X	X				X
Teacher's observational skills		X					X		X							X
Understanding of student		X	X		X		X							X		X

X = feature present.

depth than they had in the past. However, they also had to curtail the coverage of certain curricular areas, because of the time pressures resulting from implementing the assessment system. For example, at Breckenridge Middle, the eighth-grade language arts and mathematics teachers noted that they had to drop units from their curriculum in order to focus on portfolio writing and cooperative problem-solving exercises. The language arts teachers said they had stopped teaching units on grammar, sentence mechanics, and literature in order to focus on creative writing in class.

Such enhancement and curtailment of curriculum has evoked a variety of teacher responses. For example, at Hudson High, because the Regents waiver courses and assessments are locally developed, the curtailment of content coverage is by design and, therefore, is not viewed negatively by teachers. Hudson teachers are pleased about the fact that their students learn and retain in-depth knowledge of certain topics rather than encounter and often forget a wide range of topics in a given area.

At Cooper Middle School, however, full appropriation of locally developed performance assessments (and thematic teaching) led to some problems. Cooper teachers discovered that their focus on thematic units and project-based assignments took time away from certain math topics they would otherwise have covered. These teachers realized that, because they spent large amounts of time on student portfolios and on coordinating thematic lessons with other teachers, their time preparing for and teaching mathematics and science was being compromised. In the 1994–1995 school year, therefore, the problem of not covering enough mathematics was rectified by reverting to a traditional mathematics class for all students. This change from the innovative to the traditional exemplifies the difficulties inherent in creating and appropriating a new system without adequate professional support.

At Manzanita High in Arizona, changes in the classroom curriculum were not a result of appropriating and extending the assessment system. Rather, the curriculum was inadvertently affected by the logistics of implementing the on-demand, state- and district-level, external assessment systems. Manzanita teachers did not appropriate the Arizona assessments, but reported that test preparation and administration time, combined for both the state- and district-level assessment systems, robbed them of instructional time; one English teacher reported that he had to eliminate some books, such as *The Grapes of Wrath* and *The Great Gatsby*, from his curriculum.

No Curricular Changes.   At the sites where no changes to the curriculum are indicated, teachers offered two types of reasons for why their classroom curriculum had not changed as a *result* of the performance assessment system being implemented at their schools. These reasons are:

- The curriculum and the assessments were reformed in conjunction with one another (national- and school-level sites) and, therefore, no causal direction is discernible.
- The assessment systems have not permeated the classroom (state- and district-level sites).

At several sites using portfolios or extended performance tasks—Ann Chester Elementary, Niños Bonitos Elementary, Noakes Elementary, Park Elementary, Thoreau High, and Sommerville High (which are participants in national- and school-initiated assessments), and McGary Elementary and Windermere Elementary (which are participants in district-initiated assessment systems)—curricular changes did not follow changes in the assessment strategy. At these sites, assessments and curriculum were reformed, and are continuing to be reformed, in conjunction with one another. For example, at Park Elementary in New York City, teachers use the Primary Learning Record (PLeR) as an *instrument* to support the child-centered philosophy of teaching espoused at the school. At another school, Niños Bonitos Elementary, assessments were reformed in order to support changes in the curriculum. For example, for language arts, Niños Bonitos teachers first articulated the learning outcomes and, for each language developmental level, specified in detail what students should know and be able to do with regard to oral language, reading, and writing. Knowing they wanted a portfolio assessment system, teachers then spelled out what the language arts portfolio at each language development and age level should contain.

Thoreau High is unique in this group of reform-minded schools. It is a veteran of school reform whose performance assessment system was thoroughly institutionalized and integrated with its curriculum several years ago. Hence, Thoreau teachers tend not to use the assessments to drive changes in their curriculum.

In the cases of Walters Middle and Westgate Middle—sites with external, on-demand performance tasks—teachers noted no changes in their curriculum driven by the subject performance assessment, because they had not appropriated the assessment system. In both cases, on-demand performance tasks are administered once a year and, thus, have not been incorporated into the classroom on a regular basis. In the case of Walters Middle, the impact of state assessments is confounded by the fact that the district in which the school is located is implementing its own ongoing performance-based assessment system. Walters teachers mentioned that they used the curriculum-embedded district-level assessments in their classrooms. (According to district officials, the district assessments are embedded within new district curricular frameworks that are quite similar to the state curricular frameworks.) Several Manzanita teachers, too, mentioned that they had long ago adapted their teaching to the district's performance assessments. However, as noted earlier, some changes in curriculum came about due to the time involved in test preparation and administration.

In the case of Westgate Middle, PWC, the assessments are in the piloting and early implementation phase, and, hence, any impact on teaching and learning is not yet evident.

Instruction

A wide array of teaching methods, practices, and technologies fall under instruction. It is in this broad area of pedagogy that teacher appropriation of performance assessments *and* the effects of teacher appropriation are the most evident. We discuss the nature of these instructional changes under the following categories:

- Performance-based assignments
- Writing
- Group work
- Scoring rubrics
- Technology

Notice that all of these instructional methods and tools also may be integral components of the assessment process itself.

Performance-Based Assignments. The extensive use of research-based or performance-based projects that integrate writing, content knowledge, and social or scientific problem solving marks a noticeable shift away from textbook-based assignments at several schools involved in assessment systems comprising portfolios and extended performance tasks. Performance-based projects are extended tasks that typically require students to research a topic and demonstrate their understanding of the topic through essays, exhibitions, oral presentations, and experiments. Thus, students must actively seek information, exercise some judgment regarding the parameters (e.g., topic, focus, length) of the task, structure the information, and transmit the information in a comprehensible fashion. Figure 5.1 provides some examples of such tasks.

To a large extent, this project-based instructional mode is driven by the nature of the assessments themselves—portfolios and extended performance assessments require student products that are based on assignments that extend beyond writing answers to questions from the textbook. Teachers at most schools working with assessment systems that include extended performance-based tasks noted that they had changed their instructional approach as a result of using the assessment system. Through the use of performance-based pro-

An example of a performance-based task at the high-school level comes from Crandall High in Oregon. At Crandall, tenth-grade students were required, for a social science project, to weave economics terminology into a story about being stranded on a desert island. Students had to use the terms *capital, land, labor, barter, value*, and so on in their stories. In addition, they were required to use a word-processor to write their stories and to give a multimedia presentation based on their stories. However, they could determine the length of their stories and the design of their presentations. According to Crandall teachers, this project enabled their students to acquire and understand basic economic concepts and to write meaningful text.

Another example of a performance-based task comes from Cooper Middle School, which is formulating its own assessments and project-based instruction. For a thematic unit entitled, "Freedom and Responsibility," students were required to hold a mock trial: Should the United States of America ban the sale, manufacture, and use of cigarettes? To prepare for this debate, students: (a) used a variety of books and other resource materials to research the topic; (b) prepared for a role—such as a judge, a prosecutor, or a defense attorney—in the trial; (c) conducted the trial; and (d) wrote a persuasive essay for or against the ban, based on the court proceedings.

A third example comes from Ann Chester, an elementary school in Fort Worth, Texas. Ann Chester students designed their own playground, working with a budget and a building schedule and taking into consideration their play needs in the playground design specifications.

FIG. 5.1. Examples of performance-based tasks.

jects, teachers are attempting to foster in their students analytical thinking and multidisciplinary understanding.

At 5 of the 16 schools visited—Niños Bonitos Elementary, Westgate Middle, Walters Middle, Manzanita High, and Park Elementary—the use of performance-based assignments did not come about as a result of the assessment system. At at least two of these schools—Niños Bonitos and Park Elementary—teachers already were following an instructional approach that functioned independently of the assessment system.

For example, at Park Elementary in New York City, teachers observe student behavior during structured play and listen to student conversations to determine what literacy, scientific, or mathematical concepts the student might be ready to learn next. Thus, students are continually engaged in "projects"—making cookies, writing in their journals, creating Lego designs, and sewing and painting—and teachers are continually engaged in "assessing," using classroom observational methods. Thus, use of the Primary Learning Record has provided Park Elementary teachers with a powerful, nonintrusive assessment method that works synergistically with "project-based" instruction. Indeed, teachers claim that the Primary Learning Record can work as a substitute for IEPs, leading to individualization of instruction. At both Niños Bonitos and Park

Elementary, although teachers do not necessarily model their instructional strategies on the assessments, they do value the information they gain from the use of the assessment system.

At the other three sites—Westgate Middle, Walters Middle, and Manzanita High—teachers have neither appropriated the assessments nor devised performance-based projects modeled on the district- or state-level performance assessments. At Westgate Middle, PWC's Applications Assessments are still too new to have affected instruction. Westgate teachers also indicated that they were waiting for the district's new curriculum before investing much time into modifying instruction. On the other hand, at Walters Middle and at Manzanita High, the assessment systems have not permeated the classroom in any meaningful way. (All three of these assessment systems comprise on-demand tasks that are administered once a year, requiring little teacher and student involvement on a regular basis; in fact, one Westgate teacher speculated that the most likely effect of the Applications Assessments is that "there will be another test-taking strategy to be taught.")

Writing. An increased emphasis on writing skills has been especially powerful in several schools as a direct result of two factors:

- Portfolio requirements in language arts and in other subject areas.
- Writing requirements in most performance-based projects.

Not surprisingly, in classrooms where language arts portfolios are in use, both teachers and students mentioned that students are required to engage in an extensive amount of writing. For example, at Maple Leaf Middle, Vermont, and Breckenridge Middle, Kentucky, several teachers are placing more emphasis on teaching the writing process (i.e., writing, editing, and rewriting), and are including drafts of student work in portfolios. Teachers also mentioned that the current student cohort is required to write much more than were earlier student cohorts.

Teachers at these schools reported, however, that they are struggling with how to strike a balance between what they see as "the mechanics of writing" and the stylistic, communicative, and expressive aspects of writing. For example, at Maple Leaf, the eighth-grade language arts teacher switched from concentrating mostly on the creative aspects of writing in 1993–1994 to paying more attention to grammar in 1994–1995.

Whether the writing process has actually led to *good* writing, however, is still open to debate. In fact, according to teachers at Breckenridge Middle, Kentucky, because "mechanics" of writing and grammar receive minimal weighting in overall scoring of the writing portfolio, the current system actually fails to encourage writing that is good in all aspects.

At only two sites where portfolios or extended performance tasks are in use—Crandall High and Windermere Elementary—teachers and students did not mention that they were placing greater emphasis on writing skills than they previously had. It is quite conceivable that at both of these sites, the emphasis on other aspects of research-based projects overshadows the writing part of these projects.

Group Work.   Group student work is another instructional strategy and classroom organizational mode commonly employed at schools engaged in assessment systems comprising portfolios or extended performance tasks. According to teachers at these schools, group work blends in nicely with the use of extended performance-based projects that require several procedures or steps to complete. However, variation in the structure (i.e., what students do in groups) and the composition of student groups, as well as in the length of time these groups are sustained, is considerable. Cooperative exercises range from division of labor coupled with individual accountability for a common student product to peer assessments of individual student work. For example, the Pacesetter teachers at Sommerville require students to work together in groups to complete math problems; however, each student must record his or her own answer to the problem. At McGary Elementary, Harrison School District 2, students are encouraged to perform peer evaluations based on scoring rubrics specially designed for students.

At only two of the schools using portfolios or extended performance tasks—Thoreau High and Windermere Middle—have teachers not placed a premium on requiring students to work together in groups. The assessments at these sites require individual students to research a topic (or, in the case of Thoreau, topics) and to present their research findings. Hence, group work is not a natural extension of the assessment system.

At Westgate Middle, Walters Middle, and Manzanita High, teachers have not consciously decided to use group work as a result of the district- and state-level assessments systems.

Scoring Rubrics.   Our data indicate that the use of scoring rubrics for pedagogical purposes is the most visible aspect of teacher appropriation of assessment technologies. It also is the most significant, because performance assessments are the only likely pathway through which the pedagogical changes we discuss later could take place. Teachers use scoring rubrics with students to:

- Set performance standards and expectations.
- Engage and empower students in the learning process.

At state- and district-level sites, teachers use the state- and district-generated rubrics and also design their own rubrics; at school-level sites, teachers design and use their own rubrics; and at national-level sites teachers use the NSP and Pacesetter rubrics, but also design their own.

In Vygotskian terms, the scoring rubric has become a "scaffold" that teachers use for setting performance expectations and standards for their students. Prior to assigning work for extended projects or portfolios, teachers share scoring rubrics with their students to communicate the important aspects of the work to be assessed and to empower and engage students in the learning process. Thus, prior to beginning their work, students become aware of, and can take into consideration, the criteria to be used in judging the quality of their work. At sites using extended performance tasks and portfolios, the use of scoring rubrics has brought all students into the same "fold"—into the same frame of reference—for judging their own and their peers' work.

At Hudson High, Maple Leaf Middle, Crandall High, and McGary Elementary, teachers require students to assess their own and their peers' work using scoring rubrics. Teachers at these schools mentioned that students are much more engaged with the assigned task and better able to internalize performance standards and task requirements when they use the scoring rubric to judge their peers' and their own work.

In fact, at two elementary schools—Ann Chester and McGary—to truly engage students in the assessment process, teachers ask students to devise their own scoring rubrics to use with the assigned projects. One McGary teacher was pleasantly surprised by how student-empowering scoring rubrics are: "I have never before had a student come to me with a B and ask, 'How do I get an A?'"

Only at Niños Bonitos Elementary, Thoreau High, and Sommerville High do teachers not use scoring rubrics with students. Niños Bonitos's scoring rubrics may be too complicated for elementary school children, and Thoreau and Sommerville teachers have not devised any written scoring rubrics.

Our sample of assessments shows that there is a tremendous amount of variation in the quality and types of scoring rubrics in use at the classroom level. Some of the sampled assessment systems include generic rubrics that specify the dimensions of knowledge or areas of importance to be assessed in different types of student work. These systems include Kentucky's, Oregon's, Vermont's, South Brunswick's, Niños Bonitos Elementary's, and New Standards Project-influenced systems at Ann Chester Elementary and Noakes Elementary. Our data indicate that generic rubrics function as powerful pedagogical guides, because teachers must design and use assessment tasks that elicit the skills and competencies articulated in these rubrics. Other rubrics are tailored to specific performance tasks and detail the characteristics that must be present in those tasks. Assessment systems in Kentucky, Maryland, Hudson High in New York, Harrison School District 2, Prince William County, Cooper Middle, Ann Chester Elementary, Noakes Elementary, and Sommerville High (for formal Pacesetter assessment) include specific rubrics. (Note that both types of rubrics are in use at some sites.) Still other scoring rubrics (mainly devised by teachers for use at the classroom level and not a part of the formal assessment system) are more like checklists that communicate to the student the "items" that must be present in his or her work. Teachers in this case tend to use "existence proofs" (i.e., presence of such items or characteristics), rather than the quality of the information present in order to assign grades. (Such checklists are helpful to the student, but they cannot be meaningfully referred to as scoring rubrics.)

Technology.   In our sample schools, the use of technology for instructional or assessment purposes has so far been minimal. Only Cooper and Crandall are well equipped with computers, scanners, and video cameras, and regularly use these technologies for teaching and learning. Both schools have staff members who have been recently trained in the use of technology for pedagogical purposes. At Sommerville High, teachers and students in Pacesetter classes regularly use graphing calculators, because its use is a Pacesetter requirement.

At Maple Leaf Middle, Niños Bonitos, and Breckenridge Middle, teachers are attempting to integrate technology into daily teaching and learning practices by requiring their students to use a word processor on a regular basis for their portfolio writing assignments. Technology, however, has not been fully exploited and integrated into instruction to pace student work, to provide access to information, or to create a different (e.g., "floating" or "open") classroom organizational structure.

Teacher Role

The initial promise of reform included the transformation of the teacher's role, from one that conceptualized teachers as disseminators of information working in isolated, individual classrooms into one that envisioned teachers as professionals needing the feedback and support of their fellow professionals in order to competently fulfill their job of teaching *and* to advance their own learning. As discussed next, evidence indicates that the appropriation and extension of performance assessments, coupled with professional support, has facilitated some changes in that direction. We discuss these changes under the topics of:

- Teacher collaboration.
- Teacher creativity and initiative.
- Teacher observational skills and understanding of students.

Teacher Collaboration.   The necessity for devising structures and methods to establish common frames of reference for assessing student work and to discuss dilemmas associated with using performance assessments has fostered considerable teacher collaboration at schools using portfolios and extended performance tasks. Such collaboration, in fact, has been greatest in the case of assessment systems that require teachers to coordinate the work that is incorporated into student portfolios or the work that is distributed across several classes and judged by a group of teachers.

At Cooper Middle, the use of thematic units and composite student portfolios (for cross-class assignments) has compelled teachers to plan together and to discuss the types of assignments they would like their students to complete. Similarly, at Maple Leaf, Niños Bonitos, Ann Chester, Thoreau, Windermere, and Park Elementary, the necessity of coordinating student assessment has fostered collaborative activity. At Sommerville High, teachers using the Pacesetter mathematics program collaborate in order to learn Pacesetter curricular and instructional strategies from one another.

Breckenridge Middle School in Kentucky is an exception to the finding that portfolios have fostered collaboration among teachers. Although the Kentucky Department of Education encourages teachers to collaborate on scoring portfolios (through various blind scoring methods), only the language arts teachers mentioned doing so. It is unclear whether Breckenridge teachers collaborate on a regular basis for designing the assignments that must be included in student portfolios.

At three elementary schools—Ann Chester, Park Elementary, and Niños Bonitos—melding performance assessments with the philosophy of a child-centered approach to education has resulted in bringing teachers together to discuss issues of instruction and curriculum. For example, at Ann Chester, one teacher group interested in literacy read and discussed Lynn Rhodes and Nancy Shanklin's *Windows into Literacy* (1993).

Teacher collaboration, it must be noted, also is affected by another factor: It only exists in supportive environments, where time is available to teachers to discuss the implications of assessments. At Ann Chester, Park Elementary, Niños Bonitos, and Maple Leaf Middle, such seeds of collaborative efforts have been firmly planted. Teachers meet on a regular basis to discuss assessments, instruction, individual students, and the current literature on teaching and learning. In other places, however, the virtual absence of professional support for modifying and using state- or district-developed assessments and the lack of direct participation in the reform activities has translated into little collaborative effort. One-shot (i.e., performance events administered once a year), external systems in places such as Westgate Middle, Walters Middle, and Manzanita High have not accorded the ongoing opportunities needed for collaborative work. (We return to this issue of time and professional support in the final part of this chapter.)

Teacher Creativity and Initiative.   Related to teacher collaboration discussed previously, another finding is that performance assessments, when coupled with organizational and structural changes, have fueled teacher creativity and initiative in planning lessons, assessments, and classroom organization. Teacher creativity is especially evident in the variety and scope of projects these teachers assign, and in the structures they devise to learn from one another. Teacher creativity and initiative were evident at Hudson, Maple Leaf, Niños Bonitos, McGary, Cooper, Crandall, Ann Chester, Thoreau, Sommerville, Noakes, McGary, and Windermere.

For example, at Ann Chester Elementary, a math teacher uses chess as a medium for teaching problem-solving skills. At another school, Hudson High, the earth sciences teacher has devised a year-long "pet rock" assignment: Students must keep a detailed scientific journal containing their observations, inferences, and predictions about their rock's characteristics, genesis, metamorphosis, geographical location, relationship to the earth's structure and weather patterns, and commercial value.

An example of teacher initiative comes from Maple Leaf Middle. After she had become comfortable with the language arts portfolios, the eighth-grade language arts teacher took the initiative to help teachers of other subject areas move in the direction of performance-based instruction. For example, she helped the social studies teacher develop social studies performance-based assignments and a checklist for scoring the assignments.

Such effects on teacher creativity and initiative have been particularly noticeable with the use of portfolios. However, when structural changes such as provision of time for planning and collaborating with other teachers is not provided, the result is teacher frustration and exhaustion. (As noted in the previous chapter, one of the powerful facilitators of teacher appropriation of assessments is the presence of school-level support.)

Teacher Observational Skills and Understanding of Students.   As a result of collaborative efforts and effective appropriation of performance assessments, some teachers specifically mentioned that they had acquired a better understanding of some of their students through their students' performance on assessments. For example, the use of mathematics portfolios helped the eighth-grade mathematics teacher at Maple Leaf understand a child with limited facility in mathematics. Another example, albeit an atypical one, comes from Westgate, PWC. Although PWC's Applications Assessments are only in the piloting and early implementation phase and have not been adopted by Westgate teachers for instructional purposes, a special education teacher gained a better understanding of the instructional needs of her hearing-impaired students when she observed their reactions of frustration to the on-demand assessments. She realized that she had to place more emphasis on teaching her students language skills in conjunction with critical thinking skills, because the Applications Assessments require the simultaneous application of reading (and, therefore, comprehension), writing, and problem-solving skills.

In addition, teachers at three of the six elementary schools included in this study—Niños Bonitos, Ann Chester, and Park—noted that they had honed their observational skills through the use of assessments. Note that teachers at all three schools emphasize a child-centered approach to education, and observations of young children's behaviors are an important aspect of their pedagogical repertoire. Thus, the new assessment instruments fit nicely into their pedagogical framework. Pacesetter teachers at Sommerville High also noted that they had improved their observational skills.

LEARNING

The myriad influences of performance assessments on teaching are complemented by their influences on student learning (see Table 5.2). The impact of performance assessments on students is due as much to the *content* of performance-based assignments as it is to the *process* of assessment itself. Principals, teachers, students, and parents spoke primarily about the influence of performance assessments on students' motivation to learn and on their writing and thinking skills.

Impact on Motivational and Social Skills

Many interviewees reported that students exhibit a greater motivation to learn and a greater amount of engagement with performance tasks and portfolio assignments than with other types of assignments. Both teachers and students mentioned that, in large part, this effect is due to the sustained attention and effort students must invest in their educational endeavors, because they simultaneously define the parameters of their work and determine its quality.

At several schools (including Hudson High, Maple Leaf Middle, Niños Bonitos, Cooper Middle, Breckenridge Middle, Crandall High, Ann Chester Elementary, Thoreau, Sommerville, Noakes, and Windermere), teachers noted that students are more motivated to learn with performance-based tasks and writing assignments than with homework exercises out of a textbook. For example, one Crandall student described performance-based assignments as "self-motivated learning." Student engagement is particularly true in the case of the portfolio writing systems, such as the one in Vermont, where students are encouraged to reflect and write personal opinions.

Ironically enough, at Manzanita High some students reported that the on-demand assessments did not challenge them to perform at their highest levels. They said that the tests were better suited for "low-performing" students, meaning that the assessments did not require much intellectual effort.

TABLE 5.2

Impact on Learning, by Type of Assessment Task and by Site

	Portfolios				Performance Tasks and Portfolios						Extended Performance Tasks		On-Demand Performance Tasks			Teacher Observation
	Hudson High, NY	Maple Leaf Middle, VT	Niños Bonitos Elementary, CA	Cooper Middle, NM	Breckenridge Middle, KY	Crandall High, OR	Ann Chester Elementary (NSP), TX	Thoreau High, WI	Sommerville High (PS), MD	Noakes Elementary (NSP), IA	McGary Elementary, HSD2	Windermere Elementary, SB	Westgate Middle, PWC	Walters Middle, MD	Manzanita High, AZ	Park Elementary (PLeR), NY
Motivation and social skills																
Motivation to learn	X	X	X	X	X	X	X	X	X	X			X			
Acceptance and ownership of work and level of performance (grades)		X			X		X				X	X				
Ability to work cooperatively in groups				X			X		X							
Writing and thinking skills																
Development of writing skills	X	X	X	X	X			X			X					
Development of research or analytical skills	X				X				X	X	X			X		
Development of a good knowledge base	X					X	X			X	X					
Ability to generalize from one domain to another						X										

134

TABLE 5.2 (cont'd.)

	Portfolios			Performance Tasks and Portfolios							Extended Performance Tasks		On-Demand Performance Tasks			Teacher Observation
	Hudson High, NY	Maple Leaf Middle, VT	Niños Bonitos Elementary, CA	Cooper Middle, NM	Breckenridge Middle, KY	Crandall High, OR	Ann Chester Elementary (NSP), TX	Thoreau High, WI	Sommerville High (PS), MD	Noakes Elementary (NSP), IA	McGary Elementary, HSD2	Windermere Elementary, SB	Westgate Middle, PWC	Walters Middle, MD	Manzanita High, AZ	Park Elementary (PLeR), NY
Children in special education programs																
School success and enhanced learning	X	X	X							X						X
Difficulty completing tasks		X									X	X	X	X		
Sense of frustration and failure											X	X	X			
Considerable amount of "help" for special education students					X											

X = feature present.

Teachers at Maple Leaf Middle, Cooper Middle, Crandall High, Noakes Elementary, and McGary Elementary also reported that students no longer dispute the grades they receive on their assignments as much as students did in the past, and accept their assessed level of performance. Teachers attribute this effect to students' understanding of the scoring criteria; teachers in all of these schools share scoring rubrics with their students and encourage self-assessment.

Although teachers at 10 schools noted that they were assigning more group-based projects to their students than they had previously, teachers at only 3 sites—Cooper Middle, Ann Chester Elementary, and Sommerville High—specifically noted that their students' ability to work cooperatively in groups had improved as a function of such performance-based group assignments. (However, several students and teachers noted that although most students enjoyed working together in groups, some also complained that they had to be responsible for other students' work.)

Writing and Thinking Skills

Interviewees at six sites—Hudson High, Maple Leaf Middle, Niños Bonitos Elementary, Cooper Middle, Breckenridge Middle, and Thoreau High— indicated that students are improving their writing skills and habits as a function of completing written assignments. (At most of these schools, one important focus of the assessments is the development and improvement of writing skills.)

In schools where assessments are geared toward evaluating research and problem-solving skills—Hudson High, Cooper Middle, Ann Chester, Thoreau High, Sommerville High, and Windermere—students and teachers reported that students have acquired good research and analytical skills in the process of completing assessment tasks. Students are better able to use resource materials for projects and also have developed project presentation skills, such as the ability to summarize their work for an audience.

However, the development of a good base of knowledge (better than that of students not exposed to performance assessments and attendant instructional techniques) was mentioned by teachers at only five sites—Hudson High, Cooper Middle, Ann Chester Elementary, Sommerville High, and Noakes Elementary. Furthermore, student acquisition of the ability to generalize the knowledge and principles gained in one domain to another domain as a result of performance assessments and performance-based instruction was mentioned only by interviewees at Crandall High. (Indeed, several teachers agreed that teaching students to apply knowledge and skills across domains remains one of the most difficult pedagogical tasks.) On the other hand, the generalization of writing skills across different subject areas was mentioned by several teachers.

Most salutary effects on student learning were reported by respondents engaged in portfolio assessments and extended performance task assessments. Our data indicate that portfolios and extended performance tasks invite student and teacher engagement on a sustained basis, and, hence, are much more naturally integrated into instruction. Portfolios, in addition, provide an over-time record of student progress and achievement and allow reviews and revisits of old materials on a regular basis. Thus, they provide a powerful means for monitoring students' educational progress. Students themselves testified to how much "fun" it is to review their work and to see their academic progress over the year.

Impact on Children in Special Education Programs

The impacts of performance assessments on children in special education programs is not easy to assess. Because of the diversity of the categories and formats of assessment tasks used at the sample sites, and because of the diversity among the children served in special education programs (SEP), it is not feasible to report coherent findings regarding the impact of performance assessments on these students. Nonetheless, several teachers did talk specifically about the effects of assessments on some of the students in SEP.

Teachers at five sites—including Maple Leaf, Niños Bonitos, Cooper Middle, Noakes Elementary, and Park Elementary—noted a positive impact of assessments on some of their children in SEP. Respondents at these schools said that the use of portfolios and the stress on performance-based tasks has resulted in increased school success and learning for some of these students. For example, Cooper teachers noted that their children in SEP experience success with some performance assessments because many of these students are good with verbal skills and enjoy performance-based projects that allow them to do demonstrations and oral presentations. However, Cooper's special education teacher also said that assessments that place less emphasis on "show" also must be devised to capture the performance of the students in SEP who are shy and not verbal.

At both Niños Bonitos and Park Elementary, performance assessments were employed in order to individualize instruction (as much as teachers could) and also to better serve the needs of disadvantaged students and students in SEP. Hence, Niños Bonitos and Park Elementary teachers have used performance assessments primarily as diagnostic tools. In this regard, the use of performance assessments has been beneficial to children in SEP.

Teachers at several schools also noted negative effects of performance assessments on their students in SEP. Interviewees at Maple Leaf, Cooper, Windermere, Westgate, and Noakes said that their students in SEP have difficulties completing performance tasks, because these children find some of the tasks to be too complicated. Windermere teachers and parents also found that some of their students in SEP suffer a sense of failure and frustration after their oral presentations (because they were assessed by strangers who were not necessarily aware of the students' disabilities.) Similarly, teachers at Westgate and Walters remarked that their students in SEP experienced a sense of failure after taking the on-demand assessments, because on-demand situations were too complicated and stressful for them.

At Breckenridge, in order to counter the possible negative impact of portfolio tasks on their students with disabilities (and bad publicity for the school, because assessment results are used for accountability purposes), teachers admitted to completing some of these students' portfolio assignments.

BARRIERS TO EFFECTIVE CLASSROOM USE

Our data show that several barriers must be overcome before performance assessments can have a positive impact on teaching and learning. Some of these barriers have already been discussed in chapter 4. In this section, we describe the barriers perceived by teachers who are earnestly attempting to appropriate performance assessments and to change the pedagogical processes in their classrooms and, in some instances, also by teachers who like the idea of performance assessments, but have not appropriated them.

The two types of barriers to appropriation and effective classroom use of performance assessments are:

- Lack of time.
- Poorly defined (and understood) content and performance standards.

Lack of Time

Concern over the lack of time to adequately plan and score performance assessments and to use the information emanating from the assessments was voiced by virtually all teachers included in this study (see Table 5.3). Despite heroic efforts on the part of teachers who had appropriated the assessments and modeled their classroom instructional practices on these assessments, the burnout and stress generated by the lack of time could not be avoided. At Sommerville High, teachers mentioned that they had experienced this problem, but had rectified it by obtaining from their principal an additional joint planning period. In addition, Pacesetter provides teachers with a curriculum, instructional units, and curriculum-embedded assessments, reducing (although not eliminating, according to Sommerville teachers) the amount of time teachers must spend designing their own assessments.

Teachers also mentioned a lack of time for participating in professional support and development activities focused on how to effectively integrate performance assessments into instruction. (In many cases, as discussed in chapter 4, such professional development opportunities do not even exist.) This concern loomed large at Cooper, Breckenridge, Crandall, Ann Chester, and Windermere. In fact, Cooper teachers came to the conclusion that they did not possess the expertise and the know-how in teaching mathematics through performance-based methods, because their students were not learning mathematics as well as expected. Therefore, in the 1994–1995 school year, they stopped teaching mathematics through thematic, performance-based methods and reverted back to traditional teaching methods.

TABLE 5.3

Barriers to Effective Classroom Use, by Assessment Task and by Site

	Portfolios						Performance Tasks and Portfolios				Extended Performance Tasks		On-Demand Performance Tasks			Teacher Observation
	Hudson High, NY	Maple Leaf Middle, VT	Niños Bonitos Elementary, CA	Cooper Middle, NM	Breckenridge Middle, KY	Crandall High, OR	Ann Chester Elementary (NSP), TX	Thoreau High, WI	Sommerville High (PS), MD	Noakes Elementary (NSP), IA	McGary Elementary, HSD2	Windermere Elementary, SB	Westgate Middle, PWC	Walters Middle, MD	Manzanita High, AZ	Park Elementary (PLeR), NY
Time																
Lack of time to design, use, and score assessments	X	X	X	X	X	X	X	X			X	X	X	X		X
Participation of only a few teachers (creating a burden on them)		X			X											
Lack of clear and effective teaching models that integrate assessments in the classrooms					X	X	X	X				X				
Standards and performance criteria																
Lack of clearly defined content or performance standards	X	X			X	X	X	*	*						X	*
Disagreement with assessment content or scoring criteria		X				X	X		X					X	X	

X = feature present.
* = not applicable.

Content and Performance Standards

A second major concern that teachers voiced was the lack of clearly defined and understood content and performance standards. Teachers involved in using state-designed scoring rubrics were uncertain about how validly and accurately to judge student performance through these rubrics. Teachers at some state-level sites—Maple Leaf, Vermont, Breckenridge, Kentucky, and Crandall, Oregon—expressed concern over the lack of clearly defined performance standards. (Teachers at Walters Middle and Manzanita High did not mention developing and scoring assessment tasks using any state-generated rubrics.) For example, at Crandall High in Oregon, some teachers were enthusiastic about the use of portfolios and scoring rubrics, but were unsure about what constituted an acceptable level of performance in student work for outcomes such as *conceptual understanding* and *effective communication* aspects of the mathematics and science scoring rubric. At Manzanita High in Arizona, the problem of performance standards was exacerbated by the fact that Manzanita teachers do not believe that the ASAP assessments reflect the breadth of the curriculum teachers are supposed to teach.

Oregon, Vermont, and Prince William County are still defining curriculum frameworks and desired student outcomes or aligning the outcomes with concrete student performance benchmarks within the assessment system. In addition, teachers at the local level do not have sufficient information regarding the changes in the state's or district's curriculum frameworks. For example, in the case of Maryland, the state director of assessment expressed the view that Maryland teachers are still not sufficiently aware of the learning outcomes targeted by the state's assessment program.

At Hudson High and Cooper Middle, teachers were concerned about the rigorousness and fairness of the scoring criteria they had devised; they mentioned that they had little experience and professional training in designing scoring rubrics, and, hence, were not sure whether the rubrics were "good enough." However, teachers at some schools individualize performance standards and are not as concerned about scoring procedures.

A related concern was "sacrificing content to teach process"; several teachers and administrators, as well as parents and community members, believe that students are not being taught enough of the "basics" including multiplication tables, grammar, vocabulary, and "facts". For example, one Maple Leaf school board member was worried that students are not leaving the school system with " a reservoir of basic information and education that they didn't have when they first started [school]."

Teachers at Manzanita High, Maple Leaf Middle, and Westgate Middle were especially concerned that the content of mathematics assessments may not be rigorous enough. For example, one Manzanita mathematics teachers said, "The 12th-grade math assessment covers only basic math skills. In 1994, one problem required that students graph a line, but no other 1994 and no 1993 problems required students to perform any algebra, geometry, trigonometry, or calculus."

Maple Leaf teachers believe that the emphasis in Vermont's mathematics portfolios on communication and writing skills interferes with the teaching of mathematics skills. Westgate teachers believe that this same feature of the Applications Assessments in math may be inappropriate for their students. One teacher expressed especially strong reservations about "all this writing in math" and is not certain that it helps students learn math skills and concepts. (Another Westgate math teacher, however, expressed positive views about the math assessment, noting that it is aligned with the standards developed by the National Council of Teachers of Mathematics.)

In several other schools, however, the National Council of Teachers of Mathematics Standards are well accepted and have permeated the classroom. These schools include Niños Bonitos Elementary, Breckenridge Middle, and Ann Chester Elementary.

At Sommerville, teachers feel that the Pacesetter curriculum, as presented by the developers, does not adequately incorporate the teaching of "math skills" into the task sets. Task sets comprise problems students work on in small groups. Teachers determine how they score and use these task sets.

CONCLUSION

The two strongest conclusions we can draw from these findings are that: (a) students are being asked to write and to do project-based assignments due, at least in part, to the use of performance assessments; and (b) students are more motivated to learn through project-based assignments than with rote exercises out of a textbook. In addition, the teacher's role has changed significantly in some schools; teachers are collaborating more than before and are taking the initiative to create new learning environments for their students.

All of the observed and reported changes in teaching and learning were mediated to a large degree by: the type of the assessment task (e.g., portfolios or on-demand performance tasks); the degree of integration of the assessment into the classroom (i.e., appropriation); and the level of support provided to incorporate the assessment into routine classroom activities. Sites utilizing assessment systems comprised of portfolios and extended performance tasks exhibited the most extensive impacts on teaching and learning, whereas sites involved in implementing on-demand assessment systems exhibited the least number of changes.

The positive and intended changes in pedagogy are most evident for sites engaged in portfolio assessments, because the portfolio format provides teach-ers and students some measure of control over the design of assessment products within a structure for documenting student progress on an ongoing basis. In addition, assessments such as portfolios and extended performance tasks necessitate instructional change, because teachers must design and assign tasks that can be used for evaluative purposes. The use of portfolios and extended performance tasks, however, requires time and in-depth coverage of some topics and, therefore, may result in less-than-full coverage of the course curriculum.

Teachers identified two major barriers to fully appropriating and effectively using performance assessments in their classrooms. The first barrier is a lack of regular time to devise, use, and score performance-based assessments. Teachers at practically all sites voiced concerns over how little time and support they have to do justice to the pedagogical reforms they have undertaken. A second barrier is that the linkages among content, performance, and assessment strategy are not wholly clear at the local level. Thus, at this point, the quality of assessment-influenced pedagogical changes is difficult to determine.

6

Assessment Reform: Findings and Implications

Educators and policymakers across the nation have invested a fair amount of faith in performance assessments as a promising tool of education reform, the goal of which is to enhance students' development of critical thinking skills, writing skills, multidisciplinary understanding, and social competencies. We now face an essential question: Is such faith warranted?

Assessment reform—the shift toward performance-based assessments and away from multiple-choice, norm-referenced tests—is based on the assumption that performance assessments are more pedagogically valuable and more accurate reflections of student achievement than are multiple-choice tests. Specifically, assessment reform is based on the assumptions that:

- Performance assessments support the teaching and the learning of problem-solving skills, critical-thinking skills, and multidisciplinary understanding—all of which are essential for enhancing student achievement.
- Assessing student performance against established standards is better than assessing performance against group norms.
- Performance assessments provide a better measure of student strengths and weaknesses than do multiple choice tests. In addition, many educators claim that performance assessments are more interesting for students, and, therefore, engage students in the assessment process.

Findings from our study indicate that the efficacy of using performance assessments as a strategy for education reform is not unequivocally demonstrated in terms of enhanced student achievement, but that some positive changes that support student learning have, indeed, occurred in educational structures and processes. Those changes, however significant, are far from

143

spectacular. The diversity of experiences educators at our 16 school sites have had with performance assessments indicate that new approaches to student assessment alone are not sufficient to improve teaching and learning. Rather, the principles and ideas underpinning assessment reform must be clearly defined and understood at all levels of educational organization. Furthermore, if assessment reform is to meet its promise of fostering a better educational system and enhanced student achievement, other systemic reforms also must be mobilized, and several factors—including appropriate reform timelines and public information campaigns—must be purposefully incorporated in any reform plan.

The purpose of our study was to answer three basic questions:

- What are the key characteristics of performance assessments?
- What are the facilitators and barriers in assessment reform?
- What are the outcomes of assessment reform?

Next, we summarize the study's most salient findings and then go on to outline policy and research implications that emanate from those findings.

FINDINGS ABOUT THE STATUS OF ASSESSMENT REFORM

1. The assessment reform movement comprises different conceptions of and different strategies to develop and implement performance assessments.

The divergence in the paths our sites have taken in developing and implementing performance assessments does not permit us to draw a "national picture" about the status of assessment reform. We chose our sites to represent different stages of development and implementation of performance assessments and different levels of educational organization, but we found that they also represent their own constructions and understandings of assessment reform.

2. The tasks and assignments students must conduct for performance assessments take a variety of forms, including on-demand, open-ended problems; extended projects; oral presentations and demonstrations; and portfolios. In practice, any non-multiple-choice task that takes one of these forms is now referred to as a "performance assessment", whether or not the assessment possesses the other important characteristics that reformers insist assessments possess.

For all of its focus on performance assessment, the assessment reform movement is fragmented, because "performance assessment" means different things to different people. In fact, our study indicates that the assignments or tasks that students must complete range from on-demand, open-ended, timed problems to long-term research projects that culminate in oral presentations to portfolios of student work. The one feature that these different types of assessment tasks have in common is the requirement that students actively construct responses to problems or prompts. This same feature distinguishes them from multiple-choice tests. Hence, any non-multiple-choice task or assignment is, in assessment reform parlance, referred to as a "performance assessment." However, not all performance tasks are based on the principles of assessment reform (i.e., the teaching and assessing of problem-solving and critical thinking skills and mulidisciplinary understanding).

3. Scoring rubrics are an important component of performance assessments, because they articulate the criteria against which the quality of student work is evaluated. Clearly articulated generic scoring rubrics function as a powerful tool of assessment reform, because they embody the educational outcomes important to the educational organization. Their use in the classroom helps teachers and students to organize learning and teaching around those outcomes.

Student performance on assessment tasks is generally evaluated using a scoring instrument or method. These scoring instruments or methods range from checklists of the items that must be present in student work to *generic scoring rubrics* that articulate the general competency and skill outcomes that must be reflected in student work along with the criteria for judging the quality of student work.

Assessment reform to date has been served most powerfully by generic rubrics. In requiring teachers to design and use assessment tasks that elicit the skills and competency outcomes articulated in the generic scoring rubrics, states (including Kentucky and Vermont) have communicated and promoted the educational outcomes valued by the state.

4. Evidence indicates that interrater reliability on scoring performance assessments can be improved over time and with sufficient professional development opportunities. However, content validity, equity, consequential validity of performance assessments, and meaningfulness of assessment tasks to students remain to be adequately addressed and established.

Data about the technical characteristics of performance assessment systems are generally meager, but they are more likely to be available for state- and district- level systems than for school- and national-level systems. The states involved in full-scale implementation of performance assessment systems have instituted measures to investigate and ensure the content validity and interrater reliability of their systems. Such measures have yielded positive results. For example, interrater reliability for Vermont's portfolios improved between the 1992–1993 and 1993–1994 school years. Systematic information with regard to the assessment systems' consequential validity is just beginning to accrue for some schools. In some cases, surveys show that teachers have aligned their pedagogical strategies with the performance assessment systems. However, consequential validity in terms of student outcomes has not been clearly demonstrated.

On the other hand, most districts and schools involved in our study had not undertaken any formal technical evaluations of their systems. In part, this finding reflects a lack of resources or, in some cases, the developmental status of the assessment system itself. In the case of some school-level systems, teachers regard their homegrown assessments to be reliable and valid for use with their own students, and they perceive no need for an independent evaluation.

5. Performance assessment systems that are moderately prescribed and cast a wide pedagogical net are more likely to effect intended instructional and curricular changes than are those that are either loosely or tightly prescribed and those that cast a measurement net. On the other hand, tightly prescribed assessments that cast a measurement net are more likely to be useful for accountability purposes.

Our findings show that assessment systems can be characterized along two dimensions:

- Level of prescription, which refers to the degree of judgment and control a teacher exercises in implementing the performance assessment system.
- Scope of pedagogical net, which refers to the degree of student and teacher involvement in assessment systems, the representation of different types of assessments, and the frequency with which assessments are used in the classroom.

Our data support the positing of a strong hypothesis: If assessment systems are moderately prescribed—that is, if they provide a structure for implementation within a coherent educational framework and involve teachers in developing and implementing the assessments—the purpose of informing and influencing instruction is more likely to be achieved, at least in the short run.

Our findings also indicate that performance assessment systems that cast wide pedagogical nets (i.e., that involve teachers and students on an ongoing basis and utilize different types of performance assessments) also are more likely to achieve the purpose of informing and influencing instruction. Because such systems invite teacher involvement and engagement, teachers are more likely to "appropriate" the assessments, work with them, and integrate them into the classroom. On the other hand, systems that cast narrow pedagogical nets tend not to spark change in classroom instructional practices (again, at least not in the short run). That is, systems that are meant for accountability purposes tend not to affect classroom pedagogy as quickly, because these systems invite minimal teacher involvement because task specification, administration procedures, and scoring conditions are quite highly standardized.

The state-level assessment systems in our study are tightly to moderately prescribed, and the national-level and school-level systems are, more often than not, loosely prescribed. (District-level systems reflected the entire spectrum of prescription.) Kentucky's and Vermont's performance assessment systems also cast wide pedagogical nets. Both systems require students to compile language arts and mathematics portfolios based on the tasks their teachers assign to them, and both are moderately prescribed, with guidelines and scoring methods that provide the framework for teacher and student participation in the assessment system.

6. Assessment reformers identify five purposes that performance assessment systems are intended to serve. Most systems are intended to serve multiple purposes. The most frequently cited purposes are to influence instruction and curriculum and to monitor student performance. However, in some cases, failure to recognize points of conflict between the different purposes hampers assessment reform, at least in the short run.

The five purposes of performance assessment systems are:

- To influence and inform instruction and curriculum in the direction of teaching problem-solving, critical thinking, and good writing skills.
- To monitor student progress.
- To improve alignment among curriculum, instruction, and assessment.
- To hold schools accountable for student achievement.
- To certify student achievement.

Most assessment reformers involved with the 16 performance assessment systems included in this study identified multiple purposes of their assessments. However, they did not typically prioritize among purposes. Moreover, various purposes are not necessarily compatible with each other (at least not in all combinations), and emphasis on one purpose can sometimes result in an abandonment, or neglect, of another. In short, one performance assessment may not be able to serve all purposes equally well.

Perhaps the most important potential point of conflict between assessment purposes emerges when an assessment is intended both to hold schools accountable for students' performance and to improve instructional practices in the classroom. When held accountable for student performance on an assessment, teachers will teach to the test. When teaching to the test means that students are learning the valued skills, there will not necessarily be a conflict among purposes. However, the depth of the impact on teaching practices will depend on how well teachers understand the pedagogical bases of the assessment and on their own repertoire of instructional practices. Teachers may teach to the test during a finite period of the school year but may not necessarily modify regular practices, and they may not change their pedagogy.

7. State departments of education face numerous obstacles when introducing performance assessments. These obstacles include developing a technically sound system, coordinating assessment reform with other elements of education reform, communicating effectively with teachers about the purposes and value of the assessment, and selling the assessment to the public.

State departments of education in the process of introducing performance assessments (either under their own volition or in response to legislative action) are undertaking extremely complex endeavors. State-level assessments have both political and pedagogical ramifications and, thus, must pass the muster of two different sets of criteria.

Coordination among elements of education reform—most particularly coordination among assessment reform, curriculum revisions, and the development of content and performance standards—will most likely be crucial to the long-term success of assessment reform. Furthermore, this coordination is equally important from political and pedagogical perspectives. Teachers who are unaware of the connections among reforms—either because such connections are unclear or because they have not been made—are left in a quandary about how much time and effort they should invest in an evolving system. The growing emphasis on the development of standards-based curricula and assessments would seem to testify to the late recognition of the need to coordinate reforms.

8. Innovative models of professional development and support are beginning to yield results in terms of building teachers' capacity to work with performance assessment techniques.

Some states and districts are attempting to shift the focus of professional development from communication of facts to capacity building. Kentucky and Vermont in particular have expanded the traditional train-the-trainer model to vest more responsibility in individuals at the school level. They also have involved all teachers of the assessed grades in scoring activities, providing training for teachers in how to apply scoring rubrics to student work. These efforts seem to have paid off in Kentucky and Vermont, because teachers (at least those participating in this study) are becoming increasingly comfortable with both states' portfolio assessments.

National-level reform efforts—such as the New Standards Project, the Coalition of Essential Schools, and the College Board's Pacesetter Program—offer professional development opportunities unlike those typically supported by states and districts. However, the value of these conferences and workshops eventually will be measured in the classroom, where teachers must apply what they have learned to the real world of teaching and learning. Teachers participating in this study who have attended the conferences put on by these organizations have confirmed their value, but also suggest that what they learn at conferences must be modified to their own particular classrooms, schools, and districts.

In short, professional development and support activities, specifically those that focus on expanding teachers' capacity to work with performance-based assessment techniques, are crucial to realizing the purposes of assessment reform. Professional development and support is a necessary, but not sufficient, factor in the success of the reform.

9. Several types of resources, both monetary and nonmonetary, are required for developing and implementing performance assessment systems.

Although we collected information on expenditures related to developing and implementing performance assessments at different levels of educational organization, this information was not always complete. Furthermore, this information is not comparable across sites, because fiscal record keeping is not uniform across the educational organizations in our sample. Nonetheless, our data indicate that developing and implementing performance assessments is a costly venture. It requires different types of resources, not all of which are accounted for in monetary terms.

Aside from money spent on the actual development and implementation of performance assessments, assessment reform activities that require financial investments include gathering and utilizing information about assessment development; organizing and delivering professional development sessions; and disseminating information about assessments to teachers, parents, schools, and others. Yet, other cost categories include library resources and storage space for assessment products such as portfolios.

The costs that are frequently not taken into consideration at any level of educational organization are teacher time in developing, administering, and scoring assessments and student time in completing the assessments. Teachers often mentioned that the time they invested in implementing a performance assessment system over the school year or the time they spent preparing their students for a year-end assessment resulted in their having to curtail the coverage of some content areas. On the other hand, the benefits teachers saw with some of the assessments was that this necessity to do in-depth teaching resulted in enhanced student achievement in some areas.

10. The primary impetus behind the performance assessment movement—the goal of improving teaching and learning in the classroom—is best served when teachers are provided with sufficient opportunity and resources to "appropriate" the assessment technique. Teachers must use (in original or modified form) and value the assessment if they are going to shape classroom practice to reflect it.

It is self-evident that teachers are more likely to appropriate the assessment tools that they develop themselves for use in the classroom. Our findings also identify those factors that contribute to teachers' abilities to appropriate assessments they themselves do not develop. Teachers who work with moderately prescribed assessments—assessments that allow them to exercise discretion over particular aspects of the assessment within an established structure—have reacted more favorably to external assessments than have their counterparts working with assessments that do not allow that discretion. Teachers who are involved in scoring student assessments also are typically more positive about the assessments. Both of these findings illuminate the importance of giving teachers opportunities to grapple with the issues involved in assessing student performance.

11. Where teachers have appropriated performance assessments, they are asking their students to write and complete research-based assignments more often than before, but the quality of this pedagogical shift is unclear.

In several schools implementing performance assessment systems comprising portfolios, long-term research projects, or exhibitions of student work, teachers say they are asking students to write more and to conduct more research-based assignments than they did in the past. Such an instructional shift is driven by the requirements of the assessments in two ways: Teachers must design and assign tasks that enable students to demonstrate their writing capabilities or research and presentation skills, or teachers assign activities throughout the year that help their students develop the skills that a demonstration assessment might tap.

However, two related findings point to why it is difficult to judge the quality of this pedagogical shift. The first is that because teachers are still learning how to incorporate performance assessments into their classrooms, they themselves find it difficult to evaluate any relationship between the pedagogical change and students' learning. The second reason rests in unclear, unarticulated, or variable standards for performance. In the cases of several district- and state-level assessment systems, the content and performance standards associated with the systems are not clear at the local level; therefore, teachers are making a pedagogical shift, but they are uncertain as to what end. In contrast, in the cases of many school-level assessment systems or schools participating in national systems, teachers frequently individualize performance requirements for their students, making it similarly difficult to evaluate the extent to which the performance assessment system is challenging all students to meet equally high standards.

12. Both teachers and students report that students are more motivated to learn through research projects and other performance-based assignments than they are with other types of assignments, a finding that supports one of the assumptions underlying assessment reform.

Teachers and students noted that students are more motivated to learn with performance-based tasks and writing assignments than with textbook-generated homework exercises. This effect is due, they say, to the sustained effort and attention students must invest in conducting research and writing projects and in defining some of the parameters of their own work. Teachers also believe that as a result of investing in projects that require research and writing, students are developing good writing and thinking skills. However, clear, independent evidence that such is the case is not yet available.

13. Teachers have transformed scoring rubrics into pedagogical tools, using them for setting students' performance expectations. The power of this transformation has depended on how well the rubrics are constructed.

That performance assessments can fundamentally transform teaching and learning is most clearly demonstrated through the use of scoring rubrics. Teachers are using scoring rubrics as "scaffolding" to set performance standards for their students, gradually building student performance to higher levels of proficiency. In addition, teachers share scoring rubrics with their students to communicate the criteria they use in judging the quality of students' performances.

Teachers note that sharing scoring rubrics with their students has had a positive effect on students' understanding of the purposes of their assignments. Because of this better understanding, students are better able to become participants in the assessment process itself. Teachers note, too, that students internalize what they learn and develop a common framework for evaluating their own or their peers' work.

However, how well a scoring rubric serves to enhance student learning and understanding depends on how well it is constructed. Some rubrics teachers shared with their students were simply checklists, whereas others were more elaborate (and still others were developed specifically for student use). Although the former type of rubric has proven useful (according to teachers and students who use them), it is the latter type that seems to have a clear effect on students' understanding of what is expected of them.

14. The use of performance assessments with students with disabilities has yielded mixed results.

The appropriate inclusion of students with disabilities in performance assessment systems, and the appropriate accommodations that should be made to support their participation, remain controversial and unclear at the local level.

On the one hand, one justification underlying the movement toward performance assessment—to provide a forum in which students can demonstrate what they know and can do—is compatible with the goals and methods of serving students through individualized educational programs. On the other hand, our findings suggest that the format and the time and skill demands of some performance assessments have posed problems for the participation of students with disabilities in the assessment system.

On the positive side, some teachers noted that their students with disabilities experienced academic success and enhanced learning by conducting the research and writing assignments that comprise the performance assessments. At the same time, however, other teachers indicated that these students often have difficulty completing such assignments. On-demand performance tasks appear to pose the most problems for these students. Because these tasks tend to have time restrictions for completion, and because they may require higher levels of language arts skills than most multiple-choice tests require, students with disabilities often experience a sense of frustration and failure during the assessment process.

15. Although the objective of all performance assessment systems is to assess students against clearly established standards, in some cases the standards are not clear. This lack of clarity impedes teachers' ability to integrate assessments into instruction.

The lack of clearly defined content and performance standards impedes teachers' ability to use the assessments in the classroom. Teachers who make the effort to incorporate assessments into the classroom despite unclear content and performance standards are unsure of the quality of their instructional changes and of the pedagogical utility of the assessment. Indeed, most teachers who find themselves working with state- or district-level assessments for which standards are unclear simply refrain from investing much time and energy into integrating the assessments with their current teaching practices. This finding calls attention to a significant barrier to education (not just assessment) reform: Weak articulation between assessment reform and complementary reforms (particularly the development of content and performance standards) can severely compromise teachers' commitment to and investment in the reform process.

Summary

Assessment reform is occurring at all levels of educational authority—state, district, and school. It also is being spearheaded and supported by national projects and networks such as the New Standards Project and the Coalition of Essential Schools. Regardless of where it is initiated, assessment reform's predominant purpose is to enhance student achievement in terms of critical-thinking, problem-solving, and good writing skills.

Assessment reform, however, cannot be evaluated as a single entity. Current reform efforts encompass different approaches to and stages of performance assessment development and implementation. Some states, districts, and schools have developed performance assessment systems that are congruent with the original tenets of assessment reform. Others' attempts are more piecemeal than not, resulting in difficulties in institutionalizing the reform. Our study indicates that different reform initiatives have experienced varying degrees of success in transforming teaching and learning in American classrooms. It is the range of assessment reform efforts that allows us to identify some findings that illuminate both the features of performance assessment systems that offer promise and the nature of the challenges that face assessment reformers.

These findings, however, remain preliminary, for few performance assessment systems have been in place long enough to allow conclusive evaluation. In the final analysis, the success of assessment reform as a tool to enhance student achievement remains to be rigorously demonstrated.

IMPLICATIONS FOR POLICY
AND FUTURE RESEARCH

Several implications for policy and future research emerge from the present study's analysis of performance assessments and assessment systems with respect to both the intermediate purposes of assessment (i.e., monitoring student progress; alignment of curriculum, instruction, and assessment; and accountability) and the larger purpose of improving teaching and learning. Next, we discuss 14 interconnected general policy implications, followed by some implications specific to particular assessment purposes, and eight recommendations for future research that can build on our findings.

General Policy Implications

Policy implications emanate from both successes and failures that our sites experienced in developing, implementing, and institutionalizing performance assessment systems.

1. Clearly state the primary purpose of the assessment system.

The development and implementation of the performance assessment system depends heavily on the purpose of the assessment system. If the purpose is not clear, the assessment system itself will not be formulated well, and the scores deriving from the use of the assessment system will not be readily interpretable. Thus, for example, if the purpose is to affect instruction in the classroom, the assessment system must be formulated such that it enables teachers to use and to understand how performance assessments might be incorporated in their classrooms; the scores from the use of this system will be interpretable within a pedagogical framework. If the purpose is to monitor school quality and performance, the assessment system must be designed such that it yields high-quality, reliable, and valid data, especially if sanctions and rewards are to be imposed on schools based on the assessment results. If the assessment system is intended to meet multiple purposes, prioritize among the purposes, because one assessment system may not meet all purposes equally well.

2. Match the format of the assessment system with the purpose of the assessment system.

The format of the performance assessment system must be tailored to the purpose of the assessment system. For example, if the purpose of the assessment system is school accountability, the assessment system must include a battery of assessments that are comparable across schools and can be scored using the same scoring criteria. The format of the assessment system, then, has to be fairly tightly prescribed, and its reliability and validity have to be well established. If, however, the primary purpose of the assessment system is to influence pedagogy in a particular direction, the system must be moderately prescribed, allowing teachers to formulate, implement, and score the assessment tasks on an ongoing basis. A moderately prescribed format may well result in noncomparable assessments and nonstandard scoring procedures in the short term, but it will allow teachers, in the long run, to become familiar with the underpinnings and goals of the reform effort.

3. Coordinate assessment reform with other elements of education reform and with other testing requirements.

Coordinating assessment reform with other elements of education reform (in particular, the development of curriculum frameworks and content and performance standards) fosters both assessment reform specifically and education reform generally. Without such coordination, two dangers emerge. First, time and effort spent developing individual reforms is wasted when coordination is imposed late in the assessment reform process. (This effect is equally true for states, districts, and schools developing performance assessments.) Second, teachers may hesitate to invest their own scarce time to work with a new assessment technique when its connection to other planned reforms is not clear.

Coordinating the introduction of performance assessments with other testing requirements (emanating from all levels of authority—state, district, and school) is also important, because such coordination will simultaneously minimize teachers' sense of assessment "overload" and further their sense that the new assessment represents "value added" to the entire system of assessments, not just an "add on."

4. Articulate in clear and simple terms the content and performance standards the assessment system is intended to measure.

The content and performance standards on which the assessment system is to be based must be clearly and simply stated. Insofar as possible, state these standards in measurable, concrete, and content-based terms. (Standards that are stated as general outcomes and those that are perceived as having little connection to disciplinary areas create a sense of anxiety for teachers and provoke opposition on the parts of parents and school board members.) This approach will not only help teachers understand and adopt the assessment criteria, but it also will facilitate communication about the purposes of the reform with school board members, parents, and the general public.

5. Institute procedures to ensure the technical quality and fairness of the assessment system.

To ensure the technical quality of a performance assessment system, instituting procedures to monitor and confirm the continuing validity and reliability of the system is essential. Procedures to ensure validity include developing assessments based on established and accepted content standards (such as those developed by professional associations) and incorporating reviews of the assessments conducted by content area experts and classroom teachers. Procedures to ensure that scoring methods are reliable include developing scoring rubrics that state the scoring criteria in clear, simple, and unequivocal language and utilizing techniques that result in reliable scoring, including group-scoring and social-moderation methods. In the absence of such quality assurance procedures, performance assessments will likely be considered inferior to standardized multiple-choice tests, especially if they are used for high-stakes accountability purposes.

Also institute procedures to determine the fairness and consequential validity of the assessment system. Such procedures might entail investigating the performance of different gender and ethnic groups on the assessments, the effects of the use of such assessments on the education of disadvantaged groups, and the educational outcomes of all groups of students on measures other than the performance assessments themselves.

In addition, conduct small-scale pilot projects to determine the developmental appropriateness of various types of assessment tasks (particularly those intended to be administered to elementary and middle school students) and their meaningfulness to students.

6. In order to obtain a comprehensive picture of student learning, design a performance assessment system that contains a mix of different types of performance assessment tasks and scoring procedures.

Different types of assessment tasks and scoring procedures have different advantages. For example, performance assessment tasks that require students to choose the topic of the assessment reveal individual students' thinking, interests, and strengths. Such tasks, however, may not allow teachers to assess whether students have acquired a particular skill or a particular piece of knowledge that is a part of the curriculum. On the other hand, a task that poses a specific problem may allow teachers to assess whether students have acquired the understanding and skills necessary to solve the problem, but this task may not reveal much about students' interests and strengths. Hence, both types of tasks are essential for gaining a full understanding of students' skills, interests, academic development, strengths, and weaknesses. Assessment systems comprising a mix of assessment tasks and scoring procedures allow teachers, students, and education systems to evaluate more fully educational processes and students' achievements.

7. Design an assessment system composed of assessments that reinforce each other and are based on the same learning outcomes.

In order to give a consistent message to teachers and students, design an assessment system that is composed of assessments that are linked to the same curriculum and learning outcomes. The assessment system may comprise both multiple-choice tests and performance assessments. However, assessments not based on the same learning outcomes may give rise to the perception that one part of the assessment system counts and the other does not. If all parts of the assessment system are used for accountability purposes, the differences in their curricular bases may give rise to a superficial classroom curriculum.

8. Tap existing resources when developing performance-based assessments and coordinated reforms.

Using existing resources to develop performance assessment systems prevents multiple reinventions of the wheel, as it were (50 reinventions at the state level alone, as more and more states move to incorporate performance assessments in their testing systems), and the associated costs of those reinventions. Furthermore, existing resources—including work conducted by organizations such as the National Council of Teachers of Mathematics, the American Association for the Advancement of Science, and the National Council of Teachers of English—often represent the current thinking of the field about the best ways of teaching and assessing in the various disciplines. By using the work of these organizations as a springboard, assessment system developers can be assured that the work they are undertaking is in line with state of the art endeavors.

9. Plan the timeline of reform, keeping in mind the length of time required to institutionalize the change.

The timeline of reform can too often be artificial with respect to the work to be done and, consequently, serve as a barrier to reform in the long run. (This is particularly true in the case of state-initiated assessment reforms and, even more particularly, when state-level reforms are introduced in response to acts of the legislature: Mandated education reform takes place in the context of a desire for long-term change in a short-term world.)

First and foremost, the timeline for reform must be sufficient to ensure the development of a technically sound system. Performance assessments cannot compete with standardized, machine-scorable tests on certain criteria: They cannot always achieve as high levels of interrater reliability in scoring, and they cannot always achieve as high levels of standardization in administration. When performance-based assessments provoke opposition, it is on these fronts that they are particularly vulnerable. Given these disadvantages, performance assessment systems must be as technically sound as possible. Attempts to put a system in place too quickly can undermine the longevity of the system.

The timeline of reform must also be sufficient to allow for people—teachers, students, parents, and administrators, as well as the general public—to become accustomed to and develop faith in the value of the assessment. Public support will, in general, be broadened in cases in which the purposes, format, timeline, and consequences of the performance assessment are clearly communicated.

10. Communicate to the public the purposes of and the theory underlying the assessment.

A good public relations campaign can ward off negative responses to early problems in the development and implementation of the performance assessment system. Communicating to parents accurately and in sufficient detail the different purposes and the implications of the assessment for their children can serve to prevent perceptions of unfairness in the assessment. Such campaigns can include "portfolio nights" where parents are invited to browse through their children's portfolios and to ask questions about the portfolio system, or sharing the assessment with the public by inviting community leaders and legislators to complete the assessment just as students are asked to do.

Included in the public relations campaigns must be assurances to parents, school board members, and legislators that content does not have to be sacrificed with the use of performance assessments and that the format of the assessments does not imply that content knowledge cannot be adequately assessed.

11. Provide and encourage professional development activities that help teachers expand their capacity to work with performance-based assessment techniques.

For the assessment reform to be successful, teachers must develop common assumptions about teaching and learning and common frames of reference about what constitutes evidence of valued student outcomes. Innovative approaches to professional development can go a long way toward supporting teachers' understanding of assessment reform. State departments of education, whose assessment reform initiatives necessarily extend to large populations, face special challenges to ensuring high-quality, useful professional development for all teachers. However, some states have improved on the traditional train-the-trainer model by vesting more responsibility in designated individuals at the school level and by expanding the focus of professional development from communication to capacity building. Hands-on professional development—during which teachers learn to develop assessment tasks, scoring rubrics, and performance standards—increases teachers' capacity to work with performance assessments by guiding them through the issues involved in effective assessment of student growth. Opportunities for teachers to work together to understand performance assessment techniques allow teachers to broaden their thinking about the assessments. Other capacity-building approaches focus on instructional strategies and other issues in pedagogy which, in turn, allow teachers to examine their pedagogical assumptions and beliefs.

12. Involve teachers in the design and implementation of the system, and make the system as loosely prescribed as possible within the context of the purposes of the assessment.

Involving teachers in the process of designing and implementing the assessment system is likely to promote their appropriation of the assessment and, consequently, to effect meaningful changes in their pedagogical practices. Even state departments of education developing performance assessment systems can involve large numbers of teachers when the system calls for teachers to specify tasks within a given structure and to score student efforts using state-developed scoring procedures. Teachers who are involved in developing and implementing systems are more likely to appropriate the assessment technique because they have had time to work through the issues and problems associated with accurate assessment of students' knowledge and achievement.

Furthermore, by designing a loosely to moderately prescribed assessment system—one that allows teachers room to exercise their judgment in developing tasks and in setting scoring criteria and performance standards—teachers' ability to appropriate the assessment system is enhanced. The principal problem associated with assessment systems that are not tightly prescribed is that they typically lack standardization, in terms of administration procedures, standards of performance, or both. Thus, when introducing assessment systems that are to be used for accountability or certification purposes, states and districts will necessarily develop systems that are more tightly prescribed than are systems not used for these purposes. However, assessment reformers should be aware of the trade-offs between the standardization that accountability and certification purposes require and the likely effect on teachers' appropriation—and, hence, changes in teaching practices—of the assessment technique. Therefore, depending on the purposes the assessment is intended to achieve, state and district assessment reformers may want to strive to design systems that are moderately prescribed—that is, systems that allow teachers some discretion to design and administer tasks within a specified structure.

13. Encourage schools to provide teachers with time to develop assessments and to discuss their assessment experiences with colleagues.

Teachers who know that their schools, districts, and states value the time they devote to working with newly developed assessments and who, as a result, are provided with regular time to develop and discuss assessment techniques are more likely to use the assessments thoughtfully. Furthermore, they know that the school, district, or state is serious about the reform when teachers are provided with this time. Regularly provided time can take on several forms—for example, release time from the classroom, compensated time spent at weekend and summer conferences or doing independent assessment-related work, early release of students on a regular basis to provide more teacher planning time, and additional planning periods for teachers involved in developing and implementing reforms. When states and districts (even more than schools) make provisions for this time, they signal to teachers that the work the teachers are doing is important and valued.

14. Provide waivers from testing and reporting requirements to schools experimenting with innovative assessment techniques.

School-level assessment reform efforts can be hampered by state- and district-level testing and reporting requirements that are incompatible with the assessment system being developed and implemented by the school. The provision of waivers from these requirements can free up teachers to experiment in designing assessment systems that make sense to them pedagogically.

Specific Policy Implications

Although the general policy implications discussed previously are applicable to assessment systems intended for most any purpose, the degree of their importance for any given assessment system is a function of the primary purpose of that assessment system. Our research indicates that the success of assessment reform depends on aligning the format of the assessments and other aspects of education reform with the major purpose of the new assessment system. (Conversely, the major purpose of the new assessment system must be aligned with the other aspects of education reform.) Next, we discuss the two major functions of performance assessments and the development and implementation issues that must be given priority.

Improve and Inform Instruction and Curriculum. If the major purpose behind the reform is to improve and inform instruction and curriculum at the local level, the following points deserve special attention:

1. Design a moderately to loosely prescribed assessment system to enable teachers to actually work with the system in their classrooms. Also design assessments that can be easily integrated into different subject areas and into the school day.

2. Provide clearly written content frameworks, performance standards, and assessment guidelines to teachers and administrators.

3. Pay more attention to issues of content quality and curriculum and assessment coordination than to attaining interrater reliability.

4. Provide ongoing professional development in the design, use, and scoring of new assessments and also in how to use new pedagogical strategies that align with the·new assessments, how to choose new curricular materials, and how to use new pedagogies with all students.

These ongoing professional development sessions must be designed, to some extent, to fit the local-level needs, whether the "local level" is the district, the school, or the classroom. Also, information must be provided to teachers about how to explain the assessments to students and their parents.

5. Because developing and using new assessments and associated curricula requires teacher time, consider changing the structure of the school day. Devise new schedules through block scheduling, team-teaching approaches, extended school days, and other methods that allow teachers more time to learn and to teach their peers. Teachers must have the time to use, reflect on, and discuss new reforms.

School or District Accountability. If the primary purpose of a state- or district-level assessment system is to hold schools and districts accountable for student performance, assessment reformers should consider the following points:

1. To ensure the rigor of the assessment system in measuring whether or not standards have been met, design a tightly to moderately prescribed assessment system.

Accountability must be based on standards that are applied uniformly across the educational system. Thus, in order to assess whether or not standards have been met, the assessment instrument must be uniform, or comparable, across the accountability unit.

2. Institutionalize rigorous quality assurance procedures to ensure the content validity, intertask reliability, fairness, and interrater reliability of the assessments.

Use information from reputable professional organizations and from publicly recognized master teachers for developing assessment tasks and scoring methods. In addition, institutionalize procedures to evaluate the fairness of the assessment systems to schools and to individual students. Such procedures might entail evaluating whether differential performance on these assessments can be attributed to a poorly designed assessment or to opportunity-to-learn factors. The implications emanating from the two explanations of differential performance are quite distinct.

3. Public information is an important component of the accountability mechanism. The "public" includes parents, school board officers, and legislators, and information must be tailored to fit each group's information needs.

Parents typically want to know whether or not their children are receiving a good education that will provide them with the knowledge and skills they need for higher education or future employment. Therefore, information designed for parents must explain how implementing the assessment is connected to school quality and how assessment instruments are connected to the curriculum. In addition, parents must be assured that the assessment system is not biased against their schools or their children. Thus, school or district accountability scores must be contextualized within information about the assessment system's relationship to quality education.

School board members and legislators, in addition to being informed about the issues outlined previously, must see the costs of the program in relation to its benefits. Thus, information on expenditures must be contextualized within what teachers and administrators view as the short-term and long-term benefits of the use of the assessment system. Therefore, think through and clearly state the costs and benefits of the assessment system that extend beyond just the short-term accountability function.

Involve school board members in disseminating information about the assessments and about other policies to parents and legislators. They could translate the meaning of assessment scores to parents and to the general public, and explain why standards-based assessments are better than norm-referenced assessments.

4. If the assessment system is to be used for high-stakes accountability, collect information on known correlates of student performance on assessments.

If high-stakes accountability is based only on students' performance on the assessment system, the accountability system may provoke opposition on the parts of teachers and school administrators, who also may be tempted to corrupt the assessment implementation procedures. If accountability measures take into account known correlates of student performance, then this information could be used to contextualize the assessment scores and to provide help to schools in improving their scores.

Implications for Future Research

The following topics deserve the attention of future researchers.

1. Continued research into how the technical properties and fairness of perform-ance assessment systems can be improved.

Over the long run, the technical soundness will be, perhaps, the primary determinant of whether or not the movement toward performance-based assessments perseveres. Areas of concern include:

- Content validity of assessment tasks, especially for tasks that are intended to assess problem-solving skills and multidisciplinary understanding.
- Consequential validity of assessment systems, especially with regard to their effects on the teaching and learning processes in the classroom.
- Fairness of the assessment systems, especially with regard to opportu-nity-to-learn factors that might be considered in developing and imple-menting the assessment system.
- Inferences that can be drawn from scores on different types of perform-ance assessments, especially if the inferences are drawn at the individual student level.
- Features of assessment tasks that are intended to be meaningful to students, especially tasks that are intended to motivate students to engage in the task.

Further research into how technical soundness and fairness of assessment systems can be maximized is crucial to the future of the assessment reform movement.

2. Research into the most effective combinations of instructional models and assessments (including multiple choice tests) that result in improved student learning.

Our findings indicate that although teachers utilize a variety of instructional models in conjunction with performance assessments, they are not always satisfied with the fit between instruction and assessment. Some teachers have expressed the concern that the kind of instructional models that conform to performance assessments may be developmentally inappropriate and may also result in a narrowed classroom curriculum. Research programs that investigate the effectiveness of the different combinations of instructional models and student assessment systems (including different types of performance assessments) are critical for understanding the connections among instruction, assessment, and student outcomes for students at different age levels and for different subject areas.

3. Longitudinal research of facilitators and barriers in assessment reform.

The current study was able to investigate the facilitators and barriers in assessment reform only in the development and early implementation stages of reform efforts. In particular, some of the barriers identified may, over the long run, be broken down or become less significant as systems become established. Thus, the tentative set of barriers and facilitators identified here will be better understood in the light of future research that analyzes their effects in the long run.

In addition, future research must investigate further those school-level factors that hinder or facilitate the implementation of state- or district-initiated reforms at the school level.

4. Research into how different types of performance assessments are or are not appropriate for assessing the progress of children with disabilities.

Little is known about the preparedness of children with disabilities to handle performance assessments, or about how the inclusion (or lack of inclusion) of children with disabilities in large-scale performance assessment systems affects the educational experiences of these children. On the one hand, educators have long turned to "authentic" assessments to use with these children so that the time pressures of traditional methods do not hamper the child's ability to demonstrate what he or she does or does not know. On the other hand, the appropriateness of new performance assessments for use with these children has not yet been demonstrated. Topics for future research include how children with various disabilities handle portfolios and what support and accommodations they need to complete portfolio tasks; how children with disabilities respond to on-demand performance assessments and extended projects that are to be completed within a certain amount of time or require group activities; and how performance standards should or should not be adjusted for these children.

5. Research into the types of professional development and support activities that best enable teachers to understand and implement different types of performance assessments.

Our research clearly indicates that a variety of professional development and support activities is key to the successful implementation of assessment reform. However, the effectiveness of the different models of professional development aimed at teachers' understanding of assessment development procedures, validation and scoring procedures, use of assessments, and instructional models that support performance assessments is as yet poorly understood. Therefore, research that identifies professional support models for the different facets of assessment reform would help to utilize scarce time and precious resources in a more beneficial and concrete fashion.

6. Research into the impact of the use of performance assessments and related teaching strategies on student learning.

Further research must be more specific than the current study was able to be in evaluating the extent to which particular performance assessment formats promote the acquisition of particular skills and knowledge. Furthermore, it must investigate whether the acquisition of certain skills and knowledge precludes the acquisition of certain other skills and knowledge within a given domain. Research of this nature must be tailored to specific assessment systems that are carefully chosen to represent different formats but the same content areas.

7. Research into how opportunity-to-learn factors affect disadvantaged students' performance on different types of performance assessments.

Several educators have raised concerns about the performance of disadvantaged children on performance assessments. However, equity concerns are not likely to be answered without taking into consideration the opportunity-to-learn factors that affect student performance. Thus, educators and policymakers must include in their agendas research regarding the effect of opportunity-to-learn factors on disadvantaged students' performance on the newer forms of assessments. Performance assessments by themselves may not be biased against disadvantaged students.

8. Research into the long-term benefits of the use of performance assessments as compared with the long-term costs of developing and implementing performance assessments.

Long-term costs and benefits must be conceptualized on an *a priori* basis and evaluated using a longitudinal research design. The present fiscal costs of developing and implementing performance assessments are substantial, but so are the projected benefits. Whether or not such is the case must be empirically judged.

Appendix A

Study Objectives and Design

OBJECTIVES

The major objectives of the 3-year longitudinal study *Studies of Education Reform: Assessment of Student Performance* are as follows:[1]

Objective 1: Document and analyze key characteristics of performance assessments.

Objective 2: Document and analyze facilitators and barriers in assessment reform.

Objective 3: Document and assess impacts of performance assessments on teaching and learning.

Our ultimate purpose in this study was to elucidate the status of assessment reform in U.S. education systems and to offer recommendations for policy and future research.

Our approach to meeting the three objectives outlined here was driven by our conceptualization of the relationships among the factors driving and affecting assessment reform and its outcomes. We conceptualized the key characteristics of performance assessments and the facilitators and barriers in assessment reform as interdependent variables that influence teaching and learning processes and student achievement. Figure A.1 illustrates our conceptual scheme.

RESEARCH DESIGN

Our research design employed a qualitative, case-study approach to collecting data about performance assessments and their impacts at the school level. In addition, during the course of the study, we also collected a library of policy,

---

[1]The specific research questions are presented in Appendix C.

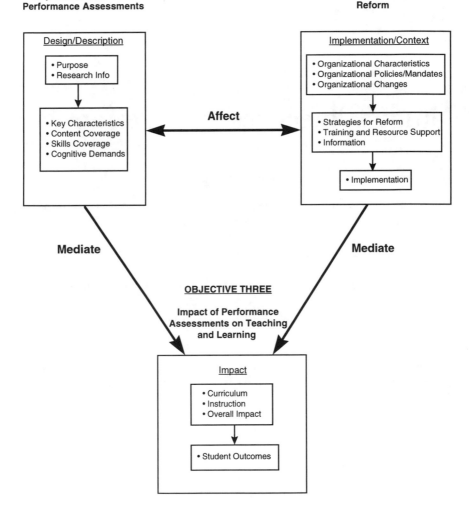

OBJECTIVE ONE

**Document
Key Characteristics of
Performance Assessments**

OBJECTIVE TWO

**Document Facilitators
and Barriers in Assessment
Reform**

Design/Description

- Purpose
- Research Info

- Key Characteristics
- Content Coverage
- Skills Coverage
- Cognitive Demands

Affect

Implementation/Context

- Organizational Characteristics
- Organizational Policies/Mandates
- Organizational Changes

- Strategies for Reform
- Training and Resource Support
- Information

- Implementation

Mediate

Mediate

OBJECTIVE THREE

**Impact of Performance
Assessments on Teaching
and Learning**

Impact

- Curriculum
- Instruction
- Overall Impact

- Student Outcomes

FIG. A. 1. Conceptual scheme of major objectives.

research, historical, and other documents on performance assessments, assessment reform, and education reform in general. Next, we describe the following aspects of our research design:

- Collection and analysis of background literature.

- The qualitative, case-study methodology.
- Sample selection criteria.
- Sample description and data collection activities.
- Data analysis procedures.

We conclude by pointing out the strengths and weaknesses of the research design employed with respect to meeting the purposes of the study.

Collection and Analysis of Background Literature

We collected the following types of documents continuously over the entire span of our study:

- *Theoretical papers* on issues dealing with all aspects, including the development and implementation of performance assessments.
- *Empirical research papers* on issues regarding effectiveness, equity, psychometrics of performance assessments, and data on student outcomes.
- *Policy papers* on the development, implementation, and uses of performance assessments.

We culled relevant information from these documents in a literature review at the beginning of the project in the fall of 1992, and again toward the close of the project in the spring of 1995. We also used these papers to deepen our understanding of the issues related to the development, implementation, and impact of performance assessments and to inform our analyses of the case-study data.

Qualitative Research Methodology: A Case-Study Approach

We employed a qualitative, case-study methodology to investigate the development and implementation of performance assessments and their impacts at the school level. We designed a modified time-series approach for gathering data, which enabled us to obtain both cross-sectional and longitudinal data. Cross-sectional data allowed us to make comparative remarks about assessments and school contexts. The longitudinal data allowed us to document the effects of and changes in performance assessments over time within sites.

We selected 16 sites (the definition of *site* for this study encompasses both a performance assessment and a single school at which it is being used), which a team of two researchers visited a single time during a 2-day site visit. We then selected a subset of seven sites, which the team returned to for a second visit (therefore, longitudinal data were collected for only 7 of the 16 sites).

We conducted the first set of site visits in the spring of 1994, and the second set of site visits in the spring of 1995. (Two of the single-time site visits were conducted in the spring of 1995.) Figure A.2 shows our site visit design.

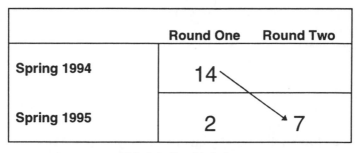

	Round One	Round Two
Spring 1994	14	
Spring 1995	2	7

FIG. A.2. Site visit design.

Sample Selection Criteria

As described previously, our research design called for two waves of data collection: a first round of visits to all sites included in the sample, followed by a second round of visits to a subset of those sites. Next, we describe the criteria we applied to select sites for inclusion in rounds one and two.

Selection Criteria: Round One Sites.   The overarching objective of our site selection process was to identify, insofar as possible, a set of school sites that exhibited the range of experiences that American schools are encountering with the development and implementation of performance assessments. For the purposes of our study, we defined a case-study site as a single school where a performance assessment was being implemented. The focus of our research was on the assessment and its implementation in the local context. To select the sites, we delineated two sets of criteria—those pertaining to performance assessments and those pertaining to schools.

Performance assessments are marked by a number of variable characteristics, and we attempted to obtain variation in our sample within each characteristic. Selection criteria pertaining to performance assessment characteristics included:

- *Type of assessment.* Performance assessments come in a variety of forms, including portfolios, on-demand assessments, demonstrations and presentations, and extended projects. We wanted our sample to include assessments that reflected this range so that we might discern variation in effects of assessment type on teaching and learning at the local level.
- *Locus of development.* The movement toward the use of performance-based assessments is taking place at all levels of educational authority. States, districts, and schools alike are developing and implementing performance assessments. Furthermore, some national-level efforts, such as the New Standards Project and the Coalition of Essential Schools, are also influencing the turn toward performance assessments. Because the pur-

poses, design, and impact of assessments developed at different levels of authority could potentially vary significantly, we wanted our sample to reflect this diversity in locus of development.

- *Status of implementation.* The entire performance assessment movement is still relatively young. However, performance assessments do vary with respect to their stage in development and implementation. Therefore, we wanted our sample to include assessments at varying stages of implementation: developmental and pilot, full-scale implementation, and maintenance.
- *Content area.* Performance assessments can be used in all subject areas, but the assessments can look different for different subject areas. We wanted our sample to include assessments that focused on a range of subject areas including language arts, mathematics, science, and social science.

Although we were less concerned with school background characteristics (e.g., size, racial and ethnic composition, and socioeconomic background of the student body) than we were with the assessment characteristics delineated previously, we attempted also to obtain variation across two school characteristics:

- *School level.* We wanted the sample to include elementary schools, middle schools, and high schools, because performance assessments might affect teachers and students differently at the various levels of schooling.
- *Geographical diversity.* Because American children are educated in schools in 50 states and the District of Columbia, and because these schools are located in urban, suburban, and rural areas, we wanted the sample to include school sites located in various regions of the country and in communities of varying urban or suburban composition.

Because the sample for this qualitative study was to include 16 schools, it is clear that not all combinations of the six factors described here could be included (if, indeed, they even exist). Rather, we aimed to create a sample in which the range of characteristics for each of the six criteria was represented.

Selection Criteria: Round Two Sites.   We chose a subset of seven sites for a second round of data collection. We based selection of the seven round two sites on one or both of the following criteria:

- It was anticipated that changes in the performance assessment design or implementation would take place between 1993-94 and 1994-95.
- Our understanding of the effects of assessment reform at the site was less than clear based on one round of data collection and was likely to improve with a second visit.

Sample Description

Sixteen performance assessments at 16 school sites were selected to comprise the study sample. The 16 sites are identified in Table A.1.

Table A.2 provides information about the characteristics of each of the 16 sites included in the study sample. As illustrated, these characteristics demonstrate the variation we achieved in our sample with respect to our selection criteria.

Table A.3 identifies the seven sites we selected for a second visit during round two of our data collection.

Data Collection Activities and Instruments

Because we were interested in obtaining information about the performance assessment, the educational context within which it was developed and implemented, and the assessment's impact at the local level, we collected documentary, phone interview, and site visit data.

TABLE A.1
16 Round One Sites*

Sites
State-level assessments:
• Arizona assessment reform, Manzanita High School.
• Kentucky assessment reform, Breckenridge Middle School.
• Maryland assessment reform, Walters Middle School.
• New York Regents portfolios, Hudson High School.
• Oregon assessment reform, Crandall High School.
• Vermont portfolios, Maple Leaf Middle School.
District-level assessments:
• Harrison School District 2's performance-based curriculum, McGary Elementary School (CO).
• South Brunswick Township Public Schools' Sixth-Grade Research Performance Assessment, Windermere Elementary School (NJ).
• Prince William County Public Schools' Applications Assessments, Westgate Middle School (VA).
School-level assessments:
• Language arts and math portfolios, Niños Bonitos Elementary School (CA).
• Primary learning record, Park Elementary School (NY).
• Rite of passage experience, Thoreau High School (WI).
National-level assessment projects:
• New Standards Project, Ann Chester Elementary School (TX).
• New Standards Project, Noakes Elementary School (IA).
• Coalition of Essential Schools, Cooper Middle School (NM).
• The College Board's Pacesetter mathematics program, Sommerville High School (MD).

*All schools have been assigned pseudonyms.

TABLE A.2
Sample Characteristics

Assessment Criterion	Sample
Type of assessment	A majority (10 of the 16) of the assessments involved multiple types of assessment tasks. The number of sites using each type of assessment is as follows:
	8 on-demand tasks
	8 extended performance tasks or projects
	10 portfolios
	3 demonstrations or presentations
	2 teacher observations
Locus of development	4 national-level assessments (3 national organizations, 4 sites)
	6 state-level assessments
	3 district-level assessments
	3 school-level assessments
Status of implementation	3 pilot and development
	12 full-scale implementation/maintenance
	1 implementation by individual teachers
Content area	Most (13 of the 16) of the assessments incorporated multiple subject areas. Some were integrated assessments, whereas others incorporated distinct assessment tasks for various subject areas. Most assessments that focused on multiple subject areas included language arts and mathematics, and some included science and social science. The number of performance assessments focusing on different subject areas is as follows:
	11 language arts
	8 mathematics
	5 science
	5 social studies
	1 practical living/vocational

School Criterion	Sample
Grade level	6 elementary schools
	5 middle schools
	5 high schools
Geographical diversity	As is demonstrated in Table A.1, our sample included schools from most regions of the country. One exception was an underrepresentation of southern states: Sites in Kentucky and Virginia were included, but no states from the deep south were represented in the sample. This was in part because, at the time of sample selection, few southern states were introducing state-level performance assessments.
	The sample is composed primarily of schools located in urban and suburban areas and small cities. Rural sites are underrepresented.

TABLE A.3
Seven Round Two Sites

Sites
State-level assessments:
• Kentucky assessment reform, Breckenridge Middle School.
• Oregon assessment reform, Crandall High School.
• Vermont portfolio assessments, Maple Leaf Middle School.
District-level assessments:
• Prince William County Public Schools' Applications Assessments, Westgate Middle School (VA).
School-level assessments:
• Language arts and math portfolios, Niños Bonitos Elementary School (CA).
• Primary learning record, Park Elementary School (NY).
National-level assessment projects:
• Coalition of Essential Schools, Cooper Middle School (NM).

Documentary Data. Prior to and during each site visit, we collected background documentary data about the subject assessment. The available data varied across assessments. Types of data collected include:

- Descriptions of performance assessments.
- Samples of performance assessments (both blank and as completed by students).
- Policy documents about the assessments.
- Policy documents about related education reform efforts.
- Evaluation and research reports regarding the assessments.
- Newspaper reports about the assessments.

These data were collected from state and local education officials, school staff members, and representatives of external groups involved in assessment reform (e.g., the New Standards Project). These data were collected throughout the life of the project.

We also collected documentary data about the school sites we visited. These data included reports describing each school's demographic composition, staff description, financial resources, and other relevant documents.

Phone Interview Data. Prior to each site visit, we also conducted initial telephone interviews with cognizant individuals in state and local education offices, the school site, and external assessment reform organizations. We used an interview protocol tailored to the role of the interviewee and to the performance assessment system under investigation.

Site Visit Data.   In the spring of 1994, we visited the first 14 schools in our sample. In the spring of 1995, we revisited seven schools and added two new ones to our sample. In total, we conducted 23 site visits.

Each site visit lasted 1½ to 2 days and was conducted by a team of two researchers. The researchers interviewed a number of individuals, observed classrooms, and, whenever possible, observed professional development sessions devoted to the development and use of performance assessments, administration of performance assessments, and other activities related to the implementation of performance assessments.

Table A.4 illustrates the roles and numbers of the individuals we interviewed during our first and second round site visits.

We used semi-structured interview protocols during our site visits. The protocols for both waves of data collection were quite similar in structure, but wave two protocols contained more probing questions about the use and effects of performance assessments on teaching and learning.

Researchers also observed various performance assessment-related activities. Table A.5 illustrates the types and numbers of assessment-related activities observed.

Data Analysis

The analyses of our data progressed in two overlapping phases. The two phases—within-case data analysis and cross-case data analysis—are detailed next. We utilized Qualitative Data Analysis (Miles & Huberman, 1994) as a sourcebook to inform our data analysis methods.

TABLE A.4

Roles and Numbers of Interviewees, by Round of Site Visit

Role of Interviewee	Number of Individuals Interviewed		
	Round One (16 Sites)	Round Two (7 Sites)	Total
Representatives of the state department of education	6	1	7
Representatives of the school district	16	7	23
Principals and assistant principals	18	6	24
Teachers	123	40	163
Other school staff (e.g., librarians, counselors)	3	2	5
Students	76	26	102
Parents	26	11	37
School board members	10	4	14

TABLE A.5

First and Second Round Site Visit Observations

Type of Observation	Number
Classroom instruction:	
• Observations ranged in length from about half an hour to a full school day	22
Assessment administration:	
• Including student presentations, group activities preliminary to assessment administration, and administration of on-demand assessment tasks	9
Professional development sessions	9
Other:	
• Including a team teaching meeting, one school's end-of-the-year "Assessment Night" when students share their portfolios with their parents, training for outside assessors, and a meeting of a district assessment committee	4

Within-Case Analysis. The first phase of our data analysis consisted of writing case studies of our sites. To reiterate, the definition of our *site* is a performance assessment and its implementation and impact at one particular school. Data from all sources—documents, interviews, and observations—were synthesized in the case-study report. One member of each site visit team wrote the case study, and the second member reviewed it for accuracy. Next, the case study was sent to the appropriate officials and school personnel for review and comments. Based on their feedback, we revised the case study writeups.

Each case study writeup is divided into the following four sections:[2]

- *Section one: school profile and introduction.* This section briefly profiles the organizational characteristics of the school, such as demographic data about its students and the community it serves. The section also presents information on the number and roles of the individuals interviewed and the types of observational data collected.
- *Section two: description of performance assessment.* This section presents a brief history of the development and implementation of the performance assessment. It also presents the key characteristics of the assessment, including purposes, content areas assessed, scoring procedures, and technical characteristics.
- *Section three: context of implementation.* This section includes a summary of the policies and procedures followed in implementing the performance assessment, the resources and help available to the education agency or school personnel for developing and implementing the assessment, and the coordination (or lack thereof) between performance assessments and

---

[2]The full case studies appear in Khattri, Reeve, Traylor, Adamson, and Levin (1995).

other tests, reforms, and organizational changes.

- *Section four: the use and impact of performance assessment.* This section describes the uses of the performance assessments by teachers and students at the sample school. In addition, it documents the school community's evaluation of the usefulness and quality of the assessments and the impact of the assessments on the teaching and learning processes at the school.

Cross-Case Analysis.   The second phase of our data analysis focused on extracting and reorganizing information from our case-study writeups into a cross-case comparative format. Based on the case-study data and the theoretical, empirical, and policy papers we collected, we developed a categorization system for each of our major variables—performance assessments, facilitators and barriers, and teaching and learning processes and outcomes. Next, we organized the data from each casestudy into the categorization system. After the categorization exercise, we identified both common patterns and unique features in our data in order to:

- Develop a taxonomy of performance assessments.
- Illustrate and discuss the facilitators and barriers in assessment reform at different levels of educational organization.
- Identify and discuss the concept of "teacher appropriation" of performance assessments as a prerequisite to meaningful changes in teaching practice.
- Catalog and describe the impact of different performance assessments on teaching and learning at sample schools.

Thus, our cross-case analysis report comprises four sections.

In the first section we organized, when appropriate, the data according to the organizational level at which the performance assessment system was initiated, developed, or implemented (national, state, district, or school). We developed this organizational scheme to enable us to identify and understand the systematic differences among performance assessments developed and implemented by different levels of education authority.

Similarly, in the second section, we organized the data by the level of initiation, development, or implementation. We isolated and analyzed the organizational factors that influenced the development and implementation of performance assessments at different levels of education authority. In the third section, we organized the data in terms of the facilitators and barriers that affect teachers' ability and willingness to work with the subject performance assessment. Teachers' "appropriation" of the assessment is seen as a necessary prerequisite of meaningful changes in teaching and, hence, learning. These two sections together are keyed to the second study objective.

In the last section (keyed to the third objective), we were interested in the impact of the performance assessment at the local school level. Thus, we organized the data according to different categories of performance assessments, because we wanted to investigate the effects of different types of performance assessments on the teaching and learning processes and outcomes at the local school. Our approach to data analysis was primarily inductive, and our findings are offered as informed hypotheses that merit further investigation.

Data Interpretation

A research design such as the one we used has strengths, but it also necessarily imposes certain limitations on the interpretations that can be drawn from the data. We briefly discuss five general limitations of our study. (Specific limitations to our analyses are discussed in the appropriate chapters in this book.)

First, our taxonomy of performance assessments is based on a limited sample of performance assessments. Although we attempted to obtain a representative sample of performance assessments, we are not certain that the assessments initiated at the district and school levels are, in fact, representative of all district- and school-initiated performance assessments. Hence, our taxonomic scheme may not be accurate and must be viewed as a work in progress.

Second, a comprehensive description and analysis of each of the performance assessments in our sample was not possible. It was beyond the scope of this study to collect the massive amounts of data required for conducting such an analysis.

Third, our findings regarding the facilitators and barriers in assessment reform, especially at the national and state levels, may be less comprehensive than for those at the district and school levels. This limitation stems from the local-level emphasis of our study. We collected information regarding national and state level assessment reform from documents and general (as opposed to detailed and probing) interviews. In addition, we did not conduct in-person interviews with state officials and researchers involved in national-level efforts as we did with district- and school-level personnel.

Fourth, our findings regarding the impact of national-, state-, and district-initiated performance assessments are valid only for the schools included in this study; the results obtained for a particular school cannot be generalized to other schools involved with the same performance assessments.

Finally, interviewees' opinions regarding impact of and problems with performance assessments signal the existence of those impacts and problems, but the absence of such opinions does not necessarily suggest the absence of impact of or problems with performance assessments.

Appendix B

Case Study Summaries

We visited 16 schools in order to study the implementation of performance assessments that were initiated at various levels of educational authority—state, district, and school—and through various national-level education reform efforts. We visited nine schools a single time during the 1993–1994 or 1994–1995 school years, and we visited seven schools twice, once during each of the two school years. The 16 case study summaries that follow are organized according to these two factors: the number of visits to the school and the level of initiation of the performance assessment under study.

Summary case studies appear as follows:

Summaries of Two-Visit Case Studies

- Coalition of Essential Schools: Cooper Middle School (Site visit dates: April 7–8, 1994, and March 23–24, 1995).
- Primary Learning Record: Park Elementary School (Site visit dates: May 5–6, 1994, and April 3–4, 1995).
- Language Arts and Math Portfolios: Niños Bonitos Elementary School (Site visit dates: April 18–19, 1994, and February 27–28, 1995).
- Prince William County Public Schools' Applications Assessments: Westgate Middle School (Site visit dates: June 6–7, 1994, and February 16–17, 1995).
- Vermont Portfolios: Maple Leaf Middle School (Site visit dates: May 10–11, 1994, and March 16–17, 1995).
- Oregon Assessment Reform: Crandall High School (Site visit dates: March 11–12, 1994, and April 17–18, 1995).
- Kentucky Assessment Reform: Breckenridge Middle School (Site visit dates: May 3–4, 1994, and March 9–10, 1995).

Summaries of Single-Visit Case Studies

- Rite of Passage Experience: Thoreau High School (Site visit dates: April 12–13, 1994).
- The College Board's Pacesetter Mathematics Program: Sommerville High School (Site visit date: May 10, 1995).
- The New Standards Project: Ann Chester Elementary School (Site visit dates: May 25–26, 1994).
- The New Standards Project: Noakes Elementary School (Site visit dates: February 21–22, 1995).
- Harrison School District 2's Performance-Based Curriculum: McGary Elementary School (Site visit dates: April 11–12, 1994).
- South Brunswick Township Public Schools' Sixth Grade Research Performance Assessment: Windermere Elementary School (Site visit dates: June 2–3, 1994).
- New York Regents Portfolios: Hudson High School (Site visit dates: May 12–13, 1994).
- Maryland Assessment Reform: Walters Middle School (Site visit dates: May 9–10, 1994).
- Arizona Assessment Reform: Manzanita High School (Site visit dates: April 27–29, 1994).

These summaries are drawn from more detailed case study reports, which can be found in the second volume of this report, *Studies of Education Reform: Assessment of Student Performance—Volume 2: Case Studies*. All participant schools have been assigned pseudonyms.

COALITION OF ESSENTIAL SCHOOLS: COOPER MIDDLE SCHOOL

In 1989, having decided that it could no longer operate Cooper Middle School as a "mini high school" and expect to meet the needs of their students, Cooper staff launched a comprehensive school reform program. As part of this program, Cooper Middle School became a member of the Coalition of Essential Schools.

Cooper's assessment reform is an integral component of its larger reform program. Cooper teachers develop and use performance assessments based on the principles and philosophy of education expounded by the Coalition.

Reflecting the Santa Fe, New Mexico, community at large, 54% of Cooper's approximately 640 students are White, 45% are Hispanic, and less than 1% are Native American.

Coalition of Essential Schools

The Coalition of Essential Schools was established in 1984, at Brown University, as a school–university partnership to help redesign schools. The reform work of member schools is guided by a set of nine "Common Principles," intended to provide a broad framework for reform activities.

One of the nine common principles pertains to assessment and states that students should be awarded a diploma only on successfully demonstrating—through an *exhibition*—that they have acquired the skills and knowledge central to the school's program.

Information from the Coalition's research and development activities is disseminated to member schools and to other interested audiences through its newsletter and other publications. The Coalition also holds regional and national conferences, as well as round-table discussions centered around a variety of reform concerns (e.g., exhibitions of student work and pedagogical strategies).

Cooper Middle School

As part of its reform program, Cooper organized itself into *family groups* comprised of a core group of teachers and students. Throughout the 1993–1994 academic year, each of the two eighth-grade "families" were composed of six teachers and a group of students, and each of the two seventh-grade families were composed of five teachers and a group of students.

For the 1994–1995 academic year, however, the family structure was altered to form three teams of teachers in the seventh-grade, and two teams of three teachers and one team of six teachers in the eighth-grade. Cooper teachers made this alteration to better represent all subject areas within each family group. In addition, teachers believed that smaller family sizes would be more conducive to planning, implementing, and evaluating the family-based curriculum and assessment systems.

Following the Coalition philosophy, each family presents its curriculum materials focused on "essential questions that lead students to final assessments centered on their abilities to use critical thinking skills in order to solve real-world problems." The focus on critical thinking and social skills is provided through thematic units integrating skills, knowledge domains, instructional strategies, and assessment systems. All thematic units and assessments are designed by teachers themselves.

In the 1994–1995 school year, in addition to changing the family structure, teachers changed the extent to which they used thematic units for covering content areas. Teachers placed less emphasis on thematic units as the preferred pedagogical strategy. This change was most significant for mathematics.

Performance Assessments

Cooper teachers design performance assessments to:

- Better capture students' learning with regard to the essential questions and the curriculum.
- Inform the student about his or her academic progress.
- Inform parents about their child's interest and progress in school.

Reportedly, assessment development is guided by the Coalition's method of *planning backwards*. Teachers first delineate the skills and knowledge they want their students to be able to demonstrate at the end of a period of time, and then design thematic units around those skills and knowledge outcomes. Next, teachers design assignments—such as essays, research projects, and debates—through which students demonstrate their proficiency with respect to those skills and knowledge outcomes.

In addition to completing the family-based projects and assessments, each student is required to keep a portfolio of his or her work, undergo the Rite of Passage Experience (ROPE), and answer an Open-Ended Interdisciplinary Question at the end of the eighth grade. None of these assessments, however, is required for graduating from the middle school.

Each assignment is scored using a scoring rubric that outlines the dimensions of the assignment to be graded and the maximum score value for each dimension. For example, for an essay entitled, "What Is a Hero?," the scoring rubric established three dimensions: writing skills—spelling, punctuation, and syntax; content—the exposition of the qualities heroes must possess; and format—an introduction and a conclusion.

Court of Law

An eighth-grade family held a mock court trial as the culminating activity of a thematic unit entitled Freedom and Responsibility. The topic of the trial was, "Should the United States ban the sale, manufacture, and use of cigarettes?" One judge, a prosecutor, a defense attorney, witnesses, a jury, a transcriber, and a court marshal, all played by eighth-grade students, constituted the "court." Other students sat in the audience. One at a time, the lawyers put forth well-informed arguments, produced expert testimony and witnesses, cross-examined one another's witnesses, and delivered closing statements. After a brief deliberation, the jury rendered its verdict. The "proceedings" lasted about 50 minutes.

At the conclusion of the mock trial, all students were required to produce a persuasive piece of writing based on the court proceedings, which was to be incorporated into individual student portfolios.

Professional Development and Support

Cooper teachers have participated in several professional development activities over the past few years. In addition, the Coalition sent researchers to help teachers develop their curriculum and instructional and assessment strategies. Few of the teachers interviewed, however, remembered receiving in-house professional support geared toward the development and use of performance assessments. Teachers during both the 1993–1994 and 1994–1995 academic years emphasized their need for more training and in-house support for the specific purpose of designing and using assessments and thematic units.

Impact of Assessment Reform

According to the principal, although Cooper teachers support the reform program, the "transition has been difficult." Teachers shoulder the demanding task of fashioning their own thematic units and assessments—a process that is time consuming and exhausting.

For many teachers, among the other issues that need further attention are the quality and design of the assessments and the appropriateness of their teaching methods. In 1993–1994, some teachers were worried that the quality of their assessments (i.e., reliability and validity) might be questionable; by the 1994–1995 school year, this worry extended to the appropriateness of their teaching methods as well, particularly for mathematics. In 1994–1995, teachers also observed that it had become increasingly difficult for many of them to be generalists and teach several subject areas.

Many of the concerns that teachers had were identified and discussed during the summer of 1994. For example, teachers discussed their students' ROPE performance and noted that students rarely mentioned mathematics in their presentations. Furthermore, many teachers were disappointed in their students' ITBS mathematics scores. Cooper teachers came to the conclusion that teaching mathematics mostly through thematic units and applied problems was not adequate for instilling in their students a good understanding of the discipline. As a result, in 1994–1995, Cooper teachers reverted to a more direct, traditional approach to the teaching of mathematics. Teachers redefined other disciplinary areas as well, and began placing more emphasis on traditional teaching methods.

In 1993–1994, according to the two students interviewed, the thematic units were enjoyable *and* confusing. They mentioned that most students were uncertain of which teacher taught what subject and that they did not understand how the subjects were interrelated within thematic units or what they were expected to know at the end of a unit. These students articulated the desire for "more organization of themes—everything is mixed up in themes; we don't know where we are."

By 1994–1995, many of these problems had been alleviated, primarily as a result of clearer identification of traditional subject areas and due to the changes in the family structure. Most students reported that their classes were "pretty separated," and they knew when they were studying mathematics, science, English, and other subjects.

Cooper enjoys a good reputation within the community. In 1993–1994, according to one school board member, the board was "very pleased and supportive of it [the school]." In 1994–1995, the school board member had a similarly high opinion of Cooper. He did, however, express the need to establish a rigorous, districtwide accountability system, because he was distressed about the fact that the district scored on the lower end of ITBS.

In both years, all parent participants were supportive of Cooper's philosophy of education and teachers' use of project-based work, but some also expressed concerns over children's exposure to content areas. Parents also expressed concern over what they perceived to be a weak scoring system, low standards, and a lack of clearly defined outcomes.

Future Plans

In the near future, Cooper staff plan to address a number of outstanding and important issues, not the least of which is to define better assessment and measurement of student outcomes.

PRIMARY LEARNING RECORD:
PARK ELEMENTARY SCHOOL

Developed in Great Britain, the Primary Language Record (PLR), and its offshoot, the Primary Learning Record (PLeR), both provide teachers with a structured method of tracking young children's academic development and planning individualized instruction to meet students' needs (the PLR does so specifically in terms of language skills, and the PLeR tracks all subject areas).

The PLR and the PLeR are being modified and adopted in several parts of the United States. In New York City, implementation of the PLR and PLeR is facilitated by the New York City Assessment Network (NYAN), a consortium of education organizations dedicated to supporting the use of performance assessments by New York City teachers.

Teachers at Park Elementary School work with one NYAN member organization to use the PLR and, beginning in the 1994–1995 school year, the PLeR with their students. Because Park teachers switched from the PLR to the PLeR during the course of this study, the combined term *PLR/PLeR* is used throughout this summary to designate facts or opinions applicable to both versions of the assessment, whereas the terms will be used separately to distinguish between the two versions.

The Primary Language Record and Primary Learning Record

As designed, the PLR/PLeR is intended to accomplish two primary purposes:

- To help the child's classroom teacher understand the child's learning style in order to tailor an educational program appropriate for the child.
- To help the teacher communicate his or her understanding of the child to the child's next teacher.

As the PLR/PLeR is implemented in schools working with NYAN, it is the first of these purposes that is of primary importance.

The developers of the PLR/PLeR recognized that teachers are not the only individuals in children's lives who have insights into their language development. Therefore, the PLR/PLeR process is designed specifically to draw on multiple perspectives of a child's development. To be as comprehensive as possible in its record, then, the PLR/PLeR process:

- Involves parents in conferences with the teacher to comment on the child's language development at home.
- Records the child's own evaluation of his or her progress.
- Includes information about a child's language development in his or her first language, if that language is not English.

The PLR/PLeR consists of two types of record forms:

- The Primary Language Record Form or the Primary Learning Record Form has sections for the teacher to record in the fall information from parent–teacher conferences, notes from conferences with the student, and other initial observations of the child's learning. In the spring, the teacher records summative observations of the student's development and notes from follow-up conferences with parents and the student.
- The Observations and Samples Form, on which the teacher notes observations of: the child's talking, listening, reading, writing, and other learning behaviors; the titles of books and other texts the student reads; and notes about the student's written work. The teacher uses this form to individualize future lessons and to aid in the end-of-the-year summary of the child's development.

New York City Assessment Network

In 1991, three organizations—the Center for Collaborative Education, the Center for Educational Options, and the Elementary Teachers Network—

joined to establish the New York City Assessment Network (NYAN). The three organizations formed NYAN because of their shared commitment to introducing their teacher colleagues to the PLR. Teachers at NYAN's member schools began using the PLR in the early 1990s, and some (but not all) of these teachers subsequently shifted to using the PLeR.

All three organizations that comprise NYAN provide extensive professional support to their member teachers. Each organization has on its staff one or more "teacher consultant," whose job it is to work with teachers who are using the PLR/PLeR in their classrooms. These teacher consultants work individually with teachers and organize and lead "study groups" devoted to enhancing teachers' ability to use the PLR/PLeR.

Park Elementary School

Park Elementary School is a magnet school in New York City's District Four. Founded 20 years ago, the school's guiding philosophy is to provide a child-centered education. During the 1993–1994 school year, Park served about 250 prekindergarten through sixth-grade students; these students were White (18%), African-American (36%), Hispanic (42%), and Asian-American (4%). Students must apply for admission to the school, but admissions are made by lottery.

About half of Park's teachers have chosen voluntarily to participate in NYAN through the Center for Collaborative Education's (CCE) Elementary School Assessment Project, whose mission is to develop the use of qualitative assessment techniques for instructing and evaluating children's learning in the

---

Using the PLeR

Yvonne Smith's pre-K/K classroom is full of energetic young students working at different work tables where they build with blocks, draw, dress up, bake, and observe the class' pet gerbils. Yvonne moves among the children, observing their activities and talking with them about what they are doing. In one instance, Yvonne watches Alberto, a Hispanic boy for whom English is a second language, working at the sand table. She asks him what he has built in the sand, and he responds, "A bump." Yvonne recognizes that this word is a new one for Alberto. She shares with him two other words he could use to describe what he has built, hill and mountain. She then asks Alberto how many words he has to describe it. He says, "Two." Yvonne holds up two fingers and asks, "Do you have this many, or," holding up three fingers, "this many?" Alberto realizes he has said "two" when he means "three," and Yvonne realizes that he is still translating numbers from Spanish to English in his mind. Yvonne says she will use what she has learned from this observation and interaction to select reading materials that reinforce Alberto's growing English vocabulary (i.e., books that have hills, mountains, and bumps in them) and that use numbers in both English and Spanish.

New York public school system, using highly detailed observations and descriptions to capture the richness of children's learning. The PLR/PLeR is the tool chosen by CCE (and NYAN) to help teachers acquire and use those techniques espoused in the mission.

Impact of the PLR/PLeR

Because the PLR/PLeR is consistent with the educational philosophy already espoused by Park teachers, its impact as a distinct educational tool on the school's teachers and students is difficult to evaluate. However, it is clear that using the PLR/PLeR requires a significant amount of time and discipline on the part of teachers, and it is equally clear that those Park teachers who have chosen to use the PLR/PLeR find it to be a valuable addition to their teaching strategies.

Park teachers vary with respect to how much they believe that using the PLR/PLeR has affected the way in which they work with children. One teacher said, "The PLR helps me individualize instruction more . . . but there is no huge change [in my instructional methods], only fine tuning." Another teacher noted that she values collaborative teaching more than she did formerly, and that the PLR has bolstered her confidence in her ability to observe accurately what her students are doing and learning. All Park teachers who use the PLR/PLeR stress its validity for individualized instruction. In the words of one teacher, "Assessment is instruction," meaning that ongoing assessment of children's progress must guide instruction, and that careful, systematic assessment designed to inform instruction (particularly because it is tailored to the individual child) is inherently valid.

Teachers at Park Elementary say that they took the switch to the PLeR in stride. In fact, just as some Park Elementary teachers said that they were "doing PLR" before there was a PLR, teachers who used the PLR also said that they had already begun to use it to track children's progress in all subject areas before they actually started working with the PLeR. Thus, the switch to the PLeR came naturally to them.

According to teachers, students take the PLR/PLeR in stride, often asking, "Are you going to write down what I did?" One significant use to which teachers at Park have put the PLR/PLeR is to aid them in their documentation while in the process of declassifying special education students. Park's special education teacher believes that the PLR/PLeR would make a good substitute for individualized educational programs as well.

Teachers report that parents like the PLR/PLeR, and that they especially like the parent–teacher–student conferences devoted to discussing the child's literacy development. Several parents have told teachers that they have never before been asked to share their knowledge of their children.

Summary

The PLR/PLeR is an example of an assessment technique designed to inform curriculum and instruction. Park is a school in which teacher inquiry and teacher collaboration are encouraged. In such an environment the interweaving of assessment with curriculum and instruction—as fostered by the PLR/PLeR or other techniques—comes naturally to teachers, at least after practice.

LANGUAGE ARTS AND MATH PORTFOLIOS: NIÑOS BONITOS ELEMENTARY SCHOOL

In 1988, after 6 months of careful observation, the principal at Niños Bonitos Elementary School in San Diego, California, determined that student's needs—particularly those for learning the English language—were not being met at the school. Students' Abbreviated Stanford Achievement Test (ASAT) scores were low, and staff morale was poor. The principal, thus, asked the full staff to take responsibility for developing the mechanisms of change.[1]

The development of the school's performance assessment system was heavily influenced by the school's demographic character. In the 1994–1995 school year, Niños Bonitos served 924 students in Grades pre-K through 6. Thirty-nine percent of the students were of Southeast Asian heritage, 46% were Hispanic, 5% were African American, and the rest were East Asians. Seventy-seven percent of the students were identified as possessing limited English proficiency (LEP).

To initiate the school (and assessment) reform process, the principal developed a site-based committee structure of governance for the school. This committee proceeded to revamp the school curriculum and to reorganize the school and the school day. Students were organized into four nongraded but age-appropriate "wings." In the morning, all students within each wing, except those who are Spanish-speaking, are assigned to one of six levels of English proficiency for language arts and mathematics course work. Spanish-speaking students are enrolled in a bilingual program.

Initially, emphasis was placed on language arts improvement, historically the area of students' greatest weakness and of staff's greatest frustration. Teachers established clear entry and exit criteria and instructional goals for each age and language development level. For each level, the learning outcomes describe in detail what students should know and be able to do in terms of oral language, reading, and writing. Using learning outcomes, assessment has become an integral, daily part of instruction.

---

[1]The Niños Bonitos principal who initiated the school's comprehensive restructuring process was chosen for the position of Principal in Residence with the U.S. Department of Education. As a result, the school acquired a new principal in 1994–1995, the second year of this study.

Written and audio portfolios of student writing, reading, and spoken language allow teachers to measure growth in language arts. Teachers have defined what each portfolio must contain for each language development level and age level. For instance, the primary-level portfolios for Spanish-speaking students should contain an audio sample of a story retold by the student, three daily journal samples, a minimum of three independent writing samples, and a reading checklist.

Teachers also developed scoring rubrics in order to objectively compare and communicate students' academic progress without having to "label" children with standard letter grades. The language arts scoring rubrics were modified and refined between the 2 years of the study; by 1994–1995, the faculty had identified five performance levels for oral language and reading and six levels for written language that cut across language development levels and age levels. The rubrics were used to redesign the student report card in language arts, which was renamed the student "growth record." Students are assigned a "growth rubric" by their language arts teacher based on a review of their written language portfolios and an assessment of their performance on reading and oral language.

In the second year of the study, teachers began to reevaluate the way in which the language arts portfolios are constructed. To date, teachers have selected the student pieces to be included in each portfolio. However, they are beginning to feel that students should have greater influence in the selection process, so that the portfolio becomes a tool for student self-reflection, as well as a method of measuring student progress from the teacher's perspective.

During the 1993–1994 school year, Niños Bonitos staff began to research and write mathematics standards and rubrics, using the same process they had followed for language arts. The full staff, meeting in groups by wing, developed learner outcomes for each age level. These outcomes identified what students should know and be able to do to demonstrate mastery of each content and process skill area in mathematics. The mathematics curriculum committee then

---

Classroom Observation: A Portfolio Task

In a third/fourth-grade ("middle-wing") classroom, groups of "transitional" students (those who are almost, but not quite, fluent in English) spent the morning working on six computers. Their teacher, who has received special training in the use of educational software, designed a performance task that required the students to describe and illustrate a book they had read about the difficulties Southeast Asian students (like themselves) experience as they assimilate into their new American culture. The teacher adopted the role of "coach" and circulated throughout the classroom as her students worked, and helped them with their writing skills as well as with their computer skills. Students saved their work in both electronic and "hard-copy" versions for their language arts portfolios, which are shared with parents at parent–teacher conferences three times a year.

developed separate "observable student behaviors"—which detailed the tasks each student must be able to perform—to accompany each set of learner outcomes.

In 1994–1995, these learner outcomes and observable student behaviors were used to develop High Expectations Learning Plans for Students (HELPS). The HELPS units require teachers to develop specific activities and assessment tools for each concept area (e.g., geometry and spatial sense or fractions and ratios) identified by the National Council of Teachers of Mathematics.

From the process and content skills they developed, the mathematics committee generated a scoring matrix that was used to evaluate student progress for the first time in 1994–1995. The school received a waiver allowing it to use the new mathematics assessment matrix as a substitute for the mathematics portion of the standard district report card. Also in 1994–1995, mathematics portfolios were introduced at all grade levels, although in differing forms and at differing paces.

Impact of Assessment Reform

Although no formal evaluations of Niños Bonitos' performance assessment system had been undertaken as of May 1995, the grassroots teacher involvement with developing learner outcomes and assessment methods seems to have ensured the success of reform efforts. Niños Bonitos' annual staff surveys indicate that, overall, teachers are very pleased with the new system and its results. The school's staff argues that their system of measuring student performance has more validity than do more traditional kinds of tests. They maintain that the portfolios and learner outcome tasks they have developed provide a complete picture of students' competencies.

In support of the central reform features (i.e., the curriculum and assessment systems), Niños Bonitos staff also have reduced individual class size and provided teachers with more weekly preparation time (teachers only teach one class during the afternoon rotation period). Some of the numerous grants the school has received allow teachers more release time.

The principal noted that the reformed system has improved classroom instruction —most teachers have moved away from the traditional teacher-centered approach and are providing more cooperative and experiential learning opportunities that focus on problem-solving skills. In addition, these new instructional and assessment methods have reduced disciplinary problems and provided teachers with a greater sense of accomplishment. One teacher noted that although the new methods may slow the pace of instruction, they reinforce the fundamentals of mathematics and language arts.

Teachers and administrators believe the effect of curricular and assessment changes on students has been noticeable. Students are doing a large amount of writing and have a greater sense of purpose, accomplishment, and enjoyment. During classroom observations, the principal has noticed a much higher degree of student engagement and "on-task" behavior. These improvements in student attitude and motivation have borne fruit in objective measures of student performance, particularly in the areas of oral and written language development for LEP students—ASAT writing scores continue to improve, and Niños Bonitos graduates are performing better at the junior high school.

Parent reaction to the new portfolio system and rubrics has been extremely positive, as measured by both the annual parent survey and the feedback received at parent outreach meetings held regularly throughout the year. The school's parent and volunteer coordinator noted that portfolios give parents a much more visual and concrete sense of their child's progress.

Future Plans

The future of Niños Bonitos' performance assessment system seems bright, because the school possesses strong leadership and has received support and accolades from the San Diego Unified School District. The school board member interviewed in 1994–1995 anticipates that, with the continued and strong support of both Niños Bonitos' new principal and the district's new superintendent, Niños Bonitos and the district as a whole will steadily expand the use of performance assessments.

PRINCE WILLIAM COUNTY PUBLIC SCHOOLS' APPLICATIONS ASSESSMENTS: WESTGATE MIDDLE SCHOOL

As part of an ongoing, districtwide restructuring effort, Prince William County (Virginia) Public Schools (PWCPS) has introduced Applications Assessments in mathematics, science, language arts, and social studies.

The district's work toward a reformed educational system has progressed rapidly. Applications Assessments in language arts, math, and science were pilot tested in the fall of 1993, and were administered districtwide in the spring of 1994. During the summer of 1994, committees of district teachers developed performance standards for the three assessments and finished revising the district's curricula in most subject areas. During the 1994–1995 school year, the new curricula began to be put in place, and the Applications Assessment in social studies was introduced.

The Prince William County Public Schools

Since the late 1980s, PWCPS has been planning and implementing a comprehensive restructuring effort encompassing:

Prince William County Public Schools' Standards of Quality

Students should be:

* *Knowledgeable and proficient in the traditional basic academic skills.*
* *Good thinkers, problem solvers, and decision makers.*
* *Effective communicators.*
* *Users of technology.*
* *Knowledgeable of various racial and ethnic cultures, as well as differences based on gender, age, and physical ability.*
* *Good citizens.*

---

* Development and adoption of the district's Quality Management Plan.
* Articulation of a set of expectations for student achievement entitled Standards of Quality (see the accompanying box).
* Expansion of the district's assessment program.
* Revision of the curriculum for all subjects at all grade levels.

The district decided to modify its assessment program when it realized that traditional methods of testing would not be able to accurately measure student progress toward the attainment of new standards. With the help of the Riverside Publishing Company, PWCPS began developing a new assessment tool—Applications Assessments. Riverside developed potential assessment items, and PWCPS teachers reviewed and revised the items. The assessment is designed to meet three additional objectives:

* To inform instruction.
* To serve as a tool for accountability (although in an as-of-yet unspecified way).
* To communicate to teachers, parents, and students what students know and are capable of doing.

The Applications Assessments, which are administered to all third, seventh, and tenth graders, constitute an on-demand performance assessment in the areas of mathematics, language arts, science, and social studies. Each assessment is contained within a booklet; a typical assessment has about a dozen tasks that call for anything from a phrase to a multiparagraph or multistep response. Each assessment task is accompanied by its own scoring rubric. The scoring is conducted by a company associated with Riverside Publishing.

Staff Development

To acquaint district teachers with the Applications Assessments, the district compiled a Resource Kit, which was distributed to all schools in March of 1994 and again in the spring of 1995. The district also held a pair of 2-day workshops for teachers who would be administering the assessments. Teachers who attended these workshops were responsible for bringing what they had learned back to other teachers at their schools. (The district did not anticipate repeating these workshops during the 1994–1995 school year.)

Other PWCPS Assessments

The district also administers a state-level, open-ended assessment and a district-level, criterion-referenced, multiple-choice assessment.

- *State level:* Virginia's Literacy Passport is a high-stakes assessment comprised of three sections—reading, writing, and mathematics—and is taken by all sixth graders. Successful completion of all three sections is intended to reflect students' mastery of basic literacy and is required by the end of eighth grade if students are to be considered "full" ninth graders.
- *District level:* Because one of the six Standards of Quality (see the accompanying box) focuses on basic skills, the district has adopted new Basic Skills Assessments. Although the Applications Assessments aim to measure students' abilities to apply knowledge, the criterion-referenced, multiple-choice Basic Skills Assessments are more traditional in their assessment of students' mastery of subject matter. The Basic Skills Assessments are administered in Grades 3, 5, 7, and 10.

The implication of the curriculum revision, completed during the summer of 1994, for the Applications Assessments is unclear. According to administrators and teachers, the Applications Assessments did not guide the curriculum revisions in any direct way. Therefore, it remains for the district's future evaluation to reveal how closely the revised curricula and the Applications Assessments correspond to one another.

Westgate Middle School

One of 12 middle schools in PWCPS, Westgate Middle School serves about 825 sixth-, seventh-, and eighth-grade students. Students come primarily from middle-class backgrounds; most students are White (81%), whereas others are African American (11%), Hispanic (5%), and Asian American (4%).

Westgate Middle School has been a central player in assessment reform and other education reform efforts introduced by the district. The school is operated by a school-based management team; over the past 6 years, the district has supported the adoption of school-based management districtwide. Westgate Middle School also has been using portfolio assessment schoolwide during the past 4 years. The portfolios are used to provide insights into students' learning processes and achievement, not for assigning grades.

Impact of Applications Assessments on Teachers, Students, and Parents

Most Westgate teachers have a favorable opinion of performance assessments in theory. However, their reactions to the Applications Assessments range from positive to ambivalent. Teachers found that the language arts and science assessments administered in 1994 were well aligned with the district's prerevision curriculum and students' actual classroom experiences. However, teachers also said that the math assessment tested skills most seventh-grade students had not yet mastered. Teachers also were unclear about the alignment between the district's new curricula and the Applications Assessments, and they expressed concerns about the subjectivity inherent in the use of scoring rubrics.

Teachers applaud the district's efforts to include them in the process of developing the Applications Assessments, setting performance standards, and revising the curricula. However, one teacher warned, "Performance assessment is not the end all and be all. Educators tend to get caught up in fads."

Students interviewed during the 1993–1994 school year said that the Applications Assessments were "easy" but that they preferred multiple-choice exams. Some students liked having the chance to express their opinions about issues on the language arts assessment, whereas others said that the themes carried throughout the assessments were "boring." Students interviewed in 1994–1995 expressed similar reactions to those cited by their classmates the previous year.

The two parents who participated in this study were not well informed about the Applications Assessments and, hence, had few opinions about them.

Summary

The Prince William County Public Schools have embarked on a comprehensive restructuring effort, simultaneously reforming curriculum, assessments, and standards. The reform effort will require several more years to bring to fruition, and the effects of the various reforms, singular or cumulative, cannot yet be determined.

VERMONT PORTFOLIOS:
MAPLE LEAF MIDDLE SCHOOL

In 1988, the Vermont Department of Education began developing an assessment system consisting of portfolios and multiple-choice, *uniform* tests in mathematics and writing. Pressure from the business community and the

Department's own belief that information on student performance is essential to improving student outcomes provided the impetus for this action. Thus, Vermont's portfolio system became the first of its kind in the United States. Although administering the assessment system was not mandated, 59 of 60 Vermont Supervisory Unions were participating in it by the 1992–1993 school year.

Vermont's portfolio system is designed to foster local involvement and initiative in assessment reform. It is intended to furnish data on student performance, to encourage effective approaches to instruction, and to foster equity in educational opportunity.

Vermont's Board of Education reasoned that the portfolio assessments would help achieve these goals by enabling schools to compare scores, building local capacity for districts to evaluate their mathematics and writing programs, and helping teachers assess their instructional methods and students' progress.

Vermont Portfolios

In the school years between 1991 and 1994, each fourth- and eighth-grade student was required to maintain both a mathematics and a writing portfolio. In the 1994–1995 school year, the writing portfolio was shifted from the fourth- to the fifth-grade level—a shift intended to lighten the portfolio burden on fourth-grade teachers.

Mathematics portfolios must contain a set of five to seven "best pieces" selected from mathematics assignments completed over the course of the school year. Exemplars of three categories of mathematics problems—puzzles, investigations, and applications—must be represented among the best pieces.

Writing portfolios must contain work in specific genres. Samples of students' writing, selected from work completed over the course of the academic year, must include: a best piece of writing; a letter from the student to the evaluator;

Maple Leaf Teachers' Assessment of Vermont's Portfolios

According to the Maple Leaf teachers present at an end-of-year scoring training session, the best aspects of the mathematics portfolios are:

- *Seeing students develop over the year.*
- *Watching students seek out and apply strategies to their work* [problems].
- *Observing student acceptance of multiple solutions and strategies.*

The best aspects of the language arts portfolios are:
- *Noticing female students' writing become natural and reflective of their experiences as females.*
- *Realizing that students feel "vested" in their writing and are motivated to complete assignments.*

a story, play, or personal narrative; a review of an event, book, or issue; and some pieces of writing from classes other than language arts or English. Each final paper must be accompanied by dated drafts that show the progress of the work.

Classroom teachers score each piece of work contained in both of these portfolios using state-generated scoring rubrics. (In the summer of 1994, the language of the writing scoring rubric was simplified, and a prompt was added to help the scorer decide whether student work should be ranked on the upper or the lower part of the rubric.) A random sample of these portfolios is subsequently rescored at the state level, and teachers receive feedback from state scorers regarding the quality of their students' portfolios. To facilitate use of the scoring rubrics, the Vermont Department of Education provides several training sessions each year to teachers through regional training networks.

Maple Leaf Middle School

One of the earliest participants in the portfolio assessment system was Maple Leaf Supervisory Union (MLSU), and Maple Leaf Middle School provides a lens through which to examine Maple Leaf teachers', students', and parents' responses to Vermont's portfolios.

In 1994–1995, Maple Leaf Middle School served about 315 students in Grades 6, 7, and 8. Ninety-eight percent of these were White. Because MLSU does not operate a public high school, about 95% of the middle school students go on to attend the local private high school (the tuition for which is paid by MLSU).

Impact of Vermont Portfolios on Teachers, Students, and Parents

Although Maple Leaf Middle School teachers included in this study expressed doubts about the use of portfolios as an assessment system, most agreed the portfolios are pedagogically useful in some ways.

The eighth-grade mathematics teacher had not integrated portfolios into his classes for one main reason: He worried that because the required portfolio tasks stress writing, students may lose basic computational skills (such as the ability to calculate fractions and to remember multiplication tables). In addition, he expressed doubts about the reliability and validity of the portfolios as an assessment instrument. He was concerned that, in the future, portfolio scores may be used for high stakes accountability purposes.

On the other hand, this same teacher said that the portfolio tasks have helped him better understand children with limited facility in mathematics. In addition, he believes that the kinds of tasks required for Vermont's mathematics portfolios are the kind that help students learn about the application of mathematical concepts.

In contrast with the eighth-grade teacher, Maple Leaf's seventh-grade mathematics teacher was sufficiently impressed with mathematics portfolios as a pedagogical tool and had incorporated them into her daily teaching routine. However, she, too, expressed concerns regarding the emphasis on writing and said that she spent a considerable amount of time teaching writing (as opposed to math) skills.

In 1994–1995, this teacher continued to use the portfolios, but with more misgivings. She concluded that teaching her students writing skills was taking time away from the teaching of mathematical skills; she was not able to devote as much time to teaching certain mathematical concepts as is required for students to truly grasp the concepts. In addition, she felt that students who were good in mathematics but not in English were beginning to develop negative attitudes toward mathematics.

The MLSU director of curriculum noted that these mathematics teachers are skeptical not so much of the portfolios per se, but of the NCTM standards—which stress communication and writing—in the mathematics scoring rubrics.

In contrast with the mathematics teachers, the language arts teacher was consistently positive about the language arts portfolios in both years. She believes that the portfolios are a powerful pedagogical tool that help teachers become better teachers.

This teacher's pedagogical approach now centers more on guiding students to think, to share thoughts through peer conferences, and to edit during the writing process. She particularly likes the voice dimension of the language arts scoring rubric, because the emphasis on this dimension of writing has especially benefited her female students. In addition, she was not at all concerned about scoring reliability.

However, in 1994–1995, this language arts teacher and another one expressed concerns regarding the articulation of language arts standards and curriculum with the local private high school. The high school had complained that Maple Leaf Middle School graduates did not possess good skills in grammar, syntax, and spelling. Therefore, in 1994–1995, these teachers began placing more emphasis on these components of writing.

In both years, students' responses to the portfolios were a blend of enjoyment and indifference. Students said that they enjoyed completing assignments for their writing portfolios. They spoke of writing more than they ever had before, and said they found the challenge stimulating. One student said, "You have to think more [about your work] to get a better grade." However, students said that the mathematics tasks were challenging but not "much fun," and they typically did not use the scoring rubric to evaluate their own work.

Teachers also noted that students felt vested in their work and were motivated to complete their portfolio assignments. One language arts teacher said that writing had become a habit with her students, and they did not think of it as being a chore.

In both years, parents interviewed said that they liked their children's portfolios but did not fully understand the purpose of the portfolio system. In 1994–1995, the school board member interviewed expressed some strong reservations about the scoring reliability and content emphasis of the portfolio system; he believes that the scoring is too subjective and the portfolio requirements underemphasize rote content knowledge.

Maple Leaf Supervisory Union

Despite being cognizant of the technical problems associated with the portfolio system, MLSU officials remain enthusiastic about its pedagogical implications. They have encouraged the use of portfolios at all grade levels. (In fact, according to one official, fourth- and eighth-grade teachers feel that they should be sharing the responsibilities of the portfolio system with teachers at other grade levels for the statewide system, largely because of the amount of work involved in instructing students in how to complete performance-based portfolio tasks.)

District officials, nonetheless, said that they realize that a tremendous investment of time, money, and support is required to implement the portfolio system. Furthermore, the new superintendent noted that the community will not continue to buy into the portfolio system if it is not used for school accountability.

Future Plans

The Vermont Department of Education is developing content and performance standards for its Common Core Framework to guide further development of its assessment system. The department also plans to extend the assessment system to other grade levels and to additional subject areas. MLSU officials also hope to incorporate the portfolio system at all grade levels.

However, teachers and officials realize that it will be difficult to achieve some of the goals of the portfolio system, for several reasons. For example, it is difficult to establish a performance baseline to monitor student progress, because the quality of the portfolio tasks teachers design is not uniform. In addition, the opportunities to learn are not uniform across the state.

Until these issues are addressed, the state's intention of monitoring student outcomes and helping districts evaluate their programs must remain on hold. On the other hand, because of teacher involvement in defining the system, portfolios are becoming more widespread and more accepted as a useful classroom instructional strategy.

OREGON ASSESSMENT REFORM:
CRANDALL HIGH SCHOOL

In 1991, the Legislative Assembly in Oregon enacted the Oregon Educational Act for the 21st Century, the primary purpose of which was to usher in a new, high-standards education system. As part of establishing the new education system, the state began defining outcome criteria for the Certificate of Initial Mastery (CIM), to be awarded at about the end of Grade 10, and the Certificate of Advanced Mastery (CAM), to be awarded at about the end of Grade 12. Students were to earn the CIM certificate by demonstrating proficiency in 11 outcome areas (as opposed to simply spending a predetermined amount of time in the classroom). CIM outcomes included: think, self-direct learning, communicate, [use] technology, quantify, collaborate, deliberate on public issues, understand diversity, interpret human experience, apply math and science, and understand positive health habits.

Part of the state's overall reform agenda was to develop an assessment system that consisted of a system of assessment tasks for each CIM and CAM outcome area, scoring rubrics, portfolios for gathering evidence of student work, and a set of criteria for determining whether a student's performance satisfies the requirements of CIM. The state initially hoped to award the first CIM in 1997.

Oregon's Educational Act for the 21st Century proved to be controversial, and, in June 1995, Oregon's governor signed into law a bill to amend the Act. Some of the major provisions of the bill included the development of an assessment system composed primarily of reliable and valid multiple-choice tests and performance assessments keyed to traditional content standards and the elimination of the CIM and CAM outcomes.

Crandall High School (the school through which this study investigated the development and implementation of some of Oregon's assessments) was involved with developing performance assessments under the 21st Century Act. However, even before Oregon's legislature amended the Act, Crandall High withdrew from full-scale participation in the reform efforts and from this study in the 1994–1995 school year. Like many individuals across the state, Crandall's principal came to oppose the outcomes incorporated in the CIM. In addition, Crandall teachers became overwhelmed and disenchanted by the pace and workload of the reform efforts they had undertaken. However, the school district (District A) of which Crandall High is a part continued to support the reform in 1994–1995.

The remainder of this case-study summary focuses on the assessment reform activities that took place at Crandall High School during the 1993–1994 school year, and in District A during the 1993–1994 and 1994–1995 school years.

Assessment Reform in District A

In 1992–1993, District A volunteered to define and field-test assessment tasks for the CIM requirement that students demonstrate proficiency in applying math and science concepts and show an understanding of how these concepts affect the world.

Most assessment development and piloting work in the district was funded by state grants. By the spring of 1994, the District Student Assessment Team (DSAT), composed of representatives from all schools in the district, had developed and field-tested several performance tasks at each CIM benchmark level (Grades 3, 5, 8, and 10). Each task had to reflect the skills and competencies articulated in the state-developed "apply math and science" scoring rubric. In 1994–1995, the district pilot effort had expanded to include a total of 150 teachers and all students at the first three benchmark levels. A new team—the Certificate of Initial Mastery Implementation Team (which replaced the DSAT)—coordinated all reform activities, and a new subcommittee—Student Performance Assessment Network— worked on developing the CIM assessments. Another team—Science and Math (SCAMA)—worked on establishing CIM math and science content standards for Grades K through 8.

According to district officials, the state-initiated reform efforts had generated considerable involvement, enthusiasm, *and* controversy on the part of teachers. Crandall High is a case in point.

Crandall High School

In 1993–1994, Crandall High School served approximately 1,250 students in Grades 9 through 12, most of whom were White. About 35% of Crandall graduates go on to attend college.

Work in developing applied math and science assessment tasks was being conducted primarily by 2 of Crandall's 15 math and science teachers. These two teachers were the first to develop and pilot assessment tasks in their classes, and they shared the results at District Student Assessment Team meetings.

Some diffusion of the design of performance assessments from math and science into other courses, such as "Tools of Our Time" (an applied technology class), was occurring through informal sharing of ideas among Crandall teachers. However, although the proposed CIM assessment system was forcing most Crandall teachers to take a look at performance assessments, only some—19 out of 75—were beginning to incorporate performance assessments into their classrooms. According to one teacher, "Most had not accepted the [reform] concept."

These teachers were experimenting with performance assessments primarily inside the schools-within-schools programs that enrolled about 23% of Crandall's students. (Crandall's high-achieving students typically did not enroll in the school-within-school programs.)

**TOOLS OF OUR TIME: Applied Technology
and Performance Assessment at Crandall High**

In "Tools of Our Time," an applied technology class, teachers often use performance assessments to evaluate their students' learning and progress. Students work in teams of two or three to complete technology-based assignments in subject areas such as economics and social studies. For example, a student demonstrated his understanding of economics by weaving economics terminology into a story entitled "What it Felt Like to Be All Alone for Three Days After a Plane Crash." Using an overhead projector connected to a computer, the student projected the text of his story (which was stored on a diskette) onto a large screen and gave an oral explanation. The story wove in concepts and terms such as capital, labor, land, barter, value, *and so on. A question-and-answer session between the student and his teacher followed the demonstration.*

Impact of Performance Assessment at Crandall High School

Teachers who were designing and using performance assessments believed that subject-integration and performance-based assessments offer students a better chance at internalizing what they are learning, and at developing higher-order thinking skills.

However, math and science teachers also expressed concerns regarding the connections between general performance criteria articulated in the Apply Math and Science scoring rubric and student work; they were unsure of how to translate the criteria into what could concretely be expected from student work. In fact, the majority of the faculty was not "buying into the concept [of reform]" largely because of a similar issue: a perceived lack of connection between the CIM outcomes and traditional content area outcomes. They viewed this lack of criteria definition (i.e., concrete content standards and related student performance standards) as a hindrance to effective teaching. In addition, most teachers were concerned about the substantial amount of time it would take to assign and assess performance-based work.

Indeed, these concerns portended Crandall's withdrawal from its CIM development and piloting responsibilities. At the end of the 1993–1994 academic year, at the request of the school's math and science teachers, Crandall's site-based committee voted down Crandall's membership in the pilot CIM assessment development program. Individual teachers, nonetheless, continued to develop and score performance tasks.

Crandall students included in this study said they enjoyed performance-based work, mostly because, in many cases, it allowed them to integrate different subject areas. In some cases, performance-based assignments gave students the opportunity to use technology to demonstrate their work. Teachers, in turn, said that their students were better able to learn and develop critical thinking skills as a result of being involved in interdisciplinary, performance-based work. Teachers also noted that the use of scoring rubrics to assess their own and their peers' work compelled students to accept more responsibility for, and take more ownership of, their grades.

Future Plans

With the amendment of Oregon's Educational Act for the 21st Century, the state eliminated the outcomes for the Certificate of Initial Mastery. The current state plan is to develop content standards in several subject areas, including mathematics, science, history, and English. The new assessment system will consist of multiple-choice and open-ended assessments that are keyed to specific subject area standards. District A, however, hopes to continue to develop its own performance assessment system.

KENTUCKY ASSESSMENT REFORM: BRECKENRIDGE MIDDLE SCHOOL

By the late 1980s, Kentucky's educational system was in crisis, with statistics showing the state ranking near the bottom among U.S. states in per-pupil expenditures on education, high school graduation rates, and adult literacy. On June 8, 1989, Kentucky's Supreme Court took official steps to remedy an educational system it perceived as inadequate and inequitable. Essentially, the court directed Kentucky's General Assembly to establish an education system that complied with Kentucky's Constitution.

In 1990, the legislature responded to the court's mandate by enacting the Kentucky Education Reform Act (KERA), which adopted six broad learning goals for all Kentucky students. This act also required that the State Board for Elementary and Secondary Education develop and implement a statewide assessment program—the Kentucky Instructional Results Information System (KIRIS)—to measure student performance with respect to four of the six goals.

Kentucky Instructional Results Information System

This KIRIS assessment system has three parts:

- Portfolios that present each student's best work in language arts and mathematics collected throughout the year.
- A small number of performance tasks that require students to solve simulated, real-life problems, working in groups for part of the tasks.
- A battery of paper-and-pencil subject tests containing multiple-choice and open-ended, short essay questions.

The assessments are administered in the fourth, eighth, and twelfth grades.[2] All schools in Kentucky are held accountable for their students' performance on these assessments; students' scores are figured into the schools' "accountability index." In order to avoid sanctions, schools must improve their accountability index by 18% of the difference between their baseline index and 100, over a 2-year period.

This study focuses on the portfolio and performance task components of the KIRIS assessments.

KIRIS Performance Assessments

Students in the assessed grade levels spend a year developing their portfolios. A language arts portfolio typically contains entries such as: a personal narrative; a piece of writing that (a) predicts an outcome, (b) defends a position, (c) solves a problem, (d) analyzes or evaluates a situation, person, place, or thing, (e) explains a process or concept, (f) draws a conclusion, or (g) creates a model; a piece of original fiction; and a letter to the reviewer discussing what the student has learned from keeping a portfolio, which entry is the best piece and why, and from which entry the most was learned. A minimum of one piece of writing must come from a subject area other than English or language arts.

For their mathematics portfolios, students must select their seven "best pieces" that "represent various types of mathematics; employ a variety of mathematics tools such as calculators, computers, or manipulatives; and integrate core concepts within mathematics and the world." In addition, students must provide a table of contents and a letter to the reviewer.

Each portfolio is scored using a holistic scoring rubric developed by the Kentucky Department of Education (KDE). Classroom teachers complete the initial scoring of portfolios, a sample of which is rescored by Advanced Systems (a private contractor to KDE) to determine scoring reliability.

Observation of Performance Events Administration

Breckenridge eighth-grade students were assigned to eight groups of four for the performance event, which required approximately 45 minutes for group discussion and 15 minutes for individual written responses. The performance tasks administered involved a short experiment or puzzle that students first investigated in groups. For instance, one group was asked to brainstorm four kinds of jobs teenagers could fill to assist the elderly. Students were then asked to construct individual responses that discussed the process their group followed and the reasoning behind the conclusions they drew. They also were asked to describe the task's application to real life, and to discuss in their responses whether and why they agreed or disagreed with their group's conclusions.

---

[2]In the 1994–1995 school year, students in both the eleventh and twelfth grades took the KIRIS assessments.

Performance events assess students in arts and humanities, mathematics, social studies, science, and practical living and vocational studies, but can incorporate knowledge and skills from more than one discipline at a time. Students work in small groups to conduct a short experiment or to solve a puzzle. Performance events are administered by Advanced Systems.

Breckenridge Middle School

Breckenridge Middle School in Lexington was chosen as a site from which to study the impact of Kentucky's performance assessments. In 1994–1995, Breckenridge served about 860 students in Grades 6 through 8, 80% of whom were White, the rest being primarily African American.

Impact of Performance Assessments

At Breckenridge, every eighth-grade teacher included in the study agreed that the new system has benefitted students but also has created a great deal of stress and extra work for the teachers. Virtually every teacher in both years of the study said that KIRIS assessments promoted among students the use of higher-level thinking skills to solve open-ended problems. Teachers also felt that students are learning to express themselves better in a variety of written genres.

At the same time, eighth-grade teachers felt that their personal and professional reputations are attached to the school scores published in the newspaper, and that they receive no recognition when the scores are good, only when they are poor.

The complaint most often voiced by teachers in 1993–1994 was the lack of adequate training in scoring, in the design of the portfolio assessments, and in ways to improve their instructional methods to be better aligned with the new assessments. However, Breckenridge teachers remarked in 1995 that the training provided by KDE had improved substantially between the 1993–1994 and 1994–1995 school years.

Despite the improved training opportunities, Breckenridge teachers in 1994–1995 raised concerns about scoring reliability. One said she didn't agree with the scores assigned to the portfolio exemplars by KDE, whereas two teachers noted that the holistic scoring guides were too complicated to be of much utility. Another felt that it was difficult to assign a reliable score to a portfolio comprised of individual pieces that may be of differing quality.

Teachers also complained vociferously about the amount of lost curriculum time the KIRIS assessments exact. In both 1993–1994 and 1994–1995, the eighth-grade language arts and mathematics teachers interviewed said they had dropped units from their curriculum in order to focus on elements of the KIRIS program (e.g., portfolio writing or cooperative problem-solving exercises). The language arts teachers said they had stopped teaching important units on grammar, sentence mechanics, and literature in order to do more creative writing in class.

Nonetheless, in 1994–1995 both the school principal and teachers themselves felt that eighth-grade instructional strategies had improved as a result of the KIRIS program. One mathematics teacher noted that "A lot of KIRIS is just what we in the math department and math community have been pushing for years." Another language arts teacher said that, as a result of KIRIS, she was learning to demonstrate to her students the real-life application and utility of the principles she taught. Another language arts teacher said that although "KIRIS implementation is very difficult, the end result is worth the effort."

In 1993–1994, opinion was divided among Breckenridge teachers about whether instructional changes had spread to sixth- and seventh-grade classrooms. Teachers also disagreed about whether the KIRIS system had affected instruction in mathematics and language arts classrooms only, or in other subject areas as well. In 1994–1995, the principal and some teachers indicated that they felt teachers in other grades and disciplines were beginning to align their instructional methods with the KIRIS philosophy, although acceptance of responsibility for KIRIS among the full faculty would take time.

In both years of the study, school and district administrators, as well as parents themselves, felt that parents had not received enough information about the KIRIS assessments. Parents receive their children's performance level in the mail, but no explanation of the performance levels or of their child's weaknesses or strengths is provided. Therefore, due to an overall lack of information, parents do not feel that the KIRIS system has improved their involvement or understanding of their child's education.

Parents interviewed in both years of the study expressed other concerns including:

- KIRIS does not prepare students for the SAT or ACT.
- Scoring is not objective.
- Students are missing curricula that they need to succeed in high school.

Students, on the other hand, enjoyed the creative nature of the assessments, noting that they are "allowed to express [themselves]" and that "personal opinions matter." Teachers at Breckenridge felt that students enjoy portfolio writing and the opportunities for group work and problem solving that KIRIS performance events allowed them. Parents concurred, suggesting that students were more invested in and concerned about their performance on the KIRIS component than they would be on multiple-choice minimum competency exams.

Future Plans

Despite its relatively promising infancy, KIRIS' future seems to be in question. Conservative groups have criticized the assessments as focusing too heavily on "liberal values" and ignoring fundamental academic skills. Although KDE has invested a considerable amount of energy and time into developing outcomes and associated assessments, there is speculation that the Kentucky legislature may abolish KIRIS before a firm judgment about its utility can be made.

RITE OF PASSAGE EXPERIENCE: THOREAU HIGH SCHOOL

Thoreau High School in Racine, Wisconsin, may be considered an example of *what* may be achieved in performance assessments, rather than as an example of *how* to achieve its goals. Thoreau was founded in 1972, setting as its goal to serve students who were not well served in traditional high schools—students who were, in the phrase of the school's founders, "knowledge heavy, but credit light." Thoreau was to be a school in which students were given "control over their academic progress and responsibility for demonstrating their knowledge."

Thoreau today comprises both a middle school and a high school and is characterized by small classes, courses designed for students of all ages, and a wide variety of course selections. Students must apply for admission, and the majority of students who enter Thoreau stay until graduation.

During the 1993–1994 school year, Thoreau served 173 middle school students and 226 high school students. At the high school, most students (88%) were White, whereas others were African American (6%), Hispanic (5%), Native American (1%), and Asian American (1%).

Rite of Passage Experience

In order to graduate, all Thoreau twelfth-grade students must complete the culminating Rite of Passage Experience (ROPE). Often referred to as the defining feature of Thoreau, ROPE requires students to construct a portfolio of essays covering a broad range of subject areas, write an autobiography and a research paper in U.S. history, and make a series of presentations to demonstrate their proficiency in 17 subject areas.

ROPE was designed to fulfill the school's objective, which is to allow students opportunities to demonstrate their knowledge and achievement through written work and oral presentation, not simply through satisfactory performance on the district's and state's standardized competency tests and the accumulation of credits. Thoreau has received a waiver from its district's testing requirements, and students' ROPE presentations serve to demonstrate their proficiency in reading, English, government, and mathematics (the four areas covered in the district's standardized tests).

ROPE is organized into two phases during a student's senior year. In the first half of the primary phase, students enroll in the "ROPE Class" to learn about the essay writing process, write an autobiography, and complete all of the short essays required for their portfolios. During the second half of this primary phase, students write U.S. history research papers and practice oral presentation strategies.

During the second phase of ROPE, students give their oral presentations before their individual ROPE committees. Each ROPE committee is comprised of two faculty members (one of whom is the student's homeroom teacher), an underclass peer (chosen by the student), and one or more adults from outside the school (most students select a parent). Committees and students are reasonably free to organize the presentations however they want. For example, some committees grade presentations on a pass-fail basis, whereas others assign letter grades; and some presentations are conducted by a group of students, whereas others are individual presentations.

Impact of ROPE

Teachers and students alike are enthusiastic about the value of ROPE as a learning experience. They are comfortable with the "loose" design of the ROPE process. Indeed, teachers say they wish the first half of ROPE—when students are writing the essays, autobiography, and research paper that comprise most of their portfolios—could be structured less formally than it is, but they recognize that their students require the structure of the ROPE class to complete the work.

The school community also is comfortable with the subjective application of standards in the grading of ROPE. Teachers acknowledge—and students recognize—that they adjust their expectations for individual student performance based on what they know of a student's aptitude, achievement, and interests. Students known to be high achievers are expected to perform at higher levels than are other students.

Teachers join the staff at Thoreau because they personally believe in Thoreau's philosophy of supporting and enhancing students' knowledge, skills, and individual interests. Although teachers quibble over the details of the process, they are uniform in their enthusiasm for ROPE and its educational value. ROPE does, however, require a tremendous amount of teachers' time. Despite this additional burden, however, teachers agree that the experience students receive with ROPE is worth the extra effort.

Thoreau students also are enthusiastic about their experiences with ROPE: It serves as a unifying force for the senior class, and students feel a real sense

---

A ROPE Presentation

For his Fine Arts and Personal Proficiency ROPE presentation, Jeremy has chosen to demonstrate his interest in music by playing a piece written by Duke Ellington and discussing Ellington's style. Witnessing Jeremy's presentation are the two teachers on his ROPE committee (his music teacher—who is also Jeremy's homeroom teacher—and another teacher with limited knowledge of music) and a group of younger students. During his presentation, Jeremy describes the history and defining characteristics of jazz and explains Ellington's contributions to the jazz form, the musical features of the piece he has chosen to play, and the technical abilities he must possess in order to play the piece successfully. After Jeremy plays the Ellington trumpet solo, his ROPE committee gives him feedback on his presentation. There is no question but that he has passed this presentation (his ROPE committee has chosen to assign only pass/fail grades), and his music teacher tells Jeremy how he measures up against a variety of standards for musical performance, noting that Jeremy "has an aesthetic sense beyond most other high school students."

---

of accomplishment on completing it. As one former Thoreau student said, the ROPE ceremony in May, when students receive certificates of completion for ROPE, "is a much more meaningful ceremony than graduation." According to the school's principal, Thoreau graduates have also found themselves ahead of their peers in college in writing and organization skills. A recent graduate concurred, adding that it is "the school as a whole, not just ROPE, that gives us an advantage."

Teachers say that parents, who are often members of their children's ROPE committees, are frequently astonished by what their children have accomplished.

Future Plans

Thoreau staff do not envision any major revisions to ROPE in upcoming years, although they will almost certainly continue to tinker with the process. Thoreau's principal and teachers believe that ROPE will continue to promote thoughtfulness in all domains of students' lives, academic and personal.

THE COLLEGE BOARD'S PACESETTER MATHEMATICS PROGRAM: SOMMERVILLE HIGH SCHOOL

Developed jointly by the College Board and the Educational Testing Service, Pacesetter programs are high school-level "integrated programs of standards, teaching, and assessment." The College Board views Pacesetter programs as one element within a strategy designed to encourage all students, particularly students who are disadvantaged or members of a minority group, to take rigorous academic courses while in secondary school. As the description of the Pacesetter programs suggests, Pacesetter assessment is integrated with the program's curriculum and instructional approach. The focus of this summary is the College Board's Pacesetter mathematics program and its implementation at one high school.

The Pacesetter Programs

The Pacesetter programs were developed to complement the College Board's existing Equity 2000 program. Together, the two programs form the core of what the College Board calls its "push-pull" reform strategy: Equity 2000 is designed to "push" students, particularly minority and disadvantaged students, into more demanding academic preparation by requiring them to take advanced math courses; Pacesetter, in turn, is designed to "pull" students toward the goal of high standards of achievement for all students before graduating from high school.[3]

All Pacesetter programs (which are currently offered in mathematics, English, and Spanish, and in the future will include science) incorporate three central components:

- Statement of Standards.
- Teacher Preparation.
- Assessments.

Pacesetter Mathematics

Pacesetter math was the first Pacesetter program to be developed. It was designed to be a "capstone" course in math, taken primarily by students in their senior year of high school. The College Board designed the curriculum as a precalculus course, with an emphasis on modeling.

The program comprises six units, each of which focuses on a particular type of mathematical function. The units include a variety of integrated instructional and assessment activities—in particular, lengthy "task sets"—that students work on guided by their teacher. Pacesetter also includes an end-of-year on-demand assessment (taken by all students across the country enrolled in Pacesetter) that assesses students' achievement in terms of "mathematical knowledge," "applied problem solving," and "communication in the language of mathematics."

Piloted in the 1993–1994 school year at 15 volunteer schools in 10 school districts across the country, the Pacesetter mathematics program provided the

---

[3]College Board (1994).

College Board with feedback about the content and implementation. Specific lessons learned from the pilot included:

- On the end-of-year assessment, students experienced the most difficulty with tasks that required them to communicate in the language of mathematics.
- The end-of-year assessment was too long and needed to be more closely aligned with Pacesetter curriculum tasks.

For the 1994–1995 school year, the College Board addressed these problems and, according to the College Board, most Pacesetter teachers agreed that the assessments were more fair.

Pacesetter Participant: Sommerville High School

Located in the suburbs of Washington, D.C., Sommerville High School serves primarily African American students (89%), with the remainder of students being White (8%), Asian American (2%), and Hispanic (1%). In addition to its regular program, Sommerville High offers programs for students who are gifted in the visual and performing arts, gifted students who are not enrolled in one of the district's two "flagship" schools for the gifted, and students in vocational education.

The school was selected by its district's mathematics supervisor to participate in Pacesetter because of its ongoing participation in the College Board's Equity 2000 program and because the school's mathematics department chair was enthusiastic about experimenting with the program. The Pacesetter course is taught by only 3 of the school's 21 math teachers and reaches only a small fraction of the school's students.

Financial Resources

The pilot implementation of Pacesetter math in 1993–1994 was funded by the College Board and the Educational Testing Service. However, beginning in 1994–1995, schools using the Pacesetter mathematics program had to pay for the curriculum and the support provided by the College Board and ETS, spending $30 per student enrolled in the Pacesetter math program.

The district provided the necessary financial support for Sommerville to participate in Pacesetter during the 1994–1995 school year and agreed to fund the program through 1995–1996. However, the math supervisor says that the program is too expensive for the district to be able to support its expansion and introduction into other high schools. "It is time to start talking with the College Board about the next steps with Pacesetter because it is too expensive the way it is now," commented the math supervisor.

Impact of Pacesetter Mathematics

The three teachers involved with Pacesetter at Sommerville High School all expressed positive comments about Pacesetter. They said that the Pacesetter approach to teaching mathematics and student assessment—which includes performance-based tasks, reflective journals, short-answer quizzes, essays, and the integrated use of technology—was already compatible with their teaching styles and philosophies.

However, they also acknowledged a real shift in their teaching strategies resulting from their participation in Pacesetter. They have honed their skills at writing performance assessment tasks for use with their Pacesetter students. Furthermore, they are applying many Pacesetter strategies in their other math classes. For example, teachers say they are using more technology, encouraging group work, and constructing more performance-based assessment tasks.

Sommerville's Pacesetter teachers also expressed some reservations about the Pacesetter curriculum. Teachers' concerns included the following:

- "Math skills" are not adequately incorporated into the curriculum.
- The curriculum is too long for a year-long class.
- Although the College Board presents the program as a precalculus course, Sommerville teachers found that the course is not adequate preparation for calculus.

However, Sommerville teachers emphasize that these concerns about Pacesetter math are minor in light of the benefits they believe the program offers their students.

All 12 students interviewed for this study were enthusiastic about Pacesetter. More than any other comment, students suggested that, for the first time, they understand, through their work on task sets, that math applications are valuable in "real life." As one student said, "You would never think it would take a function to get an interest rate. I want to go into business, and that is relevant to me." Another student said that the course had been a "confidence booster" for her; she said that she liked and understood math for the first time.

The two parents interviewed were both well informed about Pacesetter and were pleased with the impact the program had on their children. Both parents said Pacesetter had turned around their children's understanding of mathematical concepts, their attitudes toward math, and their self-esteem with respect to learning math.

One of the parents, a biology teacher at Sommerville, said she had noticed that the Pacesetter students who came to her class already knew the mathematical applications that she had always had to teach her biology students. She said, "As a parent, I give Pacesetter a 10 out of 10. As a teacher, I give it a 12 out of 10."

A Pacesetter Mathematics Class

During a 45-minute class period, Mr. Kearney taught a lesson on the hyperbolic function $f(x) = 1/x$. *After discussing the properties of the function, he asked the students (eight boys and seven girls) to turn on their graphing calculators. Using a liquid crystal display to project the output of his calculator onto a screen, he illustrated what the function looked like. He coached students as they programmed their own graphing calculators to represent the function. Then, using the calculators, the class experimented with the equation, first to see what would happen to the graph and values of the function if certain changes were made, and then to develop and test hypotheses about what would happen to the graph and values of the function if other changes were made.*

Future Plans

Sommerville teachers, students, and parents all expressed their belief that mathematics learning has improved because of their involvement with Pacesetter. Hence, they would like to continue their participation into the future. However, given the expense of using Pacesetter, expanding—and even maintaining—Sommerville's participation in the program may prove problematic.

THE NEW STANDARDS PROJECT:
ANN CHESTER ELEMENTARY SCHOOL

Ann Chester Elementary School in Fort Worth, Texas, opened its doors in the fall of 1992 with a mission to establish a "distinctive learning environment" for its students. Since then, the school has been a center of reform activity and participates in both the New Standards Project (NSP) and the district's Applied Learning Program (ALP).

Ann Chester's teachers and students are a self-selected group, as both teachers and students must apply to and be accepted by a school committee. During 1993–1994, the school enrolled 380 students in Grades K through 6. About half the students were White, 27% were African American, 20% were Hispanic, and 3% were Asian American.

NSP and ALP Partnership

Since the Fort Worth Independent School District joined the NSP in 1991, teachers at Ann Chester (and at other district schools) have been involved in developing assessment tasks and in piloting and adopting NSP assessment guidelines. In addition, Ann Chester teachers are involved in the Applied Learning Program, which encourages the use of applied, project-based instruction and performance assessments.

The goals of the two programs are compatible at Ann Chester. The goal of the NSP is to revitalize the education, using assessment as a tool for transforming teaching and learning, whereas the ALP philosophy emphasizes explicit connections between the classroom and the world of work as a central component of classroom instruction.

Since becoming involved with the NSP, Ann Chester has modeled its fourth-grade standards in reading and writing on the NSP literacy dimensions. The school also plans to adopt the NSP mathematics standards in the near future. Three of its teachers currently are developing and piloting mathematics tasks and scoring rubrics for the NSP. In addition, the school plans to develop performance standards in English language arts, social studies, mathematics, and science for all grade levels.

School-Based Performance Assessments

Because of the school's philosophy and participation in reform activities, teachers at Ann Chester enjoy the freedom to use a variety of creative, extended-response assessments on an ongoing basis. Teachers use performance assessments to inform their instructional strategies and to provide information to students and parents about students' educational progress. They make no clear distinctions between assessments and instruction, using project-based assignments for instructional as well as for evaluative purposes.

Students are assigned hands-on, inquiry-based project work that is designed to emulate the world of work. For example, for one project, students formed a "news crew" that broadcast news events every day. For another project, a team of students designed the school admission application forms and procedures. All such projects explicitly juxtapose academic learning and social problem solving to reinforce the connections between classroom and "real-life" experiences.

All students are required to keep a portfolio of their accomplishments in reading, writing, and other projects that illustrate how they are progressing as learners. In concrete terms, this means that each student's portfolio contains samples of work from all content areas. Students routinely review these portfolios to assess their progress vis-à-vis goals they set for themselves at the beginning of the year. In addition, the school invites parents to a yearly Assessment Night to examine their children's portfolios.

To enable teachers' use of project-based instruction and performance assessments, Ann Chester applied for and received a waiver from the district to replace the traditional letter-based report card with a narrative report card. Initially, teachers had described students' dispositions of character and habits of mind in the narrative report cards. However, because of requests from

---

Assessment Night At Ann Chester

Assessment night was held from 7:00 to 8:15 p.m. The school theater was packed with parents and students, and a teacher-director welcomed the group for the children's "moment of glory." After a brief talk by the NSP coordinator, parents went into classrooms to examine their children's portfolios.

Parents discussed the portfolio contents with their children, looking over each piece of work, asking questions, and providing feedback. They were clearly impressed with the work their children had done.

---

parents, teachers now describe students' progress in academic areas and include a statement about the student's rank in the classroom.

Impact on Teachers, Students, and Community

No formal evaluations of the effects of assessment reform at Ann Chester have been conducted. Yet, teachers believe that the reforms have contributed to the success of their students; they are impressed with their students' vocabulary, ability to think, and ability to work cooperatively in groups.

However, despite their commitment to the system and strong support from their peers, teachers want more time for professional activities such as learning how to write scoring rubrics. Furthermore, although much instruction is tailored to the student, many teachers believe that it could be individualized further.

Students, too, had positive reactions to project-based work and assessments. One student described the projects she had to complete as "fun activities." Students also like keeping portfolios, because it allows them to reflect on and take ownership of their work. "My portfolio has my best work and some of my favorite work," said one fifth grader. In addition, students enjoy constructing their own scoring rubrics to evaluate their progress.

Parents interviewed for this study indicated that they are generally satisfied with the school and with their children's overall progress. They like the active-learning pedagogical approach and the narrative report cards. However, they also expressed the concern that their children might not be getting enough exposure to "basic skills." This concern was echoed by a school board member: "When you do applied projects, you can't sacrifice content," he said. Parents want their children to learn multiplication tables, spelling, and grammar and to perform well on multiple-choice tests.

In response to these concerns, one teacher allows parents to take their children out of her class to drill them in multiplication tables and spelling; and the school as a whole organizes forums to inform parents about how basic skills are being taught through project-based instruction.

Future Plans

Teachers at Ann Chester plan to continue to focus on developing performance standards for each grade level in each subject area. In addition, they will collect student work that illustrates "how good is good enough."

THE NEW STANDARDS PROJECT: NOAKES ELEMENTARY SCHOOL

As part of its attempt to establish an educational system that, according to the superintendent, "makes learning real," the Anton School District in Iowa has been developing alternative forms of student assessment for over a decade. It was, in part, its long exposure to performance assessment that convinced the district to join the New Standards Project (NSP) in 1992. Iowa supported the decision and financially supports Anton's membership in the NSP. (The state supports several other districts' NSP participation as well.) The district also applied for and received a 5-year waiver for reporting yearly progress of student achievement to the state.

Jointly run by the National Center on Education and the Economy and the Learning Research and Development Center at the University of Pittsburgh, the NSP is working toward developing and adopting both a set of academic standards and new ways to measure student learning and achievement.

This case-study summary focuses on Anton's participation in the NSP and the development and implementation of NSP-influenced performance assessments at Noakes Elementary School.

Anton School District's Involvement in NSP

As part of their involvement with the NSP program, teachers throughout the Anton School District have piloted numerous NSP English language arts and mathematics assessment tasks and English language arts portfolios.

An Example of a Fourth-Grade NSP Pilot Task. For completing the NSP mathematics tasks, students are required to solve a mathematical problem, explain the method they used to solve the problem, and explain why they chose to use that method. For example, for one fourth-grade mathematics task, students are told they have $25 to buy fish for their 30-gallon classroom aquarium. Students are provided information about sizes of the fish, how much they cost, and their special needs. Then, in a letter to the principal explaining which fish they chose, students are asked to tell how many of each kind of fish they bought, give their reasons for choosing those fish, and show that they are not overspending and that the fish will not be too crowded in the aquarium.

Booklets for such tasks contain a general rubric and a rubric specific to the task for scoring students' performance.

English Language Arts Portfolios.   In addition to piloting assessment tasks such as the one described previously, several teachers also have committed to using the NSP guidelines for English language arts (ELA) portfolios. Teachers are expected to randomly select some of the portfolios and send them to an NSP benchmarking conference.

Each ELA portfolio must contain certain types of student work. For example, each elementary ELA portfolio must contain (a) a table of contents; (b) a reflection piece; (c) a response to literature; (d) some best pieces that, among other things, tell a story, demonstrate the collection and reporting of information, and show the student's best efforts in reading; and (e) four free choices. Each portfolio entry is scored using a NSP-developed scoring rubric.

Several Anton teachers have attended the NSP conferences focused on benchmarking, scoring, and developing such assessment tasks and portfolios. The district pays for teachers to attend the conferences, and the participant teachers are expected to share the information from the conferences with their peers. Teachers trained in the use of the NSP scoring rubrics said they are comfortable with scoring the NSP assessments. However, one teacher said that a clear set of anchor papers is essential to good scoring.

Noakes Elementary School

Noakes, one of the six elementary schools in the district, spans Grades K through 6, and in 1994–1995 enrolled about 565 students, 98% of whom were White.

Noakes is an enthusiastic participant in the district's assessment reform efforts. One of Noakes' 1994–1995 school year goals was to ensure that each

---

A Fourth-Grade English Language Arts NSP Pilot Task

The "Camels Task" was piloted in 4 days during 45-minute class periods. On the first day, the teacher provided her fourth-grade English Language Arts class with an overview of what the task was about, how it would be administered, and what the students should think about or concentrate on during the task. Students then read "Ships of the Desert," a short story about the history, temperament, and physical characteristics of different types of camels, and answered questions about the story. On the second day, students chose a topic, such as "Should our community have a camel in the zoo?" and began drafting their essays. Students spent the majority of the third day in small groups, discussing what they had written the day before. On the last day, students revised their essays. During the 4 days, the teacher continued to give instructions, prompts, and advice for the students to consider as they wrote their essays.

child complete a portfolio in at least one academic area. In order to fulfill this goal, all Noakes teachers received some training in how to develop and implement performance assessments, and two fourth-grade teachers received extensive training through the NSP in the development, implementation, and scoring of the NSP portfolios.

Noakes, however, does not use a standard, schoolwide portfolio system, and teachers are not required to use the NSP guidelines. Thus, teachers exercise individual control over how they develop and use portfolios in their classes.

All teachers at Noakes are committed to the use of performance assessments, albeit in different ways. Some teachers use portfolios in only one subject area, whereas others use them in all areas. In addition, some teachers do not score the portfolios, whereas others incorporate the scores they assign to the portfolios into students' final grades.

Overall, teachers—both those directly involved with the NSP and those devising and using their own performance assessments—had positive opinions about the pedagogical value of performance assessments. For example, a sixth-grade science teacher who administered a 2-hour performance task on electrical circuits said that, although the task took more time to complete than a traditional quiz covering the same topic, "it was [a] worthwhile, valuable learning experience that the students enjoyed."

One of the teachers directly involved with the NSP said that it had opened new doorways for professional growth by showing her how new units could be added to the curriculum. Other teachers pointed out that the portfolios help students demonstrate what they know, reflect on their progress, and take ownership of their work; performance-based assignments help students to gain a deeper understanding of the subject matter and to retain information longer than do other types of assignments.

Teachers also pointed out that performance tasks allow students who traditionally experience academic difficulties to perform well. On the other hand, one teacher noted that academically challenged students sometimes are unable to complete all the steps in an assessment task.

Teachers expressed concerns, however, about the lack of time and an inadequate amount of training to develop and implement performance assessments in a manner satisfactory to them. As one teacher said, "It puts stress on our free time, after school time, and weekends."

The fourth-grade students interviewed had very definite opinions about the performance task they were working on and about performance assessments in general. They found the performance task they were currently working on to be very interesting and engaging, and they enjoyed being able to write about their opinions. Students described other performance assessments they had done as learning experiences.

The district is trying to provide information about its participation in the NSP to parents and community members, most of whom are unaware of the NSP. However, according to a parent of a fourth grader, those parents who *are* aware of the changes in assessments are supportive of them. This parent said that she understands the NSP system and has seen its positive effects on her child. She has been able to see her child's progress by looking at his portfolio, and is impressed by his ability to communicate his feelings about his work.

Future Plans

The Anton School District does not plan to mandate the use of portfolios or other performance assessments. Instead, the teachers and administrators currently involved in the assessment reform process want the adoption of a performance assessment system to be a "bottom-up" decision. As a result, teachers who are using performance assessments are involving more teachers by providing in-service training and help to those who are interested. In addition, the Anton Executive Director of Instruction hopes soon to establish a professional center that will house information on student-centered learning and performance assessments.

HARRISON SCHOOL DISTRICT 2'S PERFORMANCE-BASED CURRICULUM: MCGARY ELEMENTARY SCHOOL

The development and implementation of a Literacy Performance Based Curriculum (PBC) represent a break from past practice in Colorado's Harrison School District 2 (HSD2). The new curriculum focuses on student outcomes and incorporates performance assessments.

The curriculum development process incorporates identifying, integrating, and assessing significant student outcomes for all students through the adoption of performance assessments. The district is developing its PBC in response to Colorado's House Bill 1313, which requires local education authorities to adopt standards for reading, writing, mathematics, science, history, and geography to guide curriculum, instruction, material selection, and assessment of student performance.

Performance-Based Literacy Assessments

After the development and districtwide implementation of HSD2's writing performance assessment during the 1989–1990 school year, the HSD2 began work on revising the Grade K through 12 reading and language arts (literacy) curriculum, the first curriculum area mandated by the state to undergo the standards-based change. The cornerstone of this revision was the replacement of traditional forms of assessment with performance assessments.

During the curriculum review process, members of the district's reading and language arts curriculum committee developed performance assessments and benchmarks for student achievement. The literacy PBC was piloted during the 1992–1993 school year, revised during the following summer, and implemented districtwide during 1993–1994.

The literacy PBC is designed to set achievement targets for students, classes, and grade levels; to conduct ongoing assessment throughout the year; to design and carry out lesson plans that continuously teach outcomes and target achievement indicators; to teach students to become self-assessors by providing them with ongoing feedback through rubrics; and to ensure that each unit of study has clearly stated outcomes as well as a means to assess results.

As part of achieving these goals, teachers administer three (out of five developed by the district) performance tasks each year. The performance tasks are activities that students engage in and complete to demonstrate that they can formulate the ideas and perform the skills identified in the target achievement indicator.

One of the five performance tasks (predetermined by the district) is utilized for school-building accountability purposes. Scores from the assessment are aggregated to the district, but are not high stakes. Instead, they are intended to provide instructional direction.

In some cases, especially at the elementary levels, the literacy assessment tasks have a substantive focus that overlaps with other curricular areas, such as science and history, thereby encouraging cross-disciplinary instruction.

To invite classroom participation of both teachers and students, two scoring rubrics for each assessment task are included in the literacy PBC: the teacher scoring rubric and the student scoring rubric. While students are performing the task, the teacher frequently refers to the student scoring rubric and asks the students to reflect on their performance and to evaluate other students' work based on the student scoring rubric.

A New Idea: Public Academic Performance

As part of a unit on westward expansion, students wrote a research article or kept a diary on the topic of the Oregon Trail. Teachers and students sat around mock campfires in traditional clothing and told stories based on their research article or diary entry. Parents were invited to watch the evening performance and to participate in the scoring of their child's performance using a scoring rubric. The response of teachers, parents, and students to this event was positive. Staff at McGary are planning in-services for other schools so they, too, can hold similar public academic performances.

One important feature of HSD2's assessment reform effort is its home-grown "Assessment Academy." The Academy provides all district teachers with training in how to develop, administer, and interpret performance-based student assessments. Teachers in HSD2 expressed positive reactions to the training they received through the Academy. In the words of one teacher, "I haven't had to go outside the district to get the support I need."

McGary Elementary School

A parent interviewed for this study observed that McGary Elementary School is "not your typical elementary school. It is way above average." The school has been described as an innovative school with a dynamic principal—a leader who also happens to have been one of the key figures in the adoption of performance assessments in the district. Several people in HSD2 agree that McGary has been the school in HSD2 that has most proactively embraced the new literacy curriculum, and, in fact, it is the furthest along in articulating and defining scoring rubrics and student proficiency levels beyond the literacy curriculum.

In 1993–1994, McGary enrolled about 470 students whose ethnic composition was similar to that of the district as a whole. Approximately 47% of students were White, 26% were African American, 21% Hispanic, 5% Asian American, and 1% Native American.

Impact of PBC on Teachers, Students, and Parents

One teacher related that "There was initially a mixed reaction among the faculty about the move to PBC and performance assessments. There were clearly some skeptics and some early adopters, but there was respect for the process of implementation undertaken by the district and for our principal." Most teachers interviewed agreed that PBC and performance assessments enhanced not only their pedagogical techniques, but also the very nature of instruction in the classrooms. Teachers said that the use of performance assessments gives them information about their students and a better idea of what and why they are teaching.

Although most of the impact of PBC was perceived to be positive, some teachers expressed reservations and discomfort with the changes. One point of initial resistance to this change was from teachers who were attached to favorite units they had developed and used for years. Another point of resistance came from teachers who were not as capable as others at integrating the new curriculum into their classrooms.

Most McGary teachers realize that the curriculum reform process is going to take a long time to reach even a semi-final form. So far teachers and parents see the assessment effort as a "value-added" experience that has great potential for reaching its goals, but not until the distant future. Indeed, the district is well aware of the ouster of the majority of members of the Littleton, Colorado, School Board after parents and community members reacted to their perceived rapid movement toward adopting outcomes-based education. As one teacher said, "It is important that we go slow, because of what happened in Littleton."

In general, parents expressed their support of the performance assessments. One parent said, "The performance assessments have been well accepted by 98% of the parents, but I wouldn't want to see the traditional grading system go by the wayside." In general, parents and community members are comfortable with the change and feel that HSD2 is "adding something, not taking something away" with the implementation of performance assessments.

Teachers suggest that PBC and its scoring rubrics have helped to clarify standards for their students. One student said that she liked the scoring rubrics because they helped her write advanced-level stories. She said, "I look at the rubric to make sure everything is there. Mom helps me identify where I am on the rubric sometimes." Teachers are even more enthusiastic about the impact of the PBC and performance assessments on students than the students themselves are. One teacher noted, "I have never before had a student come to me with a B and ask, 'How do I get an A?'"

Future Plans

There is much that district- and school-level participants would like to see happen in upcoming years. They would like to see more thought go into the inclusion of students with disabilities in their classrooms. They would also like to see a better articulation between the curriculum and assessment at different grade levels and the continued refinement and adoption of performance assessments.

One second-grade teacher summed up the opinions among HSD2 personnel about the reform efforts: "I think it will be worth it. I'm excited to be focusing on what we will be doing in future years. These are stressful changes, but we are getting support."

SOUTH BRUNSWICK'S SIXTH-GRADE RESEARCH PERFORMANCE ASSESSMENT: WINDERMERE ELEMENTARY SCHOOL

After realizing its students were leaving elementary school without the research skills the district wanted them to possess, the South Brunswick Township Public Schools developed the Sixth-Grade Research Performance Assessment

(RPA). Supported by the district's move toward resource-based teaching methods, the RPA helps teachers monitor student progress and provides feedback for instruction.

The Sixth-Grade Research Performance Assessment

The district drew from the work and ideas of several different organizations and individuals in developing its assessment. In 1992, following a pilot test in 1991, the assessment was implemented districtwide. The RPA, administered in May and June each year, comprises:

- *An extended performance task.* Students have 8 hours (across 2 or 4 school days) to research a question related to the "American experience" using different sources of information (e.g., encyclopedias, books, people, CD-ROM), prepare a bibliography, prepare a written report, and give a 3- to 5-minute oral presentation with at least one relevant visual.
- *A performance event.* On the day following the completion of the performance task, students present their oral reports before five or six classmates, several fourth and fifth graders, and two outside assessors.

Four components of students' work are scored:

- The written report.
- The oral presentation.
- The visual the student creates to support the oral presentation.
- The process the student follows during the eight hours he or she spends preparing the report, presentation, and visual.

Each of the four components is scored with a rubric. The rubric applied to the written report is a five-point holistic rubric: All dimensions associated with a score must be present in the written report for a student to earn that score. The other three rubrics use trait scales: Five characteristics of the component are present (1), partially present ($\frac{1}{2}$), or not present (0). The outside assessors are responsible for scoring students' reports, presentations, and visuals, whereas an adult within the school community (but not the student's classroom teacher) assigns students' process scores. Overall, a score of 12 (an average score of 3 out of 5 on each of the four components) is considered a passing score on the RPA.

Although it is not the South Brunswick Township Public Schools' only performance assessment (the district has also introduced an early childhood portfolio, and students in Grades 3 through 12 maintain a "Best Works Portfolio" that is passed on with them from year to year), the RPA is not viewed as a

---

Training of Assessors

The South Brunswick Township Public Schools invites members of the community and other interested individuals to participate in the Sixth-Grade Research Performance Assessment as assessors. Before they begin to score students' work, assessors undergo a 2-hour training session that includes:

- *Receiving an overview of the assessment process.*
- *Reviewing copies of the scoring rubrics.*
- *Reading and discussing five "benchmark" papers.*
- *Reviewing directions for using the scoring rubrics and for recording agreed-on scores.*

Based on the training they receive, assessors then work in pairs to judge the presentations of sixth-grade students. Although the assessment is popular among teachers, adequate training of the assessors remains an issue of concern.

---

part of a larger system of performance assessments. Rather, it is an assessment designed to guide curriculum and instruction and to assess specific student skills.

RPA at Windermere Elementary School

Windermere Elementary School is one of seven elementary schools in South Brunswick. During the 1993–1994 school year, the school served 500 students in Grades K through 6. Sixty-nine percent of those students were White, 12% were African American, 16% were Asian American, and 3% were Hispanic; 9% of the school's students qualified for a free or reduced-price lunch.

Teachers, students, and parents at Windermere Elementary School all have positive things to say about the RPA. Each of the three sixth-grade teachers interviewed described how he or she had modified instruction in the classroom to emphasize the skills students need to develop for the research assessment. For example, one sixth-grade teacher explained that he had held practice oral presentations throughout the school year.

In addition, the school's librarian is also very enthusiastic about the RPA and attributed increased collaboration between teachers and librarians to the adoption of the assessment. She asserted, and the school's sixth-grade teachers concurred, that "Teachers are teaching to the assessment, which is exactly what we want them to be doing."

Both the librarian and the sixth-grade teachers further reported that the school's fourth- and fifth-grade teachers also now emphasize research skills more than they did formerly. Windermere's sixth-grade teachers say that, as a result of changing instruction, their students' research skills have improved over the 3 years since the RPA was introduced. Teachers say their students typically like the research assessments because they are more "real" to the students than are multiple-choice, standardized tests.

Some students, however, find the assessment process to be very stressful. Parents and teachers share this concern, especially with respect to students with disabilities, who are assessed on the same criteria and held to the same standards of performance as their nondisabled peers.

According to Windermere teachers and students, the RPA is a valuable educational experience. However, as it exists now, the assessment is a one-time, low-stakes experience with little or no impact on the students' future educational experiences. Students move on to junior high school, where their performance on the RPA is not used for placement decisions or for identifying students who require remediation. Furthermore, the RPA provides only limited feedback for instruction. Because the assessment takes place at the end of the sixth-grade year, teachers can use the information obtained from the assessment only to modify the instructional practices they will use with their *next* group of students.

Future Plan

The district has plans to develop an eighth-grade research assessment, thereby introducing greater coordination in the teaching and assessment of research skills across elementary and junior high school. When such a plan is put into effect, the RPA promises to become an integrated feature of a more comprehensive system of performance assessment.

NEW YORK REGENTS PORTFOLIOS: HUDSON HIGH SCHOOL

New York has the oldest and largest state testing program in the nation—The Regents Examinations. The tests have long been used to maintain state-set educational standards, to influence instruction, to provide accountability (scores are reported to the public annually), to demonstrate individual competency, and to make college admissions decisions in the state of New York.

In 1992, however, the New York Commissioner of Education and the Board of Regents moved to redesign the state's testing program in recognition of the following limitations of the current system:

- It duplicates district or local testing programs.
- It provides externally scored data on a delayed time frame that cannot support teaching decisions.

- It encourages instruction that emphasizes rote-oriented tasks focused on lower-level knowledge and skills rather than rigorous content and higher-level performance abilities.
- It fails to promote linkages with the world of work and to ask students to demonstrate their proficiency as they would in the real world.

The Commissioner and Regents consequently adopted the New York New Compact for Learning, which envisions an education system in which all high school students would assemble a locally designed but state-approved K through 12 Regents Portfolio for graduation. The portfolio will include both discipline-specific and multidisciplinary student work samples (papers, projects, and exhibitions) and projects that demonstrate competence across the seven curriculum areas and the state's set of Essential Skills and Dispositions. In addition, under the New Compact for Learning, the Regents Examinations would be replaced by a set of as-of-yet unspecified performance assessments.

The state of New York intends to phase in these changes gradually. In order to support its move toward a performance-based testing system, the State Department of Education has allowed individual schools to petition for waivers from Regents Examination requirements. The waivers allow teachers to develop and use performance assessments with their students in satisfaction of the Regents requirements, in full or in part. The development work taking place at individual schools will then inform the state's development and introduction of both its locally driven portfolio assessment system and its statewide performance-based assessments.

Performance Assessment Development at Hudson High School

Located in the Hudson Valley near Albany and Schenectady, Hudson High School serves nearly 1,400 ninth through twelfth graders. In 1993–1994, the school'student body was composed primarily of White students (91%), with other students being African American (3%), Asian American (3%), Hispanic (2%), and "other" (1%).

Even prior to the state's adoption of the New Compact for Learning, two enterprising global studies and English teachers designed an interdisciplinary, team-taught course that made connections between history and literature and focused on writing assignments and performance-oriented tasks. The teachers found, however, that the current Regents Examinations, because of their content coverage emphases, prevented them from implementing their new course successfully. They petitioned the state for a waiver that would allow them to substitute for the Regents global studies and English exams a portfolio that would include a reading-response journal, a multiple-source paper, a persuasive essay, and a biography project. The request was approved in 1992.

In 1993, the state expanded schools' opportunities to apply for waivers from the Regents Examinations by formally inviting high schools to develop and pilot performance assessments in Regents subject areas. Approved pilot projects could serve as partial (up to 35%) satisfaction of the Regents Examinations.

Responding to this invitation, Hudson's principal persuaded leaders in his science, English, and social studies departments to develop proposals to take advantage of the freedom that the state's partial waiver allowed. Hudson teachers have since developed performance assessments as full or partial waivers to the Regents Examinations in tenth- and eleventh-grade English and social studies (through integrated courses), eleventh-grade English, ninth- and tenth-grade global studies, ninth-grade earth science, and tenth-grade biology.

In the integrated English/Social Studies courses, literature and writing are used to enhance and enrich the Global Studies (tenth-grade) or U.S. History and Government (eleventh-grade) programs. Issues raised in social studies provide subjects for in-depth writing and further reading. In part, the course is designed to foster writing across the curriculum and to encourage students to study different historical viewpoints and to draw their own independent conclusions.

Impact of Regents Waiver Course Performance Assessments on Teachers, Students, and Parents

Hudson teachers believe that the performance assessments they have developed provide a more realistic appraisal of students' abilities than do the Regents Examinations alone. The performance assessments provide immediate feedback about student progress, and this feedback allows teachers to modify their instructional strategies to enhance student learning.

A Regents Waiver Course in Earth Science

In Hudson's Earth Science course, students conduct a long-term study that requires understanding of key scientific and geological concepts and that promotes the development of analytical and investigative skills. At the beginning of the year, students are presented with a "pet rock" of unknown composition and origin. They learn as much as possible about their rock and keep a detailed scientific journal recording their observations, inferences, and predictions about the rock's scientific characteristics, genesis, metamorphosis, geographical location, and commercial value. In the second semester, students investigate the rock's relationship to the environment. For instance, they may take a field trip to a site where the rock might be found or interview a professional geologist. Students end their investigation with a multimedia, oral presentation summarizing their year of research.

Teachers have used the freedom the Regents waivers have provided to be more creative in developing assignments that challenge and engage their students, to make interdisciplinary and "real-world" connections, and to reinforce critical thinking skills and concepts. As one teacher remarked, "This has been the single best professional growth experience I have had in 27 years of teaching."

Despite teachers' enthusiasm about the educational value of the waiver courses they have designed, they feel the workload these courses create is "almost suicidal." Between planning and grading, teachers estimate that one section of a waiver course can create up to 3 hours of additional work each day. In addition, some Hudson teachers have said that, although they design their own assessment tasks and rubrics, they still harbor some concern about the reliability of their performance assessments because they have received no formal training in rubric development or scoring.

Finally, adequate content coverage remains a concern among some Hudson teachers. (Indeed, some teachers, particularly those who teach higher-level mathematics and science courses, have declined to join their colleagues in designing waiver courses because they feel that heavy use of time-consuming performance assessments would impede their ability to cover the breadth of material that is essential, in their minds, for preparing students for higher education.) Hudson teachers who are involved in designing performance assessments agreed that they often must sacrifice portions of their curriculum in order to provide room for the discussions, role playing, oral reports, and lengthy experimentation that performance assessments entail. However, although content coverage remains an issue, most teachers at Hudson who use performance assessments have come to the conclusion that the depth and variety of learning opportunities that performance assessments provide are more important than mastery of broad content.

Teachers at Hudson said that their students are more motivated and enjoy the learning process more when they are encouraged to express their own opinions and given the freedom to respond creatively to challenges. Students themselves also said that these exercises have helped them improve their verbal communication and persuasion skills, as well as their poise and self-confidence.

Parents interviewed for this study were unanimous in agreeing that performance assessments give them more information about their children's progress than do the traditional Regents Examinations. They noted that parents receive Regents scores months after their children take the tests, and that the scores provide no information about their children's strengths and weaknesses. In contrast, they found they more frequently saw the fruits of their children's work with performance assessment tasks, allowing them to track their children's progress.

Future Plans

The future of Hudson's performance assessment program is linked closely to the future of the Regents examination system. Meanwhile, the pilot program has worked well at Hudson, because it allows both teachers and students to participate voluntarily in the experimental waiver courses. However, extensive performance assessments clearly present extra costs in terms of teacher workload; steps also must be taken to ensure the reliability and validity of each assessment and to train teachers in the development of sound testing approaches. Successful resolution of these issues will be necessary if the reforms are to continue and ultimately to succeed.

MARYLAND ASSESSMENT REFORM: WALTERS MIDDLE SCHOOL

In 1991, the state of Maryland began developing and implementing the Maryland School Performance Assessment Program (MSPAP) as part of its Schools for Success reform initiative. MSPAP is intended to reflect standards of achievement commensurate with 21st-century expectations, and to drive the instructional changes that will help students learn how to apply their knowledge to real-world situations and become better problem solvers. This case study summary focuses on the implementation and effects of MSPAP at one Maryland middle school.

MSPAP Characteristics and Implementation

MSPAP assessments in reading, writing, language usage, mathematics, science, and social studies are administered in the spring of each school year to all students in Grades 3, 5, and 8. Typically, MSPAP tasks require students to respond to a series of questions that lead to a final problem requiring a solution, recommendation, or a decision. Students also must provide an explanation or rationale for their final response. Thus, MSPAP tasks are intended to reveal both the process and content of students' thinking.

Students' responses to the assessment tasks are scored using task-specific rubrics called "scoring keys." Each rubric provides an overview of the type of competency or skill that the task elicits, and includes a scale for scoring students' responses to the task. Scoring is performed by certified Maryland teachers during the summer, under the direction of the Maryland Department of Education and Measurement Incorporated, a private consulting firm. Based on their MSPAP scores, students are assigned to one of five proficiency levels in the assessed subject area.

Although preliminary testing began in 1991, the 1993 MSPAP results served as the baseline for school accountability reviews. For a school to achieve "satisfactory" performance in a given content area, 70% of its students must achieve the "satisfactory" proficiency level on the assessment; for a school to attain "excellent" performance in a given content area, 70% of its students must achieve the "satisfactory" proficiency level and 25% must achieve the "excellent" proficiency level. All Maryland schools are expected to reach the satisfactory standard in all subject areas by the year 2000.

MSPAP and Other Assessments at Walters Middle School

Walters Middle School serves about 860 students in Walters, Maryland, a "bedroom community" for the cities of Baltimore and Washington, D.C. Walters students come from middle- and upper-middle-class backgrounds and are predominantly White (96%), other students being African American (2%), Hispanic (2%), and Asian American (1%). In the first years of MSPAP, students at the school have scored higher than both state and district averages.

In recent years, teachers and students at Walters have begun working not only with MSPAP but also with its school district's own performance assessment system, the Criterion-Referenced Evaluation System (CRES). The CRES was developed to support the district's newly restructured Essential Curriculum. The Essential Curriculum incorporates subject area goals, individual course objectives, and five interdisciplinary outcome Learner Behaviors—effective communication skills, problem solving and critical thinking, social cooperation and self-discipline, responsible citizenship in the community and environment, and lifelong learning. The CRES is intended to monitor students' achievement of these Learner Behaviors and mastery of the Essential Curriculum.

The CRES requires students to respond to open-ended types of performance tasks that assess logic, reasoning, and comprehension skills, as well as content mastery. The system consists of both formative (ongoing) assessments and end-of-the-year summative assessments.

Formative assessments, which are used at the teacher's discretion, include a variety of extended response tasks intended to provide teachers with information about student progress so as to foster the adjustment of instruction and curriculum and the reteaching of skills over the course of the school year.

The end-of-year summative CRES assessment, required of students at all grade levels, are intended to provide information to improve instruction, help teachers measure whether the Essential Curriculum has been learned, and provide helpful information to school improvement teams. The CRES summative exams are scored by individual classroom teachers using rubrics and anchor papers to guide the scoring process.

Impact of MSPAP and CRES

According to the district administrators, the state-initiated MSPAP and the district-initiated CRES are intended to meet similar purposes, and the content and process skills they tap are also similar. For these reasons, district administrators say they are using the MSPAP, in part, as an external validation of their own CRES system, and, indeed, relative trends in MSPAP and CRES scores at the districts' schools have proven remarkably parallel. However, they harbor concerns about the implementation of MSPAP.

In fact, the implementation of two similar assessment systems is taking a toll on Walters teachers. Teachers—and administrators and school board members as well—expressed concerns about valuable instructional time lost to administering the two assessments, and a number of teachers complained about the large amounts of time required to set up the MSPAP group experiment components. One district administrator acknowledged that "There is a great need to find some relief for teachers" from the labor-intensive nature of performance assessments and to add additional staff development days to the school calendar.

Furthermore, from teachers' perspective, the value added of MSPAP is unclear, and they suggest that the impact MSPAP has had on their teaching practices has been, at most, marginal. This is because MSPAP currently is limited to just three grade levels, whereas students at every grade level take CRES. In addition, CRES assessments are administered and scored by classroom teachers, and individual students' results are available immediately. On the other hand, MSPAP assessments are not scored at the local school level, and the scores have not been received by schools until at least 6 months after the assessments were administered.

For these reasons, although they believe that MSPAP is superior to multiple-choice testing, Walters teachers identify more instructional value in their own CRES assessments than in the state's assessment. Individuals interviewed for this study suggested that CRES has encouraged teachers "to think carefully about what they want students to know" and "to bring their own critical thinking skills to bear on the teaching styles and methods [with which] they are familiar."

Although their teachers are concerned about the amount of time that MSPAP and CRES take, students at Walters Middle School expressed enthusiasm for both performance assessments. Students noted in particular that they enjoyed the group work and experimentation, and the opportunity and encouragement to express their personal opinions. Walters teachers and parents also said they believe MSPAP and CRES assessment tasks are "more interesting" and "more relevant" to students than are standard testing formats, and both groups feel that the new tests motivate students to do better work. Several teachers, however, expressed their concerns that both MSPAP and CRES tasks present too great a challenge for students with disabilities.

Parents interviewed for this study were strongly supportive of CRES, which they said provides clear information about the academic standards being set for their children and about their children's strengths and weaknesses with respect to those standards. These parents also indicated that they had received enough information about both the CRES and MSPAP assessments to inform them of assessment content and goals.

Summary

At Walters Middle School, MSPAP joins a district-initiated performance assessment quite similar in format, purpose, content, and skill coverage. Thus, at this school, it seems that perceived (and perhaps actual) redundancy among assessments has resulted in a limited impact of the state assessment on teachers' instructional strategies. However, despite concerns about redundancy and time demands of the two assessments, overall sentiment within the Walters community seems to suggest that MSPAP, as well as CRES, not only represents a departure from old ideas and policies no longer in the best interest of students, but also offers a glimpse of the future of education.

ARIZONA ASSESSMENT REFORM:
MANZANITA HIGH SCHOOL

During the late 1980s, the Arizona legislature became concerned about the quality of public education in the state. In May 1990, through the collaborative effort of Arizona's Joint Legislative Committee on Goals for Education Excellence, the State Board of Education, and the Arizona Department of Education, Governor Mofford signed into law the Arizona Student Assessment Program (ASAP), a program designed to measure students' progress toward attaining the state's curriculum standards, Essential Skills.

The Arizona Department of Education (ADE) contracted with the Riverside Publishing Company to develop the ASAP performance assessments. The assessments were piloted in all school districts during the 1991–1992 school year. (An evaluation of the validity and reliability of ASAP performance assessments was conducted by Riverside, but their report was not available.) The first full-scale administration of the ASAP was conducted in March 1993.

Arizona Student Assessment Program

ASAP tests all third-, eighth-, and twelfth-grade students who are not exempt (by virtue of provisions in their IEPs) from the program in the areas of reading, writing, and mathematics. The assessment system is comprised of an on-demand performance event, during which students are asked to construct responses to a variety of tasks. The assessment at each grade level maintains a single theme across the three subject areas. For instance, in 1994 the twelfth-grade theme focused on "consumer decisions." Students are allowed 2 hours to complete each section of the assessment.

The rubrics used to score the tasks are tailored to each individual assessment task and are printed in the response booklets for students to refer to as needed. A small percentage of the assessments are scored by Arizona teachers, with the rest being scored by Measurement, Inc.

Resource and Professional Support

The Arizona legislature allocated no new funds to support the development and implementation of ASAP. All development, training, and administration costs were supported under existing ADE testing budgets.

In the fall of 1990, Arizona conducted a statewide conference to introduce representatives from each district to ASAP. Over the course of the following school year, ADE officials traveled to regional sites to work with teachers, conducted a "trainer of trainers" seminar to teach scoring, and produced a videotape about ASAP for distribution to all districts. ADE also publishes a quarterly newsletter, *Measuring Up*, that updates teachers and administrators about developments in ASAP.

ASAP and Other Assessments at Manzanita High School

Manzanita High School is located in suburban Phoenix. The district was the highest-performing district on the twelfth-grade component of ASAP in both 1993 and 1994. One of the smaller high schools in its district, Manzanita served 1,035 ninth through twelfth graders during the 1993–1994 school year. These students were White (78%), Hispanic (15%), African American (4%), Asian American (2%), and Native American (1%).

Manzanita's district has an extensive and complex assessment program of its own. Through this program, the district administers multiple-choice, criterion-referenced tests—both pretests and posttests—in all subject areas at all grade levels (ninth through twelfth; the district is comprised only of high schools). In addition, the district administers performance assessments in several subject areas and intends to expand its use of performance assessments over the next few years to include all subjects. The centerpiece of the district's performance assessment program is the "multiparagraph essay" assessment required of all students each year. Thus, in this district, ASAP joined what was already a demanding, time-consuming assessment program.

Impact on Teachers, Students, and Parents

Although most Manzanita teachers support both the concept of performance assessment and many of its manifestations in the district's assessment program, they are, to date, less than enthusiastic about ASAP. They are critical of the current ASAP assessment instruments, because they do not believe that the assessment instruments cover the curriculum they are teaching. Even conceding that ASAP aims only to "audit" students' progress toward a subset of the state's Essential Skills, teachers dispute the validity of the instruments. One mathematics teacher said, "The twelfth-grade math assessment covers only basic math skills (adding, subtracting, multiplying, and dividing). In 1994 one problem required that students graph a line, but no other 1994 and no 1993 problems required students to perform any algebra, geometry, trigonometry, or calculus."

Manzanita teachers who have participated in ASAP scoring sessions also report difficulty in using the rubrics, finding them to be too general. Furthermore, teachers assert that the combined effect of ASAP and the district's extensive assessment program is to take a lot of instructional time out of the school year.

Students, too, are critical of their experience with ASAP. Two honors students remarked that the essay they were asked to read for the ASAP reading assessment was poorly written, illogical, and contradictory. These two students did not find the ASAP challenging, and they suggested that the assessments might have been appropriate for students at lower performance levels than their own. However, another student who struggles with his school work failed to see any relevance of ASAP to his life: "It's stupid. We don't need to do that stuff." However, one student, bound for a military career, said that, although he did not enjoy the ASAP, he could see the relevance of the skills it tested: "Writing is hard for me, but it's relevant to my future. I'll have to write a lot of reports and things like that."

One parent interviewed knew that her daughter had taken the ASAP exam, but she did not know much about the examination itself. The other parent, a member of Manzanita's site-based planning team, was better informed about ASAP. In her opinion, ASAP is a "minimum competency exam" that tells her nothing about her children's performance that she doesn't learn from their grades and their performance on Advanced Placement exams.

Future Plans

The Arizona Department of Education had originally intended to add to ASAP performance assessments in science and social studies during the next couple of years and to make satisfactory performance on the twelfth-grade ASAP a requirement for graduation. Originally, this plan was to have gone into effect in 1996, but the ADE has since extended the time line, now planning to institute ASAP as a graduation requirement for the class of 2004.

This expansion of ASAP is still officially part of the ADE's plan. However, in January 1995, the new state superintendent, citing technical problems with the assessments, temporarily postponed ASAP in order that the program in its current form could be revisited and evaluated. Consequently, the program was not administered in the winter of 1995. The superintendent intends to reinstate ASAP after the program has been reviewed and, in all likelihood, modified.

Appendix C

Research Questions

The major research questions include the following.

KEY CHARACTERISTICS OF PERFORMANCE ASSESSMENTS

- What are the key characteristics of these new assessment strategies? How do these new approaches differ from traditional practices and from prior practice in particular sites?
- What key characteristics cut across successful approaches? What characteristics are missing from less successful programs in this area? Why are particular aspects of the model approach especially important?
- What are the purposes of these new assessment approaches? Are those aims different from traditional practice and from prior practice in particular sites?
- What role was played by research, research-based knowledge, and other information in the design of these new assessment approaches? What evidence documents that role?
- What are the content and skills coverages of the assessment? What are the cognitive demands of the assessments?
- What methods are available to measure students' sustained performance? What types of material (and how much) should be kept in portfolios at what age or grade levels? What types of assessment measures can be developed from them? For example, what types of material are needed to reflect: depth and breadth of understanding in various subject matter areas, ability to use resources, ability to work productively with peers, individual productivity, and ability to respond appropriately to constructive review and criticism? What are the best arrangements for keeping portfolios or for deciding what they are to contain or when and if they should be cleaned out?

FACILITATORS AND BARRIERS IN ASSESSMENT
REFORM

- What are the circumstances that permitted or encouraged the development and implementation of new assessment strategies? To what degree and how can these or similar conditions be reproduced in other settings? How must different approaches be adapted to particular settings?
- What were the principal incentives for reform? What have been the major barriers to the initiation, development, implementation, and sustenance of the reforms, and how have those been overcome? What federal, state, district, or school policies or practices facilitate or inhibit these reforms?
- How have curriculum and instruction been affected by performance assessments? Did a drive for curricular and instructional reform give impetus to the development and adoption of performance assessments?
- Who should be involved in the development of assessments such as performance assessments or portfolios? Where is this developmental work best undertaken? School site? District? State? For example, what types of cooperation and support from the state level are most important for a district interested in developing a new assessment of student performance?
- What strategies are required to get schools organized logistically to develop and implement new forms of student assessment in the schools? What are successful strategies for involving and informing students and parents and other members of the community?
- What types of training are needed for the various individuals involved in these new assessments? What are the components of training, and what training approaches are most effective? What are the advantages and disadvantages of alternative types and sources of this training? What training and resource support are needed for change in instructional strategies and curriculum?
- What technical factors need to be considered? How have these been dealt with most successfully?
- What information sources are available for those interested in either developing their own new forms of assessment or adapting existing assessments that have been developed by others as part of their school or curriculum reform? What technical support is available? What was most helpful, and what seemed to be missing?
- What resources were required to design, develop, implement, or sustain these reforms, including staff time, staff training and support, space, materials, and supplies? If extra funds were required, how much extra was needed, what was the source of those funds, and how were they obtained? How are total costs and extra costs related to the number of pupils served?

- What role was played by research, research-based knowledge, and other information in the implementation of these reforms? What evidence documents that role?

IMPACT OF PERFORMANCE ASSESSMENTS
ON TEACHING AND LEARNING

- What strategies and approaches have been developed to assess the impact of these reforms? How do these approaches separate the impact of the reforms from the impact of other factors that might affect outcomes? How can these assessments be used to refine reforms?
- What has been the impact of these new assessments, particularly the impact on students, and especially the impact on student performance?
- What impact does the form of a test have on what students learn? What impact does the form of a test have on the quality, quantity, timeliness, and continuity of feedback to students, to their teachers, and to their parents? What information do students, teachers, and parents receive from these assessments about how students can improve their performance?
- What impact does the form of a test have on curriculum and instruction? Do tests that emphasize the mere recall of facts lead to a curriculum that emphasizes routine memorization? Do tests that require students to develop their own solutions and strategies lead to a curriculum emphasizing problem solving and higher-order thinking skills?
- What are the anticipated and unanticipated benefits and difficulties associated with this reform? How can those benefits be reproduced and those difficulties be avoided in other jurisdictions wishing to implement similar reforms?

References

American Association for the Advancement of Science. (1989). *Project 2061: Science for all Americans*. Washington, DC: Author.

American Association for the Advancement of Science. (1993). *Benchmarks for science literacy*. New York: Oxford University Press.

Bond, L. A., Roeber, E. D., King, D., & Braskamp, D. C. (1995). *The status of state student assessment programs in the United States*. Washington, DC: Council of Chief State School Officers.

Borko, H., Flory, M., & Cumbo, K. (1993). *Teachers' ideas and practices about assessment and instruction. A case study of the effects of alternative assessment in instruction, student learning, and accountability practice* (CSE Technical Report 366). Los Angeles: University of California, Center for Research on Evaluation, Standards, and Student Testing.

Bradley, A. (1994, June 1). Requiem for a reform. *Education Week*, pp. 21–25.

California Assessment Collaborative (1993). *Charting the course toward instructionally sound assessment*. San Francisco: Author.

College Board. (1994). *Facts about Pacesetter*. New York: Author.

Council of Chief State School Officers and the North Central Regional Educational Laboratory. (1994). *State student assessment programs database (1993–1994)*. Washington, DC: Author.

Evaluation Center, Western Michigan University, for the Kentucky Institute for Education Research. (1995). An independent evaluation of the Kentucky Instructional Results Information System. Frankfort, KY: Author.

Falk, B., & Darling-Hammond, L. (1993). *The Primary Language Record at P.S. 261: How assessment transforms teaching and learning*. New York: National Center for Restructuring Education, Schools, and Teaching.

Gearhart, M., Herman, J. L., Baker, E. L., & Whittaker, A. K. (1993). *Whose work is it? A question for the validity of large-scale portfolio assessment* (CSE Technical Report 363). Los Angeles: University of California, Center for Research on Evaluation, Standards, and Student Testing.

Goals 2000 will shape state, local school reform. (1994, May 27). *Education Daily* (Special Supplement).

Hansen, J. B., & Hathaway, W. E. (1991). *A survey of more authentic assessment practices*. Paper presented at the National Council for Measurement in Education/National Association of Test Directors (NCME/NATD) meeting, Chicago.

Hardy, R. (1996). Examining the costs of performance assessment. In M. B. Kane & R. Mitchell (Eds.), *Implementing performance assessment: Promises, problems, and challenges* (pp. 107–117). Mahwah, NJ: Lawrence Erlbaum Associates.

Herman, J. L. (1992). *Accountability and alternative assessment: Research and development issues* (CSE Technical Report 348). Los Angeles: University of California, Center for Research on Evaluation, Standards, and Student Testing.

Herman, J. L., Klein, D. C. D., Heath, T. M., & Wakai, S. T. (1994). *A first look: Are claims for alternative assessment holding up?* (CSE Technical Report 391). Los Angeles: University of California, Center for Research on Evaluation, Standards, and Student Testing.

Kentucky Institute for Education Research. (1995). *An independent evaluation of the Kentucky Instructional Results Information System (KIRIS)* (Executive Summary). Frankfort, KY: Author.

Khattri, N., Reeve, A. L., Traylor, K., Adamson, R. J., & Levin, D. A. (1995). *Studies of education reform: Assessment of student performance-Volume II, case studies.* Washington, DC: Pelavin Research Institute.

Khattri, N., & Sweet, D. (1996). Assessment reform: Promises and challenges. In M. B. Kane & R. Mitchell (Eds.), *Implementing performance assessment: Promises, problems, and challenges* (pp. 1–21). Mahwah, NJ: Lawrence Erlbaum Associates.

Koretz, D., Stecher, B., Klein, S., McCaffrey, D., & Diebert, E. (1993). *Can portfolios assess student performance and influence instruction? The 1991–1992 Vermont experience* (CSE Technical Report 371). Los Angeles: University of California, Center for Research on Evaluation, Standards, and Student Testing.

Linn, R. L. (1993). *Educational assessment: Expanded expectations and challenges* (CSE Technical Report 351). Los Angeles: University of California, Center for Research on Evaluation, Standards, and Student Testing.

Linn, R. L., Baker, E. L., & Dunbar, S. B. (1991). *Complex, performance-based assessment: Expectations and validation criteria. Educational Researcher, 20*(8), 15–21.

Little, J. W. (1993). Teachers' professional development in a climate of educational reform. *Educational Evaluation and Policy Analysis, 15*(2), 129–151.

Messick, S. (1994). The interplay of evidence and consequences in the validation of performance assessments. *Educational Researcher, 23*(2), 13–23.

Miles, M. B., & Huberman, A. M. (1994). *Qualitative data analysis.* Thousand Oaks, CA: Sage.

Mitchell, R. (1992). *Testing for learning.* New York: Free Press.

Monk, D. H. (1996). Conceptualizing the costs of large-scale pupil performance assessment. In M. B. Kane & R. Mitchell (Eds.), *Implementing performance assessment: promises, problems, and challenges* (pp. 119–137). Mahwah, NJ: Lawrence Erlbaum Associates.

National Council of Teachers of Mathematics. (1989). *Curriculum and evaluation standards for school mathematics.* Reston, VA: Author.

National Council of Teachers of Mathematics. (1991). *Professional standards for teaching mathematics.* Reston, VA: Author.

National Council of Teachers of Mathematics. (1995). *Assessment standards for school mathematics.* Reston, VA: Author.

Olson, L. (1995, February 1). Rules will allow district to set Title 1 measures. *Education Week,* pp. 1, 21.

Pelavin Associates and the Council of Chief State School Officers. (1991). *Performance assessments in the states.* Washington, DC: Author.

Prominent educators recommend the use of Pacesetter. (1995). *College Board News, 23*(3), 1–2.

Resnick, L., & Simmons, W. (1993). Assessment as the catalyst of school reform. *Educational Leadership, 50*(5), 11–15.

Rhodes, L. K., & Shanklin, N. (1993). *Windows into literacy: Assessing learners K–8.* Portsmouth, NH: Heinmann.

Secretary's Commission on Achieving Necessary Skills. (1991). *What work requires of schools: A SCANS report for America 2000.* Washington, DC: U. S. Department of Labor.

Sizer, T. R. (1989). Diverse practice, shared ideas: The essential school. In H. J. Walbert & J. J. Lane (Eds.), *Organizing for learning: Toward the 21st century.* Reston, VA: National Association of Secondary School Principals.

Sizer, T. R. (1992). *Horace's school.* Boston: Houghton Mifflin.

Smith, M. L., Noble, A. J., Cabay, M., Heinecke, W., Junker, M. S., & Saffron, Y. (July, 1994). *What happens when the test mandate changes? Results of a multiple case study* (CSE Technical Report 380). Los Angeles: University of California, Center for Research on Evaluation, Standards, and Student Testing.

Smith, M. S., & O'Day, J. (1990). Systemic school reform. In *Politics of education association yearbook 1990* (pp. 233–267). London: Taylor & Francis.

Specter looks to amend Goals 2000 in spending bill. (1995, September 13). *Education Daily*, pp. 1, 3.

Vermont Department of Education. (1995). *Assessment results: Writing and mathematics. 1993–1994.* Montpelier, VT: Author.

Wiley, D., & Haertel, H. (1992). *Extended assessment tasks: Purposes, definitions, scoring, and accuracy.* Paper prepared for the California Assessment Program.

Wolf, D. P. (1989). Portfolio assessment, sampling student work. *Educational Leadership, 46*(7), 35–39.

Wolf, D. P., & Pistone, N. (1991). *Taking full measure: Rethinking assessment through the arts.* New York: College Board.

Author Index

A

Adamson, R. J., 57*n*, 174*n*
American Association for the Advancement of
Science, 5

B

Baker, E. L., 11, 12
Bond, L. A., 5, 6
Borko, H., 11
Bradley, A., 10
Braskamp, D. C., 5, 6

C

Cabay, M., 11
California Assessment Collaborative, 13
College Board, 207*n*
Council of Chief State School Officers and the
North Central Regional
Educational Laboratory, 5
Cumbo, K., 11

D

Darling-Hammond, L., 11
Diebert, E., 6, 58
Dunbar, S. B., 11, 12

E

Evaluation Center, Western Michigan University
for the Kentucky
Institute for Education Research, 72*n*

F

Falk, B., 11
Flory, M., 11

G

Gearhart, M., 11

H

Haertel, H., 11
Hansen, J. B., 5, 7
Hardy, R., 13
Hathaway, W. E., 5, 7
Heath, T. M., 58
Heinecke, W., 11
Herman, J. L., 11, 29, 53, 58
Huberman, A. M., 173

J

Junker, M. S., 11

K

Kentucky Institute for Education Research, 6, 58
Khattri, N., 1*n*, 53, 57*n*, 174*n*
King, D., 5, 6
Klein, D. C. D., 58
Klein, S., 6, 58
Koretz, D., 6, 58

L

Levin, D. A., 57*n*, 174*n*
Linn, R. L., 11, 12, 53, 60
Little, J. W., 9

M

McCaffrey, D., 6, 58
Messick, S., 37, 44, 56, 58
Miles, M. B., 173
Mitchell, R., 4, 31
Monk, D. H., 13

N

National Council of Teachers of Mathematics, 5,
9
Noble, A. J., 11

O

O'Day, J., 8

Subject Index